WRITING ESSAYS
A PROCESS APPROACH

WRITING ESSAYS
A PROCESS APPROACH

Quentin L. Gehle
Duncan J. Rollo

St. Martin's Press   New York

Library of Congress Catalog Card Number: 86–60669
Copyright © 1987 by St. Martin's Press, Inc.
All rights reserved.
Manufactured in the United States of America.

10987
fedcba

For information, write St. Martin's Press, Inc.
175 Fifth Avenue
New York, NY 10010

ISBN: 0–312–89491–0

cover art: Esther Frederiksen

This book is a revised and expanded edition of *The Writing Process,* first published in 1977.

ACKNOWLEDGMENTS

Max Lerner, "Sports in America," from AMERICA AS CIVILIZATION. Copyright © 1957, 1985 by Max Lerner. Reprinted by permission of Simon & Schuster, Inc.
James Nuechterlein and Mark Gilbertson, from THE CRESSET: A Review of Literature, The Arts, and Public Affairs, published by the Valparaiso University Press.
Carl T. Rowan, "Teenagers and Booze," from JUST BETWEEN US BLACKS, by Carl T. Rowan. Copyright © 1974 by Carl T. Rowan. Reprinted by permission of Random House, Inc.
Gail Sheehy, "Jailbreak Marriage," from PASSAGES: PREDICTABLE CRISES OF ADULT LIFE. Copyright © 1974, 1976 by Gail Sheehy. Reprinted by permission of the publisher, E. P. Dutton, a division of the New American Library.

Preface

Our aim in this text is to help students become confident and effective writers. Fundamental to our approach is the knowledge that writing is hard work, but that its many interrelated tasks can be practiced and learned. We hope to take the mystery out of writing, to refute the idea held by many students that the ability to write clearly and effectively is a gift. To this end, we stress that writing involves a series of choices that a writer makes. We offer detailed explanations of what these choices consist of, and we provide insights and recommendations to help the writer make the appropriate rhetorical decisions.

Writing Essays is concerned with giving students practice in developing papers not only for a course in English composition but for courses in any other discipline. Learning how to produce effective essays is one of the most important and necessary goals in a student's academic life. It will continue to serve and reward in the professional world as well. But to make writing *manageable* for many students requires that they understand the relation between a finished essay and the individual tasks by which it was developed. We believe this aim is best accomplished by focusing on the process by which an essay is created, from an initial consideration of topic, purpose, and audience to a finished product that has the effect its author intended. In broad terms, we see the process evolving through certain tasks within three stages of writing: planning, developing, and revising. The process as we present it is orderly and flexible and, above all, recursive.

As we did in our earlier rhetoric, *The Writing Process,* we have organized *Writing Essays* according to the three stages of writing. At the same time, we emphasize throughout that the writer's goal is ultimately to produce an effective essay. We therefore begin with an overview of the essay and its major elements, and we explain how the various tasks within each stage of the writing process contribute to an essay's overall effectiveness. With the goal thus established, we turn to planning, the first stage. The first of three chapters in this part of the text involves students in considering subjects to write about; in understanding how the four types of nonfiction prose can help them achieve their purposes; and in analyzing and approaching the audiences for their writing. The remaining chapters provide students with practice in narrowing broad subject areas into manageable topics and, finally, in creating thesis statements that will guide and control their essays.

We devote six chapters to the second stage, "Development." The first of these chapters provides instruction and practice in constructing effective paragraphs. We begin with attention to the topic sentence and its relation to the thesis, and go on to discuss the qualities of effective paragraphs. In the next chapter we discuss special purpose paragraphs, specifically introductory, transitional, and concluding paragraphs. The remaining four chapters in this stage involve students in developing their essays using narration, description, exposition, and argumentation.

Revision is at once the third stage and an ongoing stage. We devote five chapters to revision, beginning with one on revising the larger elements of content and organization. In this chapter we illustrate revision by reproducing and discussing the first, second, and third drafts of essays written by students. The remaining chapters in this stage address revising stylistic features, including variety and emphasis, sentence construction, and diction. We conclude with a discussion of punctuation and mechanics.

It is important to note here that our treatment of revision is not limited to these five chapters. In fact, revision is presented as an integral, ongoing part of writing throughout the text. To this end, we include in every chapter "Revision Exercises" that are designed to reinforce the chapter's discussion of writing tools and techniques and to encourage students to think of writing and revising as simultaneous tasks for which the tools and techniques can be equally useful. The emphasis on revision continues into our appendix on writing research papers.

As it did in *The Writing Process,* reinforcement remains a major means of helping students develop necessary skills and gain confidence. Thus, in addition to the "Revision Exercises" in *Writing Essays* we provide scores of other exercises that invite students to apply what they have just read and discussed. These exercises are not arbitrarily grouped at the ends of chapters but are placed within the text at the points where they will do the most good. Moreover, we avoid the abstract by providing abundant examples—from individual sentences to paragraphs to complete essays— more than half of them written by students. In this way, students using this text are presented with models that guide and instruct, but do not intimidate. At the same time, they learn that effective writing is not the sole province of the professional and, indeed, that professionals experience many of the same problems that students encounter. Finally, to facilitate students' using and reviewing writing principles and processes, we have produced boxed summaries throughout the chapters, a visual device that again aids in reinforcement.

Expressing gratitude for assistance in producing a book is always one of the more pleasurable parts of writing. In this instance, much of our debt must go to Nancy Perry, Senior Editor at St. Martin's. Her guidance, insight, and determination that this text would expand and extend many of the principles we initially advocated in *The Writing Process* have been invaluable. We are also indebted to Barbara Hoffert, Agnes Greenhall, and Richard Steins for their advice and attention to the manuscript.

Numerous composition instructors from across the country have contributed their expertise to help make *Writing Essays* a better book. For their insightful reviews of *The Writing Process* or their generous criticism and suggestions for *Writing Essays,* we would like to thank Sheila Bowler,

University of Wisconsin—Milwaukee; Harry Brent, Baruch College, CUNY; Patricia Burnes, University of Maine—Orono; Cyndia Clegg, Pepperdine University; Carmine Dandrea, Lake Michigan College; Jean English, Tallahassee Community College; Kathleen Greenfield, Drexel University; George Hayhoe, Virginia Polytechnic Institute and State University; Mary Hyatt, Spokane Falls Community College; Deborah Shaller, Towson State University; Kathleen L. Steele, DePauw University; George Tylutki, Marywood College; Barbara Weaver, Ball State University; and Linda Young, California State University—Sacramento.

Finally, we owe a special thanks to our wives, Linda Gehle and Paula Rollo, for their patience and sound critical suggestions. And to our children—Bruce, Ben, and Karen Gehle and Elizabeth and Katherine Rollo—a special debt is owed, for they ultimately provide our inspiration and delight.

Quentin L. Gehle
Duncan J. Rollo

Contents

15 CHECKING MECHANICS 243

APPENDIX A   UNDERSTANDING GRAMMAR   262

APPENDIX B WRITING THE RESEARCH PAPER 283

WRITING ESSAYS
A PROCESS APPROACH

1

Understanding the Writing Process

Effective communication is the main goal of any kind of writing, whether it be an essay, letter, lab report, or résumé. Your success in writing will be measured by how well you achieve this goal. You already possess one essential ingredient, your knowledge of language.

To become a good writer, however, you must also learn to use intelligently the many tools and techniques of language and composition. Mastering these will enable you to present your thoughts clearly, logically, and convincingly. You will thus acquire a skill essential to your academic and professional success.

Effective writing can also shape your intellectual growth. Ideas that are fresh, thoughts that are developed, relationships that are explored—these hallmarks of effective writing do not simply flow from a pen. They are products of the insights gained from the writing process, a process that helps you discover, explore, and refine *what* you think and *why*.

The writing process involves mastering a series of tasks. Although the steps are *recursive,* we shall explore them in turn. Identifying the tasks and exploring each separately will provide a reassuring amount of order in your writing. In addition, by gaining a hold on one aspect of the process at a time, you will grow to appreciate how the various tasks are interconnected and interchanging. As you consider each stage, you will find that there is no one method for executing it. Just as there are perhaps ten ways to build a bridge, there may be ten ways to develop a paragraph. The successful engineer makes the choices that will *best* achieve his purpose. As a writer, you, too, must constantly make appropriate choices. You do not simply develop a paragraph; you find the *best* way to develop it in accordance with your particular purpose. Thus, underlying the entire writing process is your knowledge of the many choices available to you at any given stage. A major goal of this text is to make you aware of what those choices are and to advise you in making them.

1

This book is organized so as to parallel the writing process by exploring specific tasks that fall within the three major stages necessary for effective writing. The first section of the book, "Planning," discusses getting off to a good start, often the most difficult task for inexperienced writers. It describes how to determine your purpose and consider your audience; how to expand, shape, and limit an idea; and how to create a generalization called a *thesis statement* that will guide you and later the reader through the development of your essay.

The second section, "Development," shows how you can deliver on the promise your thesis makes by constructing a network of paragraphs that support it. Each paragraph must contain a topic sentence that sums up its content and, if your entire essay is to be effective, each paragraph itself must be effective. This section teaches you how to write topic sentences and effective paragraphs. It also explores writing special-purpose paragraphs—the introductory, transitional, and concluding paragraphs that will give your essay its final shape.

The chapters in the third section, "Revision," offer guidance on assessing your essay as a whole; on improving style; and on checking for appropriate sentence structure, mechanics, and grammar. Exercises giving you practice in revision appear throughout the text. Their pervasiveness illustrates an important point. Revision itself pervades the writing process; you revise continually even as you plan and develop an essay. For instance, when planning an essay, you may find that there is little information on the topic you have chosen and that you must therefore revise your topic. Or, while checking for spelling and punctuation errors, you may realize that you need to rework your thesis; your idea has grown and changed as you worked on it, and the point you are now communicating is slightly different from the point you originally intended. Because writing is an ongoing and fundamentally creative activity, *continual revision* is part of the writing process—no less important than the planning and actual writing itself.

Many of the models used for illustration and discussion throughout this book are essays written by college students in introductory composition courses. You will note that these essays vary widely in subject and writing style. They are not meant to represent separate approaches to a single implied standard of correctness but simply to be interesting and helpful examples of the particular writing task under discussion. Some essays and paragraphs, you will realize, have been thoroughly revised, while others have not.

SEEING THE WHOLE ESSAY

Before considering the major stages of the writing process and the tasks that each entails, you should be aware that these tasks and stages are important individually only insofar as they lead to your writing complete essays. A complete essay has a definite shape or structure that helps an audience understand the ideas and information you, the writer, wish to convey. At its most basic level, the structure of a complete essay usually involves a beginning, middle, and end. The beginning, or *introduction,* attracts the reader's attention and states the main point of your essay. In the middle, or *body,* you provide convincing support for your main point. The end, or *conclusion,* is your opportunity to draw the essay to a close by reinforcing your point.

In subsequent chapters, you will find full discussions of this basic three-part structure. For now, however, it is enough to keep before you the goal of writing complete essays. By working through the stages and tasks of the writing process, by completing the many trial-and-error writing exercises in this text, and especially by paying attention to your instructor's comments, you will make your writing more effective.

THE ESSENTIAL ELEMENTS

The three-part structure of introduction, body, and conclusion that shapes most essays will give your writing unity (harmony and agreement of interdependent parts) and emphasis (stress on a single purpose). By keeping the whole essay in mind as you write, and by seeing that the essay reveals the following key qualities in its progression, you reduce the chances of inadvertently moving away from your subject matter and hence losing your audience.

The most important element in the **introduction** is the *thesis statement.* The thesis statement is a generalization that states your topic precisely. It also indicates how you have limited your topic and how you will organize your presentation. The thesis may be presented in one sentence, or it may consist of several sentences, depending on the complexity of your topic.

Paragraphs in the **body** of the essay usually offer *topic sentences.* A topic sentence suggests which aspect of the thesis statement you are covering in that particular paragraph. The topic sentence is usually most effective when it is placed at the beginning of the paragraph, though it may also appear in the middle or at the end. Sometimes the topic sentence is merely implied, not stated.

Normally, each paragraph in the body of an essay provides *support* for the thesis. Support usually consists of *details,* which form the evidence needed to persuade the audience to believe what you are saying. Various methods of development, such as narration, analogy, classification, and definition are used to present these details. (Methods of development are discussed later in the text.) Details offer *specific* evidence; that is, they are items that can be mistaken for no others. For example, "Many children have been immunized against polio" is not specific, but "One hundred children in Plantagenet County have been immunized against polio" is. "Dogs" is not specific; "Irish setters" is more specific but could use further clarification; "Mr. Johnson's pair of Irish setters" is unmistakable. A fully developed paragraph in the body of an essay is one that has sufficient

support to make the topic sentence—
and thereby that aspect of the thesis statement—convincing.

The **conclusion** of the essay reinforces your thesis statement. In it, you may offer a *summary, recommendation, question,* or *prediction.* You may also conclude with a quotation you find particularly apt. Your conclusion should usually be brief and to the point.

Writing that follows the three-part structure and contains these key elements will be effective whether it is an English composition, a lab report, a sales survey, or a business letter. The student essay that follows is a good example of effective writing. As you read it, pay attention to the way the elements discussed earlier are used in the introduction, body, and conclusion.

THE HYPOCRISY OF THE COLLEGE GRADING SYSTEM

State University's grading system is designed "to show how much a student has learned in each course and to motivate **INTRODUCTION** him through competition with other students"—at least that

Thesis Statement is what the school catalogue says. Since I have been here, though, I've found that this system is illogical and its motivation is misdirected.

What makes the grading system illogical is that professors **BODY**
Topic Sentence teaching the same course often have different goals. For example, my roommate Gail and I are both taking U.S. History I, but all my examinations are essay and hers are multiple-choice. All she has to do to get an "A" is to memorize information. On the other hand, I'm required to explain why certain conflicts
Supporting Details and changes took place and to do it in "good, clear English." Not only does my professor take off for content, but he also drops the grade for writing errors, or what he calls "lack of clarity." In addition, I'm expected to read two history books, while Gail has to use just one for her class. In a way, I really shouldn't complain. Gail and I both realize that I'm learning much more than she is about U.S. history. Nevertheless, that isn't going to show up in the grade reports. As of last week, she was averaging a "B" (she isn't memorizing everything) compared to my "C."

Topic Sentence The other thing that undermines the grade system logic is the different standards that individual professors have. For
Supporting Details instance, two of my closest friends—Beth and Jerry—took first-year French, used the same textbooks, and were each required to cover the same material. Professor Erikson, however, counted simple vocabulary quizzes and short translations much more heavily than did Professor DuBois, who relied

mainly on oral examinations for determining grades. Having had four years of high school French, I realized that both Beth and Jerry's knowledge of the language was about the same at the end of their courses. Beth received a "B." Meanwhile, poor Jerry, who became very nervous during oral recitations, had earned only a "D."

Jerry's anger at the grade is understandable, as, I think, is mine with regard to my U.S. History I class. But this anger

Supporting Details points up the other problem with the grading system: because students know that others will immediately measure their knowledge by the grades they have received, they are liable to become more interested in "A"s and "B"s than in learning. I admit that the grading system is likely to motivate students,

Topic Sentence but not in the way the university intends. Instead, it will motivate them away from the pursuit of knowledge and toward the pursuit of the easy "A," the simple course, and the most lenient professor. Jerry has already signed up for Professor Erickson next term, and I am planning to take U.S. History II from the professor Gail has this semester.

What are the solutions to the problems created by the present **CONCLUSION**

Question Recommendations grading system? Standardizing course requirements in each department is a first step. More important, though, is that each teacher enthusiastically stress the benefits to be gained from the material in his or her course.

EXERCISE

The following student essay contains a thesis statement, topic sentences, specific support, and a conclusion. Identify these and be prepared to discuss how they lend unity and emphasis to the essay:

ILLEGAL IMMIGRANTS: A BETTER APPROACH

Complaints about illegal immigrants have been increasing in the past few years. Thousands regularly stream across the southern border of the United States, some fleeing political repression and others fleeing economic hardship. Our current immigration and visa policies offer some relief for these immigrants, but these inadequate policies now exist alongside several other unsatisfactory and sometimes illegal solutions.

Current policies for granting visas permit entry to the United States for several purposes but do not address the problems of most illegal immigrants. A limited number of visas for purposes of immigration are available each year, with most going to persons who have waited for years to gain permission for entry or to persons who have critically needed professional and technical skills. Other visas are issued to students who have been accepted into study programs at American universities. Still other visas are issued to tourists and diplomats. A small number are issued to persons designated refugees, who are undeniably in danger of political repression and possible imprisonment or death for their political views. Judging from newspaper reports, however, most illegal aliens do not qualify as refugees, nor do they have sufficient money or education to qualify for student or tourist visas. Their suffering and poverty need immediate relief—they do not have time to wait in the long queues for immigrant visas, which can take years rather than a few weeks.

In response to the problem of large numbers of illegal immigrants, several unsatisfactory solutions are at hand or are already being applied. One solution has been the forming of the "sanctuary movement," which involves groups of Americans illegally giving aid and shelter to the immigrants. Forced repatriation is also being tried, but as the U.S. border patrol rounds up the aliens and sends them back, they simply return a few days later, and the numbers of those entering the country illegally has reached such proportions that the border patrol force is overwhelmed. Another possible solution is the addition of physical barriers to the border. That solution, however, could result in a national image that would do more damage than good, and comparisons to the Iron Curtain and the Berlin Wall would undoubtedly appear prominently in world media.

Though no solution will apparently be ideal, it should be possible to develop a new visa system that would ease the problem. Would-be immigrants who are poor and uneducated and who are clearly subject to severe economic or political problems could be granted temporary visas and be restricted to certain agricultural or industrial areas where they could find employment at wages below our national standards but higher than the standards in their home countries. Perhaps some of the technical jobs that our manufacturers have "exported" could return in this way. After a certain period, the immigrants could be repatriated. The nation would benefit by having a source of less expensive labor, and the aliens' needs for temporary economic or political shelter would be met.

ADDITIONAL GUIDELINES

The two preceding essays succeed because they present worthwhile ideas developed logically. The writers lead the reader through their development of each idea by using a *thesis statement, topic sentences, specific support,* and a *conclusion* that reaffirms the main point. In addition, both writers followed some commonsense guidelines that helped ensure that their messages would be understood. These guidelines, which are discussed fully in subsequent chapters, include the following points:

1. *Respect Yourself.* Present the reader with thoughts that are worth your time to write. Do more than echo common, unexamined views. Even if you are assigned a subject, take the time to explore it carefully so that you can present a unique point of view.
2. *Respect the Audience.* Use words that will be understandable and appropriate to your audience. Organize and develop your main point logically and emphatically. Check to make sure that you have followed acceptable standards of usage.
3. *Respect the Language.* Be precise in your choice and arrangement of words and be highly specific in your supporting material. State your message so that your audience *cannot* misunderstand you. Do not quit work when it is merely possible that the reader might understand.
4. *Respect Logic and Grammar.* Whatever your subject, avoid introducing irrelevancies. Present all your points clearly, with sentence and paragraph elements arranged in a unified, coherent fashion. Strive to create sentences consisting of the fewest number of words necessary to convey your meaning.
5. *Respect the Conventions of Grammar, Spelling, and Punctuation.* If your essay is worth the reader's attention, it is worth your own. When you reduce your reader to proofreader by ignoring spelling, grammar, and punctuation errors, you risk incurring resentment and alienation. Therefore, you should allow adequate time for careful proofreading.

Like virtually all other aspects of writing, adhering to the above guidelines requires conscious effort on your part. It also requires continual revision, as you rewrite to sharpen words, sentences, and paragraphs. Your goal is effective writing. Now let us discuss in greater detail how this goal is to be achieved.

REVISION EXERCISE

The following student essay would profit from careful revision. Read it two or three times, keeping in mind the three-part structure of an essay, its essential elements—thesis statement, topic sentences, details, and conclusion—and the guidelines just discussed. Then revise the essay.

FOOD WORLD'S MADDING CROWD

I spent the summer bagging groceries at a large supermarket. I saw the usual mix of American suburban humanity—young, single people buying brie and white wine, old people buying bread and beans, middle-aged people buying tons of everything to feed themselves and their teenaged kids. Some were rude, some were polite, but most were withdrawn, preferring to remain nameless and faceless. What interested me more was not the customers but the way that the employees at Food World reacted to the different kinds of customers.

The cashiers, who had the most contact, may have been friendly people once, but they seemed to have grown indifferent to the customers, probably because few of them ever responded when wished a friendly "Good afternoon" or "Have a nice day." The manager and assistant manager, who saw the customers only to approve checks, were much friendlier. The bag boys, including me, were somewhere in between, and of course we had an in between amount of contact compared to the managers and the cashiers. So maybe it is the amount of contact an employee has with a customer that determines whether the employee becomes "burned out" in the realm of friendliness.

Anyway, there are the three types of employees when it comes to how they treat the customers.

Howard is typical of the cashiers, the first type, which is sort of robot-like when it comes to customer relations. Let me give you an example. I bagged for Howard and watched him all one Saturday morning. The first customer was an elderly lady, who made three or four attempts to chat with him, asking him whether he hated to work on Saturdays and didn't he think it was a lovely day. Howard never even answered her. I don't think he ever made eye-contact with any of the customers. He just kept looking at the individual grocery items coming down the conveyor belt of the check-out counter, pulling them across the price-scanner, and dropping them back for me to put in bags. About the only thing I ever heard him say was a mechanical "thank-you" as he handed change and receipts to customers.

The second type of employee is the friendliest. These are the managers. They have two reasons for being friendly. Less frequent contact with the public than the cashiers have allows the managers not to become burned out greeting people who are usually unresponsive, and the managers have a greater interest in promoting the success of the store than the cashiers do. Ursilla, for example, who is the assistant manager, always has a smile and cheery greeting for everyone, even with the people whose checks she says she cannot approve and to whom she apologizes profusely.

The baggers, including me, tend to be inbetween. We have less contact with the public than the cashiers do but more than the managers do. We tend to be friendly to the people who answer when we say "How are you." Other customers, especially the ones who won't make eye-contact, we tend to ignore.

Maybe the answer to better customer relations is to work especially on ways to improve the cashiers' attitudes. That could be done through training sessions and frequent reminders to be friendly, even to customers who look like they won't be responsive. The way the three types of employees are able to show friendliness in proportion to their lack of public contact also says to me that China isn't the only place suffering from overcrowding, and maybe the only way a busy retail business is going to preserve politeness is to give frequent breaks or split schedules to the employees who have to have the most contact with the public.

student essay

PLANNING

Planning is the first stage of writing. It requires that you make rational, conscious choices about your essay before you begin writing—that you decide where you are going before you set out. Planning also allows for an interplay between your conscious self and your imagination that brings out aspects of your experience, personality, and memory you can use in your writing.

This part of the text gets you off to a good start. It begins with a discussion of why you write and how you analyze an audience so that you can get your message across. The discussion then helps you consider what to write about—that is, how to find a subject and how to explore your subject to arrive at a manageable topic. Planning culminates with the creation of a thesis statement that announces the main idea of the essay and indicates how the essay will be organized and developed.

Part I discusses these aspects of planning:

> considering subject, purpose, and audience
> moving from subject to topic
> the thesis statement

2

Considering Subject, Purpose, and Audience

If you were to list all the things at which you excel, chances are that you would overlook a major area of expertise: your mastery of communication. Your conversation is probably full of interesting stories and insights, humorous anecdotes, and vivid descriptions. You know how to ask directions of a stranger and how to give them. You can argue persuasively for or against something, and you know how to explain an idea or process to someone. You are, moreover, something of a psychologist. You have learned that what you say and how you say it depend to a great extent on your listener—that some subjects are best avoided when talking with a grandparent, that the casual and familiar language you use with your friends is sometimes misunderstood by your parents.

Like many people, however, you may find that your skill in communicating seems to disappear when you begin to write. Seldom at a loss for something to say, you find writing much more difficult. Usually sure of the importance of your ideas and opinions, your confidence seems to slip away along with the minutes on the clock as you confront a blank piece of paper. Why is it, you may have wondered, that talking seems so much easier than writing?

The answer is that talking *is* easier, for when you converse, you are responding to a particular set of circumstances that automatically provides you with a context—a subject to discuss, a purpose to achieve, an audience to address. The interaction of subject, purpose, and audience is essential to any form of communication, oral or written. Assume, for example, that you are talking with a friend who wants to know how you managed on Professor Baker's zoology exam. Your response is likely to be quick because the context has been established. Your subject is the exam, your purpose is to answer your friend's question, and your audience is the friend. Your response will take other factors into account. If your friend is not enrolled in the same course, you would probably describe the content of the exam in some detail. If, on the other hand, your friend is enrolled in the same class and received a higher grade than you, you might alter your purpose to justify your grade or to question the fairness of the exam. And almost certainly your response would reflect, if only subconsciously, your analysis of the friend's motive for asking in the first place. But whatever the extent of analysis and the ultimate direction and scope of the conversation, communication proceeds only after its context has been established.

As with oral communication, written communication proceeds only when the context is clear. It is this context—subject, purpose, and audience—that is your initial consideration as a writer.

DETERMINING A SUBJECT

Throughout your college and professional life, you will generally find yourself writing in response to specific assignments. You might, for instance, write an essay explaining a major theme in three Steven Spielberg movies, addressing a specific question posed by the professor in your Modern Film 201 course. Similarly, a prospective employer might want to know in writing why you think you are uniquely qualified for a particular job, or a boss might want you to analyze the prospects for computer sales in Martin County, Minnesota. In each case, the subject is given. Your task will be to narrow the subject to a suitable topic—an issue that will be addressed in the next chapter.

Even if you are not assigned a subject to write about, you should have little difficulty finding one that you can develop in an essay. As you consider subject choice, keep in mind that your goal is to write about what you know. Do not assume that you know little that could possibly interest a reader; do not assume that you should leave writing to people who lead exciting lives.

The question of what to write about requires honesty and ego. Certainly, admit the limitations of your experience, but recognize also that no one else sees the world exactly as you do. Your experiences are probably shared by many persons, but because your perception of them is original, you can transform these experiences into interesting, worthwhile, and even exciting essays.

Finding material is an active process. Probe your mind to discover what and why you believe as you do. What is your experience? What are your interests, opinions, goals? Why did you vote for a particular candidate in the last election? What bothers you about certain fashions or customs or regulations? Finally, realize that no one wants to read the same thing over and over. Instead of writing generally about how some people are bored by spectator sports, describe your own reactions as you sat through an afternoon watching a football game in which the final score was 77–0.

WRITING WITH A PURPOSE

You write to give an audience something it previously did not have. Whether you narrate an event, describe an object or a person, explain how something works, or argue for a point, at the very least you give an audience a perspective it did not have before. This is not to say that writing is entirely selfless; obviously you, the writer, gain insight from grappling with your thoughts and experiences, and you are likely to be prompted by academic or professional demands. You will become more conscious of the specific purposes of writing by considering your experience as a reader. When you read a textbook, a repair manual, or even a recipe, you expect to be informed. You examine an article in a newspaper or magazine to find out what is going on outside your immediate experience— in effect, you invite the writer to expand your world. You anticipate that editorials and opinion columns will reinforce or challenge your ideas and beliefs. Sometimes your expectations are lighter. You may read works to stimulate your intellect or aesthetic senses, or humor or fantasy for entertainment. Naturally, some of these expectations overlap. You read certain columnists such as Art Buchwald or Erma Bombeck expecting to be not only informed but also entertained, and you expect that the writer of a recipe will not only explain the steps in the process but also describe exactly how finely the cheese must be grated or the nuts chopped.

When reading a book or an article, you need not be particularly conscious of your specific expectations. As a writer, however, you must be aware of your purpose, because understanding *why* you are writing an essay ultimately governs the decisions you will make regarding *how* you will achieve that purpose. Assume, for example, that you are writing about boxing, specifically a match that you have just witnessed. The purpose that you have decided on is simply to inform, to provide information. This decision will, among other things, dictate both the content and the organization of your essay. You would probably describe what happened and to whom; you might narrate the event, starting, say, from round one and moving to the knockout in round four. On the other hand, if you choose to analyze the result of the match, the content and organization would be significantly different. Rather than presenting a blow-by-blow account, you most likely would explain what happened, comparing and contrasting the skills of the two fighters and supporting your analysis by specific references to individual moves that one fighter made and the other failed to detect. And if you decide that your purpose is to persuade your audience that boxing should be banned because of its brutality, your essay would most likely be given over to graphic descriptions of the punishment endured by one of the fighters, and perhaps to depictions of the spectators responding to the events in the ring. Both descriptions would give you a basic organizational plan for your essay.

WRITING TYPES

Your purpose probably will be reflected in the type of essay you choose to write. Nonfiction prose types include *narration, description, exposition,* and *argumentation.* Each type has certain uses and thus lends itself to certain purposes. Understanding these types will give you greater insight into the purposes each can serve, thereby assisting you in the decisions you will make regarding content, organization, and even style.

Narration

Writers use narration to recount an event or a series of events, usually in chronological order. Often, as in newspaper writing, narration is designed to provide specific information regarding what happened, where, to whom, when, and why. Narratives in the press are often unmixed with other forms, such as exposition, but writers frequently employ narration in combination with an argument or exposition. Narration is used in college, general, and business writing, usually as a means of supporting an idea—that is, of providing an answer to the anticipated question, "For instance?" Narration is also the dominant means of development in fiction. You will rely on narration extensively in your academic work, using it to recount everything from historic events to the evolution of scientific principles or schools of thought.

Here is an example of a narrative passage from a work by a neurologist, who uses case histories to illustrate particular kinds of brain disorders in his patients.

> Mrs. O'C. was somewhat deaf, but otherwise in good health. She lived in an old people's home. One night, in January 1979, she dreamed vividly, nostalgically, of her childhood in Ireland, and especially of the songs they danced to and sang. When she woke up, the music was still going, very loud and clear. 'I must still be dreaming,' she thought, but this was not so. She got up, roused and puzzled. It was the middle of the night. Someone, she assumed, must have left a radio playing. But why was she the only person to be disturbed by it?
>
> Oliver Sacks, *The Man Who Mistook His Wife for a Hat and Other Clinical Tales*

In *The Informed Heart,* psychologist Bruno Bettelheim illustrates the effects of social pressure on dissenters by use of narration:

I once spoke with a young German psychologist who was a child at the beginning of the Hitler regime. Her father was a strong opponent of the Nazi movement and she felt as he did. But life went on and she had to go to school. At school she had to swear allegiance to the Fuhrer, to give the Hitler salute repeatedly. For a long time she mentally crossed her fingers. She told herself that the oath and salute didn't count because she didn't mean them. But each time it became more difficult to hang on to her self respect and still keep up the pretense, until finally she gave up her mental reservation and swore allegiance like anybody else.

Description

Writers use description to portray in words a person, place, or object or a combination of persons, places, or objects. In some instances, description is designed to persuade an audience to buy something, as in the advertisement for a Calvin Klein outfit presented as "a sweatery little tank and slouchy cardigan over flowing silk foulard." In other instances, description may be intended to help a reader envision a scene that is central to a point the writer is making. Consider what a description would be like if the writer had no idea of its purpose, no guiding principle for what details to choose for presentation to the reader. Should a description of a house, for example, include details about each nail and each brick? Should the description mention only the amount of sunlight that reaches the various rooms of the house? Many writers select details for a description according to the *dominant impression* they wish to establish. A dominant impression is the most significant *effect, feeling,* or *image* that the writer has about the object of the description, the effect, feeling, or image that the writer wants to leave with the audience. A dominant impression, for example, may be fear, glee, or reverence. Whether strong or vague, the dominant impression guides the writer's selection of detail. The impression may even be compound, as is the passage below, which shows a selection of details to present an image of violence and beauty.

> Another time I saw another wonder: sharks off the Atlantic coast of Florida. There is a way a wave rises above the ocean horizon, a triangular wedge against the sky. If you stand where the ocean breaks on a shallow beach, you see the raised water in a wave is translucent, shot with lights. One late afternoon at low tide a hundred big sharks passed . . . in a feeding frenzy. As each green wave rose from the churning water, it illuminated within itself the six- or eight-foot-long bodies of twisting sharks. The sharks disappeared as each wave rolled toward me; then a new wave would swell above the horizon, containing in it, like scorpions in amber, sharks that roiled and heaved. The sight held awesome wonders: power and beauty, grace tangled in a rapture with violence.

Annie Dillard, *Pilgrim at Tinker Creek*

In the academic and professional worlds, description is frequently a major tool, as in the writing of biology and geology reports, in historical analyses, and in market surveys of potential consumer groups. You are likely to find, however, that description is most often a key means of providing persuasive supporting detail in writing that is predominantly argument, narration, or exposition. In the following paragraph, a student writer uses description to buttress her assertion about the aims of some late nineteenth-century photographers:

> Documentary photographers at the turn of the century frequently turned their attention to persuading society of the necessity of providing for the poor. Typical of them was Jacob Riis. His photograph of Baxter Street Alley in 1888 shows tenements on either side of the narrow passage, crowding so close as to shut out the daylight. On one side the tenements are brick and on the other wood, but they appear rickety and squalid. Bags of rags and bones and paper are stacked in the alley. A small child stands beside the bags, in front of a pile of scrap wood she apparently has gathered for fuel.

Exposition

The type of writing you will use most often in your academic career is exposition, which clarifies or explains. Science reports, responses to reading assignments, and explications of literature are all examples of exposition. Analysis also sometimes groups elements into categories for the purpose of explaining or clarifying, as in the following analysis of the force of nationalism:

> Nationalism is an amalgam of two elements; an ideology embroidered about the idea of nationality, and the political institutionalization of that ideology into the national state. The strength of nationalism rests on a consensus of national unity which may stem from race, language, common history and experiences, religion, territory, or other interests. The national state, reflecting the political and social organization of the individuals which comprise it and having coercive power over them, claims, in their name, sovereignty over the territory in which they live.
>
> Norman J. Padelford and George A. Lincoln,
> *The Dynamics of International Politics*

Exposition has various forms, which include exemplification, process, comparison/contrast, analogy, classification, definition, and causal analysis. Process, for example, explains to an audience how to do something. The following is an explanation of how to play the children's card game, "Old Maid."

> The dealer shuffles and distributes the cards, one at a time, facedown. Each player examines his or her cards and places all matched pairs faceup on the

table in front of him or her. The dealer begins play by drawing a card from the hand of the player to the left. If the drawn card matches one in the dealer's hand, the matched pair is placed on the table; if not, the card remains in the dealer's hand. The player to the dealer's left follows the same procedure. The game ends once all the pairs of cards are matched, and the loser is left holding the Old Maid card.

Argumentation

The purpose of an argument is to convince an audience through a sequence of reasoning supported by evidence, including examples, statistics, testimony from experts, and research reports. This brief paragraph, written by a student, illustrates how argumentation works:

> According to the Environmental Protection Agency's most recent report on pollution and clean air standards, the air in Chicago is 25 percent less polluted than it was a year ago. This improvement follows the introduction of an Illinois state law requiring strict emission standards for automobiles. According to the EPA study, 90 percent of the hydrocarbons that pollute the air come from automobile emissions. Therefore, if we want to continue to have clean air, we should support the enforcement of this law.

Throughout your academic career you will use argumentation when writing papers that defend or develop a position, particularly on a controversial subject. Here, for example, is a selection from a book arguing against sex discrimination in the corporate world:

> The stronger the personal identification of a top business executive to his football past, the more violent his antipathy to women managers is apt to be. He will be so convinced business (management-football) is the apogee of a man's game (great men against great men) that he will feel that women are positively unqualified to compete against the strongest, most powerful, best-trained men in the world. Such affectations are managerial daydreams, of course, because the game of business is not a literal physical clash between male brutes. It is a symbol, a computer model, a paper game, a psychological contest. Competitive large-scale business does resemble football contests, but the business game is a mental competition—it's played in the head not the stadium. Not a single technique needed for the game is inherited or inborn—the talents, mental agility, abilities, attitudes are learned. Men teach them to each other but adamantly refuse to teach them to women. Too bad about them; women are smart enough to teach themselves, and their practice field can be everyday situations confronted on every job.

> Betty Lehan Harragan, *Games Mother Never Taught You*

We will have more to say in later chapters about argumentation and about various combinations of types of writing. For now, keep in mind that, in the broadest sense, the basic purpose of all writing is to *persuade*—to bring your reader to accept the ideas you develop in your writing.

The uses of nonfiction prose types:

- NARRATION: *recounts* an event or series of events.
- DESCRIPTION: *portrays* a person, place, or object.
- EXPOSITION: *explains* or *clarifies.*
- ARGUMENTATION: *convinces* through a sequence of reasoning.

EXERCISES

1. Write a narrative paragraph in which you tell an audience of your classmates of an event that happened in your family. Try to provide answers to the following questions: what happened? where? to whom? when? and why?
2. Write a narrative paragraph for the same audience recounting what you have done so far today.
3. In a short paragraph describe one item of apparel you are wearing.
4. Describe vividly your favorite food or beverage.
5. Write an expository paragraph in which you explain how to carry out a simple process such as changing a tire or selecting jogging shoes.
6. In an expository paragraph or two, explain some of the reasons why rock stars or other entertainers such as Bob Geldorf are sometimes able to make a major political impact on a society.
7. Examine the following excerpt from *Dombey and Son,* in which Charles Dickens argues that the building of a railroad (likened in the first line to an "earthquake") has a destructive effect on society. List the specific evidence that Dickens provides to support his claim that the "progress" usually associated with the railroad in the nineteenth century is really nothing but "dire disorder."

    The first shock of a great earthquake had . . . rent the whole neighborhood to its center. Traces of its course were visible on every side. Houses were knocked down; streets broken through and stopped; deep pits and trenches dug in the ground. . . . Here, a chaos of carts, overthrown and jumbled together, lay topsy-turvy at the bottom of a steep unnatural hill; there, confused treasures of iron soaked and rusted in something that had accidentally become a pond. . . . There were a hundred thousand shapes and substances of incompleteness . . . burrowing in the earth, aspiring in the air, mouldering in the water, and unintelligible as any dream. Hot springs and fiery eruptions, the usual attendants upon earthquakes, lent their contributions of confusion to the scene. Boiling water hissed and heaved within dilapidated walls; whence, also, the glare and roar of flames came issuing forth; and mounds of ashes blocked up rights of way, and wholly changed the law and custom of the neighborhood.

In short, the yet unfinished and unopened Railroad was in progress; and, from the very core of all this dire disorder, trailed smoothly away, upon its mighty course of civilization and improvement.

8. Form a conclusion about neighborhood zoning laws, mass transit, acid rain, or some other issue, and then organize the evidence into an essay that supports your conclusion.

USING THE WRITING TYPES

The four basic types of nonfiction prose will usually appear in combination, although one type probably will dominate according to your purpose in a specific essay. Experienced writers know, however, that using types in combination with each other will strengthen their essays—that argumentation can make use of exposition as part of the supporting evidence, that exposition is often further clarified by description, and so on.

Each of the following essays, written by students, uses a dominant writing type in combination with other types to achieve a specific purpose. By way of review, notice that each essay contains the elements essential to effective writing: thesis statement, topic sentences, specific support, and conclusion. You may wish to look back at these essays from time to time as you work through the text and write essays of your own.

Student Essay #1: Narration

Notice that the unifying concept expressed in the thesis statement of this narrative is an impression the writer formed about the events recounted. The progression is chronological, and the impression is reinforced through the use of description.

HUMAN DIGNITY DENIED

When I visited Mr. Kessler, a neighbor of mine, in the hospital, I began to realize that a sick person is sometimes treated by hospital personnel as if he or she were no more important than a piece of furniture. I found this attitude in one of the nurses, whom I knew from my church. Even worse, I found it also in Mr. Kessler's doctor.

Though a stroke had left Mr. Kessler in a condition something like a piece of furniture—he could not see or speak, and he was paralyzed from the neck down—he did not deserve the impersonal treatment he got from Mrs. Kraft, the nurse. I went to the hospital to visit him after he had been removed from the intensive care unit. I decided to sit by his bed for a few minutes, just to give him some moral support. During the half hour I was there, Mrs. Kraft, whom I had known from church as a normally kind person, appeared. She greeted me warmly. Then, as if she were straightening the cushions on a sofa, she rearranged the pillows under Mr. Kessler's head so that the tube in his mouth was better positioned. Raising his head with her left hand, she plumped up the pillow with her right. Then, instead of gently letting his head down again, she simply withdrew her hand and let his head drop.

A few minutes later, Dr. Cox came in. Without a word to me or to the patient, he briskly placed his thumb on Mr. Kessler's eye and pushed up the eyelid. The doctor's manner suggested that he might as well have been readjusting a loose button on an upholstered cushion. Dr. Cox left as swiftly as he had entered. Neither he nor Mrs. Kraft had noticed the empty intravenous fluid bottle or the wilting flowers in need of water beside the bed.

I left a few minutes later. Stopping at the nurse's desk on the way out, I mentioned the empty IV bottle to Mrs. Kraft, but I said nothing about the flowers. Mrs. Kraft, however, was engrossed in a Rosemary Rogers novel and, without looking up, muttered, "I'll see to it."

EXERCISES

1. What is the writer's purpose in this narrative? What, specifically, is she informing her audience about?
2. Identify the thesis statement. What is the writer's attitude toward the people in the narrative? How does she suggest this attitude?
3. Briefly explain what happened, where, to whom, when, and why.
4. Identify the topic sentence of each body paragraph. How does each topic sentence help guide the organization of the narrative?
5. How does description enhance the overall impression of the narrative? Which descriptive elements are particularly effective? Why?

Student Essay #2: Description

This essay is description, but you will also notice that the writer uses narration to help develop his attitude toward his topic as suggested in the thesis statement.

GEOMETRY IN THE DEAN'S OFFICE

When I wanted to get permission to move out of a dormitory and into a private apartment with three friends, I was told that I had to get the approval of the dean of students. The office and the dean looked so rigid that I immediately knew that my request would be turned down.

Dean Pullman's office was arranged for the love of geometry, not for a visitor's comfort. In the front half of the office were four straight-backed armchairs—all the joints were perfect right angles—two against opposite walls. All of the chairs were at right angles to the dean's huge, rectangular desk. Once seated, I could not face him without turning awkwardly in the chair. So, twisting unnaturally in the hard wooden seat, I saw that each item on the desk was geometrically arranged. There were no papers on the dust-free rectangular glass that covered his desk top. As if to give geometrical balance to that top, a dictionary (still wrapped in cellophane) was set directly opposite the telephone. The dean sat squarely behind the desk.

Dean Pullman looked as cold, hard, and exact as his furniture. His thin gray hair seemed cemented in place, with no two hairs crossing. He looked like a man as lively as a Calvin Coolidge—many years dead. His well-polished glasses revealed no speck of dust, and his clear gray eyes never blinked. I thought to myself that the taxidermist had done a good job. Below the dean's glasses and around the corners of his mouth ran lines probably formed from years of scowling. His suit, like his furniture, was a solid dark brown. Even though he was seated, his coat was completely buttoned, and it had been pulled and straightened so that no fold or wrinkle appeared. His spotless white shirt looked starched, and a solid brown tie, which might have been made from the same material as his suit, lay flat and straight against the shirt front. He didn't move or speak when I came in. His hands were folded on his desk top lightly, as if he feared smudging the polished glass.

Dean Pullman turned down my request with a soft monosyllable, "no." As I left his office, I imagined him rising to dust the chair I had sat in and straighten it ever so slightly. It was with intense pleasure that I dropped a crumpled chewing gum wrapper in his doorway as I stepped out.

EXERCISES

1. Discuss the writer's purpose in this descriptive essay.
2. Identify the thesis statement and the dominant impression.
3. Does the dominant impression serve as the selection principle for the detail? Explain how. Do you find detail that does not support the dominant impression?
4. Identify the topic sentence for each body paragraph. How does each reinforce the thesis? Do you find detail in a body paragraph that does not support its topic sentence?
5. Although most of the essay consists of a description of the dean and his office, there is also a narrative element. Briefly summarize what happened, what the narrative is about.

Student Essay #3: Exposition

This essay is primarily exposition, but you will also notice some descriptive and narrative elements that help the writer achieve his purpose.

MONSTER WATCH

Whether through fear or curiosity, people have long been fascinated by monsters. Each year, there are a number of accounts of sightings of the yeti, Tibet's Abominable Snowman, and Big Foot, an apelike creature that reportedly haunts the California redwood country. Yet the most famous creature is Scotland's Loch Ness Monster ("Nessie"), and the number of sightings each year (coupled with some rather convincing photographs) has resulted in serious scientific inquiry. When I visited Loch Ness last year, I learned of two scientific theories that attempt to explain the existence of this creature.

Even in the bright summer sunlight, Loch Ness is a foreboding place. The loch itself stretches and winds for miles, and its waters are cloudy, a result of the peat that permeates it. The cloudiness of the water is significant for the first theory: that prehistoric sea creatures were trapped in the loch by earth shifts that sealed their passageway to the ocean. Over the centuries, these creatures adapted to fresh water, but were concealed from man's eyes by the peat in the water and by the loch's isolated geographic position. The trailers that house the Loch Ness Inquiry surround the loch, and I was shown a number of pictures that testify to the existence of a large-bodied, long-necked, small-headed creature that looks very much like the prehistoric plesiosaur. The most interesting of these was taken at night in 1936, and although the picture is murky, a rather large creature is visible.

The second theory is also credible, though not nearly so exotic as the first. Some scientists claim that the monster is really a giant squid, similar to those that inhabit the ocean depths. It, too, was allegedly trapped by earth shifts. The squid, these scientists claim, is used to darkness and would have little trouble navigating in the loch's murky waters. Again, an assortment of pictures lends credibility to this theory.

Proponents of both theories agree on one thing: there is more than one monster in the loch. Many scientists claim that nine individual creatures would be necessary to continue the species in an area the size of Loch Ness. This multiple monster idea helps explain why there have been simultaneous sightings at different ends of the lake, some of which go back to the ninth century.

Whether or not "Nessie" exists is still open to debate. And if it does, it is still uncertain which theory, if either, is correct. After seeing the evidence, my fascination with the unknown has been further aroused, and I would be the last person to rule out the existence of the Loch Ness Monster.

EXERCISES

1. What is the writer's purpose in this essay? What, specifically, is the writer attempting to explain or clarify?
2. Identify the thesis statement. Does it reflect the writer's purpose?
3. How does the writer's purpose affect the organization of the essay?
4. Identify the topic sentences of each body paragraph. How do these sentences serve the writer's purpose?

5. Explain how the use of description enhances the writer's expository purpose. Which descriptive elements are particularly effective? Why?
6. Identify any elements of narration that you find. How do these contribute to the exposition?
7. Why does the writer introduce the yeti and Big Foot?
8. Is this an effective expository essay? Why, or why not? Would you make greater use of description or narration to further the exposition? Explain.

Student Essay #4: Argumentation

The following essay is essentially argumentation, although the writer uses elements of exposition and narration to support the argument. Notice how the introduction identifies the basis for the writer's stand.

THERE'S NO BUSINESS LIKE SHOW BUSINESS

The American public is in danger of losing one of its great institutions, the theater. This doesn't mean that Broadway no longer boasts comedies, dramas, and musicals in its many theaters. Rather, it means that entrance to them is confined to an elite group able to afford the outrageous prices of tickets. Such exclusivity especially penalizes students, whose education—whenever possible and regardless of their majors—should certainly expose them to an art form as old as modern man himself.

During a recent visit to New York to see some friends, I decided to spend an evening on the "Great White Way." Anticipating transport to another time, another place, I wandered about Broadway faced with the choice of a score of productions. I finally settled on *Les Misérables,* a hit musical based on the novel by Victor Hugo. Believing that I would be able to pick up one ticket for the performance that night (a weekday and therefore with greater availability of tickets), I approached the box office only to be staggered by the prices, which ranged from $22.50 to $45.00. I departed and tried two other musicals, which were only slightly less expensive. Musicals, I concluded, were too rich for my blood. Comedies and dramas, however, were bound to be much more affordable.

I was wrong. Ticket prices for comedies, such as *Brighton Beach Memoirs* or a revival of *Barefoot in the Park,* still ranged from the low teens to $30. Those for dramas such as *Benefactors* or *The Cherry Orchard* were about the same. In addition, I realized that most people had to pay for transportation into the city, parking, and dinner. It began to dawn on me that an evening at the theater for two could run between $100 and $200. And for a student such as me, even doing it with a stop at McDonald's and a bus ride back to my friends' house outside the city was still way beyond my budget.

My disappointment was lessened, however, by my belief that I still had an option in the form of Lincoln Center, whose costs are reduced by some assistance from the state. Walking the twenty-odd blocks from Broadway to the center, I felt grateful that I had such an option. Wrong again. I found ticket prices to be only slightly less than those of many of the Broadway productions; apparently, the amount of public funding is inadequate to offset rising production costs. Anger mingled with curiosity compelled me also to check ticket prices for the opera while at Lincoln Center. They, it turned out, dwarfed even the prices for Broadway musicals.

Before you assume that such high costs are common only to New York, guess again. I have since found that this kind of price scale is repeated in my hometown, Washington, D.C., whose Kennedy Center also seems to cater largely to the economic elite. Friends have since confirmed that theater in their various parts of the country is, for them, equally out of reach.

The elitist caste of American theater today means that entire generations will be brought up to believe that the drama is to be equated with television series like *Dallas,* that comedy means a thirty-minute sitcom on CBS, and that the musical is alive and well in a Bruce Springsteen video. Something can, however, be done: the establishment of subsidized theaters similar to those that abound in many parts of Europe, where the theater is viewed as an art form. But if we continue in this country to allow theater to be reduced to a business, we will be depriving an overwhelming number of Americans of something that for thousands of years has been accessible and civilizing.

EXERCISES

1. What is the purpose of the argument?
2. Identify the thesis statement. How does the thesis establish the essential elements of the argument? How does the thesis help organize the argument in the rest of the essay?
3. Identify the topic sentence in each body paragraph. How are these topic sentences related to the argument?
4. Elements of exposition and narration appear in the development of the essay. Identify them.
5. How do the expository elements contribute to the argument?
6. How do the narrative elements contribute to the argument?
7. Do you find the argument convincing? Explain.

SEEING YOUR AUDIENCE

Writing, a scholar once noted, is an inward craft that must look outward. Implicit in this assertion are two points that you, as a writer, should keep in mind: (1) that *whom* you are writing for—your audience—is the ultimate judge of anything you write, and (2) that your ability to envision a specific audience will affect your manner of presentation.

You can appreciate the importance of an audience by examining its role in your conversations. Over the past week, you may have discussed a number of subjects such as love, equality of the sexes, a particular college course, or even nuclear disarmament with your friends. You would not, however, talk about these subjects with your seven-year-old brother, Billy, because he would not be interested, nor would he have sufficient knowledge to understand them. Instead, your conversations with Billy might more realistically deal with sports or "Spiderman" or a recent visit to the zoo, thus reflecting your understanding of his interests and the limits of his experience. When talking, you also tailor your manner of presentation—that is, your language—to your audience. Think, for example, how you would express yourself to your roommate after receiving a grade lower than you anticipated and then how you would articulate your complaint to the professor involved.

Your success in conversation shows your ability to analyze a specific audience and to use that analysis to help you select language *appropriate* to that audience. Your analytic skill in conversation is one that you are probably not especially conscious of, simply because you use it each time you speak with someone. Nevertheless, it is central to effective communication.

The same holds true in writing. But if you do not know who your audience is, you are ignorant of what would or would not be appropriate and are thus unable to anticipate and deal with possible negative reactions. Of course, many writing situations will specify a particular audience. In college, for example, your instructor may tell you to write for your classmates, or the National Audubon Society, or the Policemen's Benevolent League. Or she may indicate that she is your audience, and that she will approach your essay in the role of an unbiased, generally educated reader. And in your professional life, you can usually assume that your audience is your boss or a managerial committee. Even when a particular audience is named, however, you still need to analyze that audience carefully in order to choose an appropriate means of expression and not offend needlessly.

ANALYZING AN AUDIENCE

Communicating effectively with an audience requires that you consider what gives it a specific identity. Your initial goal should be to gain an appreciation of an audience's probable interests and attitudes, for these will be central to what you hope to achieve. Don't, however, believe that you should tell an audience what you think it wants to hear; audiences are generally very good at spotting intellectual dishonesty. But if you are going to write an essay advocating the expansion of day-care centers for an audience of conservative county politicians, your understanding of their point of view and political convictions will at least enable you to avoid alienating them unnecessarily, and it may also help you to get a fair hearing.

Analyzing an audience is especially important, not only to gauge its interests but also to understand its unique perspectives and thus its particular biases. The term "bias" refers to an audience's opinion or outlook; all of us have certain biases that reflect our backgrounds, perspectives, and concerns. As a writer, your analysis of an audience's bias will help keep your writing appropriate. For instance, many audiences would probably be interested in an essay on unemployment, but each will examine it in relation to its own experience and concerns. Thus, if you were addressing a group of auto industry workers, you would need to consider how they perceive unemployment and what effect unemployment has had on their community. You might, for example, choose especially tactful language to introduce the issue of foreign imports.

Bear in mind that people usually belong to an organization because they share certain concerns and attitudes about a particular issue. Sierra Club members, for example, are vitally concerned with conservation, National Organization for Women members with equal rights for the sexes, and National Rifle Association members with laws governing guns. An audience's philosophical affiliation helps you to select an appropriate subject and the appropriate way to handle that subject. It also presents you with certain challenges, not the least of which is the likelihood that, because of its bias, the audience will be well informed on the issue you are discussing. If you appear to know less about the subject than does the audience, your chances of achieving your purpose will be small.

Despite the fact that everyone has biases, occasionally the question of bias is irrelevant. Should you, for instance, write an essay explaining how automobile manufacturers spend millions of dollars each year on unnecessary style changes while ignoring the need for passive safety devices, you are addressing the audience in its role as consumer, not as members of B'nai B'rith or the National Education Association. If you somehow attempted to infuse bias-related material into this subject, that material would most likely detract from—because it is irrelevent to—your purpose, as in the case of the student who, having discussed Polish folk dancing, concluded by railing against Soviet domination of his forefathers' homeland.

Below is a list of questions that will assist you in analyzing an audience's background:

1. How old is the audience?
2. Is the audience made up primarily of males or females?
3. What is the audience's economic background?
4. What is its religious affiliation(s)?
5. What is its ethnic orientation?
6. What is its educational level?
7. What professions does it include?
8. Does the audience have a particular organizational or political affiliation?
9. What philosophical biases might this audience have?
10. What role(s) could you assign to this audience that would make its bias irrelevent?

Considerations of audience:

- *Understand* your audience's interests, perspectives, and biases.
- *Evaluate* your topic in relation to your audience.
- *Adapt* your topic, examples, and language so that they are appropriate to your audience.

EXERCISE

Each of the five selections that follow succeeds in part because its author tailored the presentation to a specific audience. Examine the excerpts carefully and respond to the following questions:

1. Using the audience analysis questions previously detailed, identify the audience each writer was addressing.
2. What, specifically, seems especially appropriate about the author's tailoring of subject and language for that audience? Cite examples.
3. What philosophical biases might the authors have assumed on the parts of their audiences? What were probably the bases for these assumptions?

A. The following passage is from Bruno Bettelheim's *The Uses of Enchantment: The Meaning and Importance of Fairy Tales.*

As an educator and therapist of severely disturbed children, my main task was to restore meaning to their lives. This work made it obvious to me that if children were reared so that life was meaningful to them, they would not need special help. I was confronted with the problem of deducing what experiences in a child's life are most suited to promote his ability to find meaning in his life; to endow life in general with more meaning. Regarding this task, nothing is more important than the impact of parents and others who take care of the child; second in importance is our cultural heritage, then transmitted to the child in the right manner. When children are young, it is literature that carries such information best.

B. This excerpt is from Linda Brent's preface to her account of her life in slavery, *Incidents in the Life of a Slave Girl.*

When I first arrived in Philadelphia, Bishop Pain advised me to publish a sketch of my life, but I told him I was altogether incompetent to such an undertaking. Though I have improved my mind somewhat since that time, I still remain of the same opinion; but I trust my motives will excuse what might otherwise seem presumptuous. I have not written my experiences in order to attract attention to myself; on the contrary, it would have been more pleasant to me to have been silent about my own history. Neither do I care to excite sympathy for my own sufferings. But I do earnestly desire to arouse the women of the North to a realizing sense of the condition of two millions of women at the South, still in bondage, suffering what I suffered, and most of them far worse. I want to add my testimony to that of abler pens to convince the people of the Free States what Slavery really is. Only by experience can any one realize how deep, and dark, and foul is that pit of abominations. May the blessing of God rest on this imperfect effort in behalf of my persecuted people!

C. The passage that follows is from a scholarly work by Walt Wolfram and Ralph W. Fasold, *The Study of Social Dialects in American English.*

Although interference from a foreign language may be quite obvious in the speech of first-generation immigrants, straightforward interference from another language is of little or no significance for the second- and third-generation immigrant. In fact, the occurrences of this interference are so rare that we have referred to them as matters of *vestigial interference.* The lack of straightforward interference does not, however, rule out the possibility of a more subtle substratal effect on language. For example, Labov observes that the vowel patterns for the Jewish and Italian communities do not coincide with that of other New Yorkers, and reasons that this may be because of a *substratum language* effect from the languages spoken by previous generations. With reference to the vowel systems of these two groups, Labov concludes that "ethnic differentiation is seen to be a more powerful factor than social class, though both exist in addition to a marked stylistic variation" (1966: 306).

D. The following excerpt is from *A Vindication of the Rights of Women,* by Mary Wollstonecraft. It was published in 1792.

My own sex, I hope, will excuse me, if I treat them like rational creatures, instead of flattering their *fascinating* graces, and viewing them as if they were in a state of perpetual childhood, unable to stand alone. I earnestly wish to point out in what true dignity and human happiness consists—I wish to persuade women to endeavour to acquire strength, both of mind and body, and to convince them that the soft phrases, susceptibility of heart, delicacy of sentiment, and refinement of taste, are almost synonymous with epithets of weakness, and that those beings who are only the objects of pity and that kind of love, which has been termed its sister, will soon become objects of contempt.

Dismissing then those pretty feminine phrases, which the men condescendingly use to soften our slavish dependence, and despising that weak elegancy of mind, exquisite sensibility, and sweet docility of manners, supposed to be the sexual characteristics of the weaker vessel, I wish to shew that elegance is inferior to virtue, that the first object of laudable ambition is to obtain a character as a human being, regardless of the distinction of sex. . . .

E. In the following excerpt from *Walden,* Henry David Thoreau explains why he went to live in the woods by himself.

I went to the woods because I wished to live deliberately, to front only the essential facts of life, and to see if I could not learn what it had to teach, and not, when I came to die, discover that I had not lived. I did not wish to live what was not life, living is so dear; nor did I wish to practise resignation, unless it was quite necessary. I wanted to live deep and suck out all the marrow of life, to live so sturdily and Spartan-like as to put to rout all that was not life, to cut a broad swath and shave close, to drive life into a corner, and reduce it to its lowest terms, and, if it proved to be mean, why then to get the whole and genuine meanness of it, and publish its meanness to the world; or if it were sublime, to know it by experience, and be able to give a true account of it in my next excursion. For most men, it appears to me, are in a strange uncertainty about it, whether it is of the devil or of God, and have *somewhat hastily* concluded that it is the chief end of man here to "glorify God and enjoy him forever."

APPROACHING YOUR AUDIENCE

Analyzing your audience will enable you to decide how best to present your material. Your first consideration in approaching your audience is to determine how familiar the audience is with your subject, and therefore how much explanatory material you will need to provide so that it can follow your discussion. If you assume too much knowledge on the audience's part, you run the risk of writing *above* it and thus losing it. But if you give it information it already has, the audience may feel insulted and conclude that you are writing *down* to it.

Dealing with this problem is simple, providing that you pause during writing and revising to remember whom you are addressing. For example, if you plan to write an expository essay for a general audience on types of sailboats, you probably would not refer to a "ketch" or a "sloop" without explaining the design of these sailboat types, nor would you use highly technical sailing jargon. For an audience of sailing enthusiasts, however, you could legitimately assume a degree of expertise, and you could use technical boating terminology freely—in fact, your audience might feel insulted if you bothered to explain "ketch" or "sloop." Similarly, if you were arguing that an IBM personal computer is superior to the latest Apple model, you would use terms such as "scrolling" and "disks" without explanation if you were addressing persons who were already familiar with personal computers. But if your audience were generally unfamiliar with these devices, you would need to provide simple definitions of most technical terms.

Your second consideration in approaching your audience involves the degree of formality you choose to use. Formal usage is usually marked by at least some of the following qualities: intricate sentences, use of the passive voice, learned word choice, and absence of the first-person singular ("I") point of view, for which the first-person plural ("we") or the third-person ("one") is substituted. Serious occasions, such as those pertaining to death and war, are normally treated formally. For example, a death notice in a newspaper, an argument for erecting a war memorial, and an essay or editorial in observance of the anniversary of the bombing of Hiroshima are likely to be written with formal usage. Critiques of literary, dramatic, and musical productions are also often written formally. Here is an example of a formal passage from an essay by poet and critic T.S. Eliot:

> Mr. Joyce's book has been out long enough for no more general expression of praise, or expostulation with its detractors, to be necessary; and it has not been out long enough for any attempt at a complete measurement of its place and significance to be possible. All that one can usefully do at this time, and it is a great deal to do, for such a book, is to elucidate any aspect of the book—and the number of aspects is indefinite—which has not yet been fixed.
>
> *"Ulysses*, Order, and Myth"

Informal usage usually has at least some of the following characteristics: relatively short, compact sentences; frequent use of the active voice; simple diction; and the use of the first-person singular point of view. In the following paragraph, author and critic Langston Hughes employs informal usage to describe an early experience with religion:

> Then I was left all alone on the mourners' bench. My aunt came and knelt at my knees and cried, while players and songs swirled all around me in the little church. The whole congregation prayed for me alone, in a mighty wail of moans and voices. And I kept waiting serenely for Jesus, waiting, waiting— but he didn't come. I wanted to see him, but nothing happened to me. Nothing! I wanted something to happen to me, but nothing happened.
>
> *The Big Sea: An Autobiography*

As a general rule, you will capture the widest audience by striving for a manner of presentation that is neither too formal nor too informal. Although some less experienced writers seem to believe that formality "sounds" impressive, it too frequently leads to wordiness and pretentiousness—characteristics that can bore and sometimes annoy an audience. At the same time, however, you should avoid being carried away by informality. Slang, dialect, and abbreviations or symbols are usually appropriate only for writing to a close friend or in keeping a personal journal.

Ultimately, of course, the matching of your subject and purpose with your audience will determine the level of formality you will use. Subjects such as death or war, and purposes such as those inherent in a history term paper or an argument concerning the creation of a Palestinian state generally do not lend themselves to highly informal presentations. On the other hand, a highly formal defense of the new morality or nude beaches probably would be inappropriate. Readers will expect a manner of presentation that they are comfortable with. You can best gauge expectations by carefully examining what *you* know about the audience and what you know about the subject and what you intend to do with this knowledge.

A third consideration when approaching your audience is to choose words that will give your subject an appropriate *tone*. Tone reveals your attitude not only toward your subject but also toward your audience. Just as you show anger, disappointment, happiness, cynicism, and many other feelings when you talk, these attitudes can be projected when you write.

Although much more will be said about word choice and tone later in the text, for now be aware that one of your many tasks is making sure that your tone is appropriate to your subject and audience and that it complements your purpose. Thus, a paper on the horrors of a Nazi concentration camp that employed a light, frivolous tone would seem tasteless; a letter to your beloved that sounded like a chemistry lab report would be offensive; and a letter of application for a job that began with "Hi" would be ludicrous. Furthermore, remember that while sarcasm or tongue-in-cheek humor might be appropriate and even effective when addressing a sympathetic or well-informed audience, an unsympathetic audience might not understand it.

Your final consideration in approaching *any* audience is to treat it with the respect that you would desire were you part of it. You do this by carefully revising your essay to make sure that there are no errors of fact, vague wording, contradictions, or anything else that would act as a barrier between your thoughts and the audience's reception of them. And you check your paper carefully for errors in grammar, usage, spelling, and punctuation. Do not reduce your reader to proofreader.

EXERCISES

1. Assume you are writing an argumentative essay advocating the abolition of handguns to be presented to the local chapter of the National Rifle Association. What could you logically assume about that audience in relation to your subject? Your point of view? The amount of supporting information you would need to provide? The appropriateness of technical terminology?

2. Now assume that you will take the same subject and tailor it for a college audience. How would you analyze that audience? What would you assume about its members? How would you change the essay before presenting it to an organization called Victims of Violent Crimes?

3. Choose a subject for an essay, determine a purpose, and envision three separate audiences. Specify how your analyses of these audiences would determine questions of the amount of information you would provide, the level of formality you would use, and the tone you would strive for.

REVISION EXERCISE

Revise the following letter to make it informal.

Dear Sir or Madame,

   It is incumbent upon me to respond to your recently advertised position for summer employment concerning the need of your respected company for a cashier. It is my privilege to inform you that I have sufficient qualifications based on previous positions of employment and mathematical course work that I can assume my availability for your position will meet with your expeditious and confirmatory response.

   Thus, one can but await a response—affirmative, one most surely hopes—at your earliest convenience, in fulfillment and confirmation of my expressed hope for gainful occupation in your employ.

Sincerely yours,

April-Dawn Hooverdale

3

Moving from Subject to Topic

In chapter two, subject was underscored as one of the three important elements to consider early in the writing process. However, if you were to try to write about all aspects of a subject, you would quickly find yourself writing a book—and a long one at that. *Subject* is simply a general area of knowledge or experience. If you were to try to write all about the subject of, say, "tennis," you would find yourself tracing its history, cataloging its rules, explaining the fundamental tennis strokes, distinguishing between types of tennis rackets, examining various tennis associations, and exploring many additional components that together make up "tennis." And if you were somehow able to pack all these components into a twenty- or even a thirty-page paper, its content would be so general as to have little value for your audience.

Obviously, then, finding a subject is only a starting point. Before you begin writing about "tennis" or any other subject, you have to decide what, specifically, you wish to treat within the general area of the subject, how you wish to shape that material, and what your purpose is. In other words, you must explore the subject and select an aspect of it that is manageable and controllable—what we call a *topic*. A topic is the specific focus or point that you, the writer, give to a subject. The following example indicates the difference between the subject and the topic:

SUBJECT	TOPIC
tennis	The basic differences between wooden and metal tennis rackets

Any subject can lead to a number of topics suitable for an essay. The example below illustrates some additional topics derived from the subject "tennis":

SUBJECT	TOPIC
tennis	how to select tennis shoes
	basic tennis equipment
	a memorable tennis match
	advantages of indoor tennis

Note that a topic is more specific than a subject. In the examples above, the topics sharpen the focus of the subject.

Because experience and perception differ from person to person, there is no one method that all writers use in arriving at topics. Some writers may begin by listing any idea that comes to mind; some may simply jot down thoughts and the feelings they engender in a random manner; others may use their own writing as well as reading and observation to help them recall and reflect on personal experiences; and still others may begin with a more structured approach by asking themselves basic questions about a general subject or by discussing it with someone else. Whatever the mechanics of their search, all writers proceed with the knowledge that the process of finding topics within experience is one of exploring a subject and then of sharpening the focus.

BRAINSTORMING

As the term implies, brainstorming is a solitary method of free association in which you first think of a general subject and then make a list of anything that pops into your mind in connection with it. Here is a list generated by thoughts on the general subject "disease":

DISEASE

inoculations
vaccines
colds
vitamins
AIDS
cancer
chemotherapy
hospices for the terminally ill
heart disease
nursing care
insurance
doctors' fees
medicare

Consideration of these and related ideas could eventually lead to topics concerning the need for expanding (or limiting) the government's role in health care or on the qualities that make a person a good nurse. Similarly, the general subject "war" could, through brainstorming, generate a list of related ideas:

WAR

arms
swords
tanks
missiles
disarmament
Geneva talks
Civil War
Robert E. Lee
Gettysburg
tactics
propaganda

Exploring some of these could lead to a topic concerning General Lee as a strategist or an instance of Soviet propaganda in connection with the disarmament talks.

Of course, there is a big jump between a brainstorming list and the actual emergence of a topic. Your mind helps you make that jump by focusing on certain aspects of the general subject as you list them, and perhaps by rejecting others. As your list grows, you (consciously or subconsciously) reexamine individual aspects, select those that are most promising insofar as they trigger additional, related ideas, sort them, and gradually shape them into a suitable topic. The following illustration shows a basic brainstorming process generated by the subject "animals":

ANIMALS

lions
tigers
whales   ## DOGS
raccoons
zebras   husky
dogs   golden retriever
cats   Samoyed   ## SPANIEL
apes   Old English sheepdog
horses   poodle   physical characteristics
sheep   spaniel   temperament
                 terrier   breeding
                 boxer   buying
                                feeding
                                grooming

When you are ready to impose limitations on your material, you are ready to define your *topic*. For instance, further focusing on "physical characteristics" in the above diagram may lead to an essay on "The characteristics of a champion springer spaniel" (description). Consideration of "grooming" may result in an essay on "How to groom a springer spaniel" (exposition). Additional brainstorming on "buying" may enable you to write an essay advocating "Buying a puppy from a breeder rather than from a pet store" (argumentation). And consideration of "temperament" may enable you to write on "The day my spaniel bit my rich Uncle Fred" (narration).

The process of moving from subject to topic by brainstorming is basically the same for any subject area, that is, a process of exploration and ever-sharpening focus. For example, here is a somewhat streamlined diagram illustrating the process as generated by the subject "education":

EDUCATION

at-home
preschool
primary
secondary
college
postgraduate
continuing

COLLEGE

professors
administrators
buildings
classes
grades
friends
fraternities
sororities

GRADES

great emphasis
measure progress
competition
incentive
pressure
memorize
regurgitate

TOPIC

Should we abolish the grading system at State University?

By exploring another aspect of "education" through brainstorming, we can create an entirely different topic:

EDUCATION

at home
preschool
primary
secondary
college
postgraduate
continuing

COLLEGE

professors
administrators
buildings
classes
grades
friends
fraternities
sororities

SORORITIES

socialization
sense of belonging
identity
help with studies
professional contacts

TOPIC

Why a sorority enhances career prospects for the professional woman

EXERCISES

1. Reexamine the list of aspects under "education." If additional aspects occur to you, add them to the list. Then focus your attention on one aspect and create from it a topic suitable for a 300- to 500-word essay.
2. Create a diagram similar to those above in which you employ brainstorming to evolve a topic from the general subject "music."

3. Through brainstorming, create topics from each of the following subject areas:
   a. food
   b. nature
   c. television
   d. the Olympics
   e. travel

Keep in mind these steps for reaching a topic through brainstorming:

- *Think* of a general subject.
- *List* anything that comes to mind in connection with the subject.
- *Reexamine* individual aspects of the subject.
- *Select* one that triggers additional, related ideas.
- *Sort* and *shape* them into a suitable topic.

FREEWRITING

Freewriting, another method of finding topics, is similar to brainstorming insofar as it involves putting words and phrases on paper in a spontaneous fashion. You begin by writing down seemingly random words and phrases concerning anything from a personal experience to an object or an idea found in a magazine article. In putting down the words and phrases, you may trigger related ideas and feelings. As implied by its name, freewriting removes such concerns and restrictions as logical order, form, and even grammar, spelling, and punctuation. The "freedom" from those concerns enables you to concentrate exclusively on substance.

The association of situation, ideas, and feelings common to freewriting is evident in the following student example:

> The day I got my driver's license. Cloudy. Raining. Crummy taste in mouth. Nervous stomach. Sweaty hands. DMV exam room. Crowded. People pushing. Smoking. Stale air. Loud laughter and kids crying. Waiting in line for eternity. Dirty floor, carved up desk tops. Waiting and waiting. Still in line. Candy wrappers on floor. People next to me looked poor. Dirty T-shirts. Foreigners having trouble understanding written test. Lots of luck. Everyone seems older than me. Cop graded written test. Passed. Knew I would. Studied hard for weeks. Only missed two questions. Don't know why, knew the answers. Here, said the cop. Thanks I said. He ignored me, just looked straight ahead. Next,

he mumbled. Big beer gut. Gray face. Smoking. More lines. Wait again, again, again. Cigarette butts everywhere. Wait in line for vision test. People loud, rude, nervous in line. Getting angry at waiting. Been here three hours said a scruffy looking kid. Tough. Faceless eye examiner. Passed. Go to the next line. Thank you. No response. Thanks a lot. Still no response. Big moment—driving test. Hi I said. Cop looked at me. Get in the car. Almost a growl. Thinks he's doing me a favor. Dealing with a robot. Important moment for me. Must of been for him when he was my age. Guess he doesn't remember. Why not? Driving. Doing well. Don't hit the curb when parking. Eyes front. Freedom. License. I can escape any time. New responsibilities, decisions. Money for insurance. OK cop says. Passed. One more line. Waiting. Had to get picture taken. How do I look—who cares? Not me. Palms still wet, eyes burning. Why do people smoke? Dumb. Why do they let them in DMV office? Look at the birdie. Got it. Thanks. Silence. Outside. Free at last.

Within the situation described are a number of general subjects: frustration, official behavior, growing up, impersonalization, freedom, prejudice. The day the writer got his license thus becomes a catalyst for ideas and feelings that, once discovered through freewriting, may evolve into a topic.

At this point, however, all we have is the recreation of a situation and loosely associated thoughts. To develop a topic requires examining one of the subject areas, sorting details, and then extracting those that are closely related to that subject. For example, there are over eighty phrases, details, and bits of information in the freewriting passage. By examining the passage, you will see that some of these seem related to one major subject area, some to others. By focusing on one of these subjects, say, the general behavior of the licensing officials, you can select details from the freewriting that will help you explore that subject, sharpen your focus, and shape the material into a topic. A diagram depicting this process may look something like this:

SITUATION

The

Day   SUBJECTS

            Growing up   OFFICIAL
I   impersonalization   BEHAVIOR
            freedom   nonprofessional
Got   official behavior   setting   TOPIC
            prejudice   poorly regulated
My   anger   administration   The lack of
                                  discourteous   professionalism
Driver's   police   in the local
                                  bored officials   Department of
License   Motor Vehicles

Consideration of other details related to the general subject "official behavior" could just as easily have led to topics such as "the mind-numbing routine of the DMV official" or "are our unprofessional DMV officers licensing unqualified drivers?"

As you can see, a major advantage in using freewriting—as with self-brainstorming—is its lack of form, which, in turn, fosters free association. You may wish to experiment with freewriting in an effort to find a means of exploring subjects and sharpening focus that works best for you.

EXERCISES

1. Reexamine the freewriting passage above and list all the subject areas it contains. Choose one and then identify all the closely related details that help you explore the subject.
2. Repeat exercise one, this time by focusing on a different subject area. After identifying appropriate details, construct a table beginning with the situation and culminating in a topic.
3. Create a freewriting passage that explores an experience you have had. List all subject areas it helps you uncover. Then, by repeating the process of narrowing focus discussed above, evolve at least three topics from one of those subjects.

Keep in mind the following steps for reaching a topic through freewriting:

- *Consider* a situation.

- Without concern for order, grammar, or spelling, *write* down related ideas and feelings that the situation aroused.

- *Examine* these thoughts to find those that are closely associated and can be shaped into a topic, and *sift* and *develop* appropriate details.

KEEPING A PERSONAL JOURNAL

Another means of discovering essay topics is to keep a personal journal, that is, a regular record of your experiences. If you get into the habit every day or at least a few times a week of recording what you have seen, heard, felt, and considered, reflecting briefly on the *why* or *how* of your experience, you will have a rich source of material and a head start on calling to mind details essential for developing topics for your writing. Insofar as a journal entry functions as a means of helping you evolve topics and because its audience is generally only you, the writer, it is similar to freewriting, though with greater structure and focus.

The following entry is from a student's journal:

> Friday I got lost in the College of Architecture classroom building, of all places. I had gone there to find Mary. I was supposed to meet her for coffee right after her two o'clock class . . . Room 2101A. I wandered around for fifteen minutes—and got misleading directions from two students and a janitor—before I found her room. By then she thought I had forgotten her, and she had left. At least now I know that the stupid building is arranged so that all the odd-numbered rooms are on the west side, and the even-numbered on the east. And that the "A" and "C" corridors are on the west, and the "B" and "D" corridors on the east. What a mess!

Consideration of the information in the journal entry reveals a number of possible topics that the student may draw from it:

> A confused classroom layout
> Friends who do not wait
> How to give clear directions
> Feeling enslaved by the clock

In addition to providing a continuing source of material, keeping a journal helps instill writing discipline by providing an impetus to write regularly. Through the ages writers have recognized the value of recording immediate impressions as a means of helping them reflect on the significance of experience. The following excerpt from the journal of John Woolman, an eighteenth-century Quaker preacher and writer, illustrates how a personal journal can be a source of reflective and insightful topics.

> . . . going to a neighbour's house, I saw, on the way, a robin sitting on her nest, and as I came near she went off, but, having young ones, flew about, and with many cries expressed her concern for them; I stood and threw stones at her, till, one striking her, she fell down dead: at first I was pleased with the exploit, but after a few minutes was seized with horror, as having, in a sportive way, killed an innocent creature while she was careful for her young: I beheld her lying dead, and thought those young ones, for which she was so careful, must now perish for want of their dam to nourish them; and, after some painful considerations on the subject, I climbed up the tree, took all the young birds, and killed them; supposing that better than to leave them to pine away and die miserably: and believed, in this case, that scripture-proverb was fulfilled, "The tender mercies of the wicked are cruel."
>
> *The Journal of John Woolman*

Woolman's focus on a single incident and its vivid details enables him to relive a thoughtless boyhood prank and to recreate a sense of disgust. Out of a painful lesson learned through experience he evolves a provocative topic: man's unsuccessful effort to reconcile cruelty with his conscience.

A personal journal can serve as a rich source of writing topics. In keeping your journal:

- *Write* entries that focus on single, recent events.
- *Reflect* on what you have written. Identify your feelings concerning the event.
- *Study* an entry to find a writing topic based on a generalization about the experience recorded in the entry.

EXERCISES

1. Even though you may not now be keeping a personal journal, write a journal entry similar to the two above in which you focus on one event—however minor—that you have experienced today or within the last week.
2. Reflect on what you have written. Have you learned anything from the event or experienced a particular feeling because of it?
3. After studying your entry, formulate a topic from it that you could use to write a 300- to 500-word essay.

TAPPING YOUR IMAGINATION AND MEMORY

In moving from subject to topic, your goal is to find an idea that is worth writing about. One of the best means of discovering good ideas is to tap your own experiences of reading, watching, and listening. Some of the knowledge you have gained from these experiences you have already assimilated, or made part of your personal body of knowledge, and other experience is easily accessible. Among the resources available are books, periodicals, encyclopedias, other library resources of all kinds, lectures and speeches, plays, radio and television programs, and movies.

One way to narrow subjects is simply to use these resources to jog your memory of personal experiences. For example, one student spent fifteen minutes thumbing through a dictionary and then compiled the following list of words that held some importance for her:

art	automobile	bourbon
cafeteria	gun	king
optometrist	pizza	restaurant
umbrella	vacation	zoo

Thinking about these words triggered the student's imagination and memory. The word "umbrella" prompted her to recall attending her grandfather's funeral on a rainy day and ultimately led her to write an essay analyzing changes in the way the members of her family got along with one another after the death.

Jogging your memory can be just as effective in relation to specific texts. Thus, if your art history professor were to assign a paper on ideas in painting, you might look through your text for that class; jot down words like "abstract" and "modern," which would bring to mind a Picasso exhibit you had just attended; and then write an essay on your difficulty in understanding modern art. Similarly, simply looking through an encyclopedia; the table of contents in magazines like *Newsweek, Time, Consumer Reports, Smithsonian, Psychology Today,* and *Travel and Leisure;* or the subject headings in a library's list of holdings and in periodical indexes like the *New York Times Index* and the *Reader's Guide to Periodical Literature* are all ways to get a better understanding of several broad subjects, thereby allowing you to select one and narrow it effectively.

Exploring your subject can lead you to deepen or extend knowledge or beliefs that you already have. You may, for example, be reading several articles on crime in preparation for a paper assigned by your sociology or psychology professor. Reading a rape victim's account of her experience is likely to bring you closer to the subject of rape, sharpen your attitudes, and possibly provide you with statistics that would enhance your appreciation of the enormity of this problem. Your greater familiarity will help you define a topic for your paper.

Of course, you might have read the rape victim's account in passing and then seen its relevance to a current assignment. It is therefore important to keep an open mind: you may get a good idea even when you are not looking for one. Pay close attention to newspapers, magazines, television newscasts, specials, and talk shows; you may suddenly see a subject you are considering in a new light. A casual conversation with a friend might do the same. Remember that you are participating in the experiences of others—experiences that could be useful in fulfilling an assignment. (As one scholar noted, this kind of vicarious experience enables you to live "lives you have not time to live yourself," and to travel into worlds "you have not time to travel in literal time.") Ideas often come from unexpected sources, and you should never miss an opportunity to uncover a unique and interesting approach to a subject area you have been assigned.

You can find a topic by jogging your memory of personal experiences.

- Among your resources are conversations, books, periodicals, encyclopedias, other library resources, talks, plays, radio and television, movies.

- *Deepen* or *extend* your knowledge of a subject by reading or developing conversations. Make use of the experience of others.

- The greater your familiarity with a subject, the easier it will be to select a worthwhile topic.

EXERCISES

1. Leaf through a dictionary and make a list of ten words that have some personal importance to you. Examine the words carefully, and jot down the specific memories and experiences each triggers. Then, keeping in mind a course you are currently taking, choose one word you have explored and see whether you can narrow your explorations to fit an essay assignment you could receive in that course.
2. Compile an additional list (ten items) from a textbook you are using for another of your courses. Repeat exercise 1, focusing on an assignment for this particular course.
3. Think of a contemporary issue you consider especially important. Consider how your opinions and attitudes on this issue have been affected by reading, watching, and listening. Try to recall specific sources that have been instrumental in forming your opinions on this issue, and think of others that would be of additional benefit.

ASKING JOURNALISTIC QUESTIONS

The traditional questions of the journalist can help you explore a subject and make it more and more specific until you have arrived at a suitable topic. The questions are *what? who? when? where? why?* and *how?* The goal is to work toward detailed, precise answers rather than vague, general ones.

Probing a subject with any of the following questions will bring that subject into sharper focus:

> What are its characteristics?
> What does it look like?
> What makes it work?
> How does it work?
> Why does it work?

Who is involved?
When did it happen?
Where did it happen?
To whom did it happen?
Why did it happen?

There are, of course, many additional questions that you can frame, depending on the subject you are probing (*What* was the cause? *What* was the effect? *How* do you build a bridge? *When* is the best time to plant corn?).

To illustrate how the process of asking journalistic questions works, assume that you are interested in camping and that you wish to write on the subject of campsites. Applying a *what* question to the subject may generate a process that we can diagram as follows:

JOURNALISTIC QUESTION	ANSWERS
What makes a good campsite?	clean water
	relatively flat ground
	trees for shade
	available firewood
	toilet facilities
	access to electrical power
	recreation facilities

Naturally, your answers to certain questions may lead to additional questions. For example, *why* is relatively flat ground important? *Why* is access to electrical power necessary? *What* kind of recreation facilities do you envision? You should continue asking questions until your answers are specific and you are ready to assert your topic. A diagram of the process from subject to topic using journalistic questions might look as follows:

SUBJECT

C
A
M   **JOURNALISTIC QUESTION**
P   What
S   makes
         a   **ANSWERS**
I   good
T   campsite?   clean water
E   relatively flat
S   ground   **TOPIC**
                        trees for shade
                        available firewood   Seven essential
                        toilet facilities   qualities of a
                        access to electrical good campsite
                           power
                        recreation
                           facilities

In addition to helping you move from subject to topic, journalistic questions can assist you in writing a particular kind of essay. As illustrated above, the question "*What* makes a good campsite?" leads to a topic for an *expository* essay. A related but different question such as "*Why* is Bear Mountain a good campsite?" would likely generate a *description* or *argumentation* essay. Should you ask the question "*When* did I discover that camping is so much fun?" Your answer probably would result in a topic appropriate to *narration;* assuming that you did not go camping alone, you might also ask questions about *who* accompanied you and *why* they added to your enjoyment, with the answers to these questions most likely involving *description.* Finally, *how* questions such as "*How* do I set up a campsite?" will usually lead to *exposition,* particularly *process-oriented* exposition.

Journalistic questions can also guide you in developing the finished essay. In the following essay written for the op-ed page of a college newspaper, a student writer laments the encroachment of a new athletic complex on a woodland area at the edge of the campus. As you read through the essay, note how the student's efforts to answer journalistic questions helped him shape his argument.

FOR OTHER VALUES

Groundbreaking at the Barber Athletic Complex, scheduled to begin in six months and to be completed in two years, has been hailed by college and town officials as one of the most significant events in the school's recent history and as a further indication that we are about to move into "big time" athletic competition. I do not dispute the significance of the event, the fact that the complex will benefit our athletes, or that the college will reap financial rewards from the new basketball pavilion, the wrestling center, and the Olympic-size pool. I do, however, take issue with the cost—not in dollars, but in the elimination of O'Connel Park, which will be subsumed by the Barber Complex, thus taking away from the college as a whole one of the few remaining areas where students and faculty can find the tranquility that is just as essential to the academic life as is a sports complex.

The facts behind the Barber Complex are generally well known and require only the merest mention: $16 million, main basketball arena holding eight thousand spectators, potential for generating thousands of dollars in revenue for the college. The facts about the loss of O'Connel Park apparently are less well known. Situated at the south end of the campus, the land for the park was donated to the college in 1935 by Patrick O'Connel, who retired to the town following a long career as an industrialist in the northeast. In deeding the 200 acres, O'Connel lauded the humanistic tradition of the college and offered the park as a means of contributing to that tradition.

O'Connel's plan succeeded. Since 1935, the park has been the scene of countless activities central to the life of the college: a place of paths where students and faculty may walk and contemplate; a place of flowers that remind us of nature's order and beauty; a place for meeting a special friend, perhaps by the pond, or for holding a session of any of the college's many small clubs. Picnics, lounging about in the sun, the annual snowman-building contest—the list of activities in the park could go on and on, and should remind us of the magnitude of what we are about to lose. Most of all, however, we are losing a place of tranquility, a quality said by the ancients to be necessary for putting a person in touch with his inner being.

The loss would not be so dramatic were it not set against other, similar losses. My research shows that in the last ten years, the college has added six new buildings without acquiring any additional land. Beyond dollars and cents, the cost has been four quadrangles, the twenty-five acres around the old duck pond, and an area in the northwest corner of the campus that used to be called Taylor's Downs. It is now called the Sunderson Computer Center. In short, the pending loss of O'Connel Park takes away from the college its *last* park area. True, we are to receive in return something we do not have, but it is also something that many of us may not want or need.

The episode with O'Connel takes on even more troubling dimensions if we recall the failure of the administration to look for additional land. College officials have downplayed the loss of O'Connel Park as something necessitated by progress. But it seems to me that progress and tradition should be able to coexist. Our administrators, however, have chosen one over the other and in so doing are changing the fundamental nature of the college itself.

EXERCISES

1. Formulate as many journalistic questions as possible for three of the following general subjects:
   a. soap operas
   b. railroads
   c. success
   d. exams
   e. inflation
   f. volunteer army
   g. my hometown
2. Choose one of the subjects above and create a diagram showing how your journalistic questions have moved it from subject to topic.
3. Repeat exercise two, this time starting with a subject of your own choice.
4. List the specific journalistic questions asked and answered by the student writer in "For Other Values."
5. Are there other questions the writer should have asked and answered? Why? Why not?
6. Assume that the writer wanted to develop a descriptive essay on "O'Connel Park." What questions would he then need to ask and answer?

INTERVIEWING

You can also develop and shape your ideas for an essay topic by talking with another person. For instance, a conversation with a friend about why she displays a family crest on the cover of her notebook could lead you to consider such topics as snobbery, family ancestry, ethnic foods, or even the rights of adopted children to seek out their biological parents. A discussion on the pressures of exam week could lead to such topics as school grading policies, the availability and effectiveness of counseling, or the ways in which different students prepare for exams or relax and break preexam tension. Sometimes, however, talking is not enough. When you need to narrow a subject, *guiding* a conversation will more likely lead you to suitable topics for development. You guide a conversation by asking someone to expand on an idea or by asking increasingly incisive questions on a subject. The following is a set of questions you might use to explore the topic, "enduring the pressures of exam week"; the answers are from a fellow student.

INTERVIEW: NARROWING AND EXPANDING FOCUS

Q: How did you get through exam week last year?

A: With a lot of hard work.

Q: You couldn't have worked all the time. What else did you do?

A: Well, I got some physical exercise, and I slept a lot.

Q: What kind of exercise?

A: Ping-Pong. It was too cold to play tennis, which is what I prefer to do.

Q: Did you play Ping-Pong often?

A: After about every three hours of studying in the evening.

Q: What else did you do to ease pressure?

A: The only way I could really begin to feel relaxed was to study enough so I felt secure about taking each test. Then I'd reward myself by going out for a snack and maybe watching a TV show or two. I also liked to play my stereo at a low volume so it wouldn't distract me but so there was something to fill the silence and let me daydream when I paused during my reading.

As you can see, as long as the interviewer picks up on ideas voiced by the other person and encourages him or her to elaborate, the answers often become more expansive and more specific. Sometimes a repetition of the main question, slightly reworded, will serve to bring out an expanded answer, as in the interview above. With an expanded answer to work from, the interviewer could proceed by drawing out answers on what kind of music provides a person with the greatest relaxation or on what kinds of sports are also effective for relaxing, and exactly why. Thus, one or more topics, such as the following, can be drawn from the interview above:

Three effective ways to relax during exam week
How certain eating habits help me get through exam week
Music to study math by

Of course, if interviewed, other people could give a variety of perspectives on enduring exam week. For example, a guidance counselor would be likely to provide views differing from those of a student. A failing student would give answers much different from those of a successful student. And the responses of a physical education instructor would differ from those of a psychology instructor.

In the following essay from her book on adult crises, *Passages,* the reporter Gail Sheehy uses an interview to develop and shape her topic.

JAILBREAK MARRIAGE

Although the most commonplace reason women marry young is to "complete" themselves, a good many spirited young women gave another reason: "I did it to get away from my parents." Particularly for girls whose educations and privileges are limited, a *jailbreak marriage* is the usual thing. What might appear to be an act of rebellion usually turns out to be a transfer of dependence.

A lifer: that is how it felt to be Simone at 17, how it often feels for girls in authoritarian homes. The last of six children, she was caught in the nest vacated by the others and expected to "keep the family together." Simone was the last domain where her mother could play out the maternal role and where her father could exercise full control. That meant good-bye to the university scholarship.

Although the family was not altogether poor, Simone had tried to make a point of her independence by earning her own money since the age of 14. Now she thrust out her bankbook. Would two thousand dollars in savings buy her freedom?

"We want you home until you're 21."

Work, her father insisted. But the job she got was another closed gate. It was in the knitting machine firm where her father worked, an extension of his control. Simone knuckled under for a year until she met Franz. A zero. An egocentric Hungarian of pointless aristocracy, a man for whom she had total disregard. Except for one attraction. He asked her to marry him. Franz would be the getaway vehicle in her jailbreak marriage scheme: "I decided the best way to get out was to get married and divorce him a year later. That was my whole program."

Anatomy, uncontrolled, sabotaged her program. Nine months after the honeymoon, Simone was a mother. Resigning herself, she was pregnant with her second child at 20.

One day, her husband called with the news, the marker event to blast her out of the drift. His firm had offered him a job in New York City.

"Then and there, I decided that before the month was out I would have the baby, find a lawyer, and start divorce proceedings." The next five years were like twenty. It took every particle of her will and patience to defeat Franz, who wouldn't hear of a separation, and to ignore the ostracism of her family.

At the age of 25, on the seventh anniversary of her jailbreak marriage (revealed too late as just another form of entrapment), Simone finally escaped her parents. Describing the day of her decree, the divorcée sounds like so many women whose identity was foreclosed by marriage: "It was like having ten tons of chains removed from my mind, my body—the most exhilarating day of my life."

EXERCISES

1. Specifically, what questions do you think Sheehy asked in her interview? Make a list of these questions, being as exact as possible.
2. Explain how the answers to these questions helped shape the topic.
3. Explain what you believe to be Sheehy's attitude toward the topic. How might the answers provided by "Simone" have influenced Sheehy's attitude?

There are, as you now understand, many methods for finding an essay topic worth developing. As you experiment with these and perhaps other methods, you will probably find the ones that work best for you. The methods themselves are unimportant. What they lead to—what they unlock—is.

Once you have arrived at your topic, combining it with considerations of purpose and audience, your next step will be to formulate your thesis statement, the topic of our next chapter.

Some methods of moving from subject to topic include:

- Brainstorming
- Freewriting
- Keeping a personal journal
- Tapping imagination and memory
- Asking journalistic questions
- Interviewing

EXERCISES

1. The following topics are all aspects of the subject "ecology." Which of them require further exploration and sharpening or limitation in order to be suitable for a short essay?
   a. The poor quality of air in my hometown
   b. Smokers' rights
   c. Why automobile traffic should be banned in the downtown area of _____
   d. The importance of antipollution laws
   e. A history of the U.S. steel industry
   f. Famous conservationists of the twentieth century
   g. Toxic wastes: what they can do to your neighborhood
   h. Industry, not government, should clean up toxic waste dumps
   i. The ineffectiveness of federal environmental laws
   j. What nuclear war can do to you
2. Make a brief list of recreation spots. Select one item from the list and apply journalistic questions until you arrive at three writing topics suitable for a short essay.
3. Select a subject touched on in a recent conversation, and by means of interviewing explore it and narrow it to a topic.
4. Select another subject and by means of brainstorming explore it and narrow it to a topic.
5. Select still another subject and by means of freewriting explore it and narrow it to a topic.
6. Begin a personal journal. Write a paragraph on something that happened to you today, and add a couple of sentences of reflection on why or how it happened. Select a writing topic from the ideas that develop.

REVISION EXERCISE

Reexamine the list of topics in exercise one above. Through the process of ever-narrowing focus, further limit those topics you judged as too broad. Your final list should be appropriate for essays of no more than 500 words.

4

Formulating the
Thesis Statement

The thesis is the intellectual center of an essay. It is a statement that reveals the major decisions you have made during planning. In a broad sense, your thesis offers a controlling generalization that informs your audience of the main idea you will develop. It is also a statement of purpose by which you present a specific topic, impose limits on that topic, and suggest its subsequent development. Your thesis may be expressed in a single sentence, or more than one sentence if your topic is complex. It will usually appear in the introduction of your essay. (We shall have more to say about the introduction in chapter six.)

A thesis is formulated from a topic. Topics such as "Many Americans are buying foreign cars," "San Francisco is an interesting place to visit," "The Old English sheepdog makes a good pet," or "Inflation is one of Detroit's major problems" are beginning theses insofar as each informs your audience of the main idea controlling the essay that is to follow. You may find it useful to begin writing your essay by using a tentative thesis, for your idea can change shape as you write about it. Revision is essential in producing an effective thesis.

Any audience is going to expect you to do more than simply present a generalization. For example, even though any of the beginning theses above could get you started on a first draft, none of them accomplishes as much as a thesis should. In fact, each immediately forces a reader to ask questions. "Many Americans are buying foreign cars" is hardly new information to most people, so the thesis may lead to a legitimate audience response of "So what?" or "Why?" An audience would, among other things, want to know why San Francisco is interesting, what makes Old English sheepdogs such good pets, and what kind of inflation Detroit is suffering from. A thesis that omits vital information—causing a reader immediately to question or shrug with indifference—hinders communication because it breaks the reader's concentration. As a writer, realize that writing, unlike talking, does not give you the opportunity to stop in order to clarify a point. What you are going to discuss, how you will proceed, and why your discussion is worth reading should be clear from the beginning. Thus, your beginning—the thesis—may require more care and revision than any other part of your essay.

OBJECTIVES OF A THESIS

Careful attention to the major tasks of planning will help you to form an *exact* thesis statement, one that goes well beyond a generalization that only announces the main idea of your essay. The following discussion focuses on what many writers agree to be the three objectives of a thesis: (1) to indicate the *specific topic* you will address; (2) to impose *manageable limits* on that topic; (3) to suggest the *organization* of your essay. Through the thesis, you say to your audience, "I have thought about this topic and know what I believe about it. I have a specific purpose in mind that I have examined in relation to you, my audience, and I have decided how I can best organize my discussion." You may find that you have to revise your thesis several times.

By examining the thesis on foreign cars in light of the three previously stated objectives—specific topic, manageable limits, and organizational approach—you will see that it needs exactness.

THESIS: Many Americans are buying foreign cars.

The first problem with this thesis is that it fails to define a specific topic. This failure leads to troublesome questions for an audience. For example, which foreign cars are Americans buying? Why? The thesis could go in several directions, from the economic impact of foreign cars on United States manufacturers to the reasons behind consumer choices. If you choose the latter direction, your understanding of the need for topic specificity may lead you further to conclude that, at least in a short essay, you would do better to limit your topic to one make of car, say, Toyota. But even after resolving this problem, you will notice that the topic still remains too broad. You would, for example, find it unmanageable to deal with all the reasons for buying Toyotas. Furthermore, there are many differences in the various Toyota models. You could, however, limit your topic to make it manageable by selecting only a few major reasons for buying one particular model of Toyota—the Corolla, let's say. Finally, by stating several of the specific reasons some people have for buying the Corolla, you would overcome another problem—the failure of the original thesis to suggest how the essay will be organized.

Thus, by keeping in mind the criteria of specific topic, manageable limits, and indication of organizational approach, you will be able to sharpen the thesis to make it more exact. Note the difference between the original thesis statement and the revised thesis statement, which reflects these criteria:

ORIGINAL THESIS	REVISED THESIS
Many Americans are buying foreign cars.	Many Americans are buying the Toyota Corolla because of its competitive price, fuel economy, and high resale value.

The revised thesis accomplishes the following: it treats a specific topic (why some people buy a particular foreign car); it limits the topic to a manageable length (by considering only economic factors and a single car model); and it establishes the essay's organizational approach by indicating the order that the discussion will have (three specific reasons for the model's popularity). Such exactness helps assure that you will not lose your audience. Equally important, it gives you, the writer, a map that not only indicates where you are going but also how you will get there.

By giving attention to the criteria for exactness, you can see how the three remaining theses have been revised and sharpened:

ORIGINAL THESIS	REVISED THESIS
San Francisco is an interesting place to visit.	San Francisco is a stimulating place to visit because of its magnificent location, its theaters and art galleries, and its many fine restaurants.
The Old English sheepdog makes a good pet.	Because of its placid nature, even temper, unswerving loyalty, and high intelligence, the Old English sheepdog deserves consideration if you are looking for a pet.
Inflation is one of Detroit's major problems.	Inflation is having a serious effect on Detoit's housing industry: many people are no longer able to afford to buy single-family houses; builders are going bankrupt; and consumers are forced into renting apartments, often at very high rates.

An exact thesis accomplishes the following:

- It indicates the *specific topic* you will deal with.
- It imposes *manageable limits* on that topic.
- It suggests the *organization* of your essay.

EXERCISES

Discuss the following questions. Make specific reference to the preceding three thesis statements.

1. Explain the reasons for the changes in each of the revised thesis statements.
2. Explain how each revised thesis statement satisfies the criteria of specific topic, manageable limitation, and organizational approach.
3. The thesis on inflation differs from the other two theses. Explain the differences.

REVISION EXERCISES

The following theses are too general and thus weak. Revise them according to the criteria for exactness.

1. College administrators are impersonal.
2. A good restaurant is hard to find.
3. Drugs are dangerous.
4. A career in the civil service can be worthwhile.
5. The kitchen is a hazardous room.
6. Drinking diet soft drinks can be advantageous to your health.
7. Obscenity laws threaten all of us.
8. Forced busing is a good way (or is not a good way) to solve the nation's racial problems.
9. Illegal aliens are straining the nation's already overburdened social welfare agencies.
10. Consumer legislation is inadequate.

ARRIVING AT A THESIS

An exact thesis reflects initially the care that you have given to planning your essay and later to revision. With an exact thesis, you are, in effect, answering three questions that are outgrowths of your attention to subject, purpose, and audience: (1) *What* is my point? (2) *How* will I present it? (3) *Why* is my point important? (The last is often only implied in the thesis.) Answering these questions will enable you to create an exact thesis statement that will identify a specific topic, impose manageable limits on that topic, and suggest the organization of the body of your essay.

The following diagram illustrates how you can evolve a topic into an exact thesis statement by means of these three questions. For purposes of illustration, assume that planning has led you to the topic, "What to look for in a good stereo receiver":

QUESTIONS

WHAT IS MY POINT?

To instruct a general audience on the qualities of a good stereo receiver.

TOPIC	HOW WILL I PRESENT IT?	THESIS
What to look for in a stereo receiver.	By explaining the necessity for (1) appropriate wattage; (2) usable sensitivity; (3) frequency response.	If you are in the market for a good stereo receiver, you should select one that provides adequate wattage or power to drive your speakers, high usable sensitivity to capture all the sounds from your listening source, and wide frequency response to capture distant radio stations.

WHY IS MY POINT IMPORTANT?

It will help the audience select a good stereo receiver.

In the following diagram, assume that planning has led you to the topic, "Why going home may be the most difficult part of a freshman's adjustment to college life":

QUESTIONS

WHAT IS MY POINT?

To suggest to an audience of college freshmen that, contrary to popular opinion, going home after being away for one semester may be the most difficult part of adjusting to college.

HOW WILL I PRESENT IT?

TOPIC

Why going home may be the most difficult part of a freshman's adjustment to college life.

By explaining that a college assumes that I am an adult and therefore gives me much freedom to supervise my own life; and that when I returned home, my parents still saw me as a child and thus wanted to continue restrictions on my independence.

THESIS

When I left for college, many people warned me that learning to assume responsibility for my actions would be the most challenging part of adjusting to college life. They failed to explain that no matter how capably I made this adjustment to adulthood, my parents would continue to view me as a child.

WHY IS MY POINT IMPORTANT?

It develops an idea that helps me and my audience understand how our personalities are developing.

Both of the preceding illustrations reveal how answering the three thesis questions leads to exact theses suitable for controlling short essays dealing with relatively simple topics. As the following illustrations indicate, these same questions can also enable you to deal with more complex topics in longer essays. In the next example, assume that planning has led you to the topic, "Why the public should be skeptical of entertainers who publicly advocate particular social or political points of view":

QUESTIONS

WHAT IS MY POINT?

To argue that if my audience
is interested in certain social
or political issues, it should
be skeptical of entertainers
who use their high public
profiles to advocate
particular stands on issues
that they often know little
about.

TOPIC	HOW WILL I PRESENT IT?	THESIS
Why the public should be skeptical of entertainers who publicly advocate particular social or political points of view.	By showing that some entertainers are unfairly using their popularity with the public to influence attitudes, that these entertainers frequently have no expertise on the issues in question, and that people who are thus influenced are being manipulated by illogic.	If you had a toothache or wanted information on ten-speed bicycles or computers, common sense would tell you to consult experts. Yet this rule of common sense increasingly is being challenged by entertainers who use their popularity and skill in one field to advocate social or political positions outside their area of expertise. This is both illogical and, as a look at ecent history will show, dangerous.

WHY IS MY POINT IMPORTANT?

It will prompt the audience
to evaluate the positions of
such entertainers more
critically.

   In the final example, assume that planning has led to the complex topic,
"How the nation's political parties, contrary to democratic principles, give
the voter no choice in the selection of the vice president of the United
States":

QUESTIONS

WHAT IS MY POINT?

To argue that a party's
presidential nominee should
not have what is, in essence,
the power to appoint a vice
presidential nominee;
rather, each presidential

TOPIC

How the nation's political parties, contrary to democratic principles, give the voter no choice in the selection of the vice president of the United States.

WHAT IS MY POINT

candidate should indicate prior to the national convention whom he or she wishes for a running mate.

HOW WILL I PRESENT IT?

By explaining that the present system makes the vice presidency, in effect, an appointed rather than an elected office, and by also suggesting that this practice is unconstitutional.

WHY IS MY POINT IMPORTANT?

It calls attention to the need for election reform.

THESIS

Both the delegates to national political conventions and the people voting in an election deserve a voice in deciding who will be their vice president. But since the tradition is to give the presidential nominee the power to appoint a running mate, neither the delegates nor the people have any say in the selection. Thus, the present process of selecting a vice presidential nominee contradicts basic democratic principles, while it also violates the Constitution.

Answering the following questions will enable you to arrive at an exact thesis:

- *What* is my point?
- *How* will I present it?
- *Why* is my point important?

EXERCISES

1. Respond to the following questions with regard to the preceding four topic-thesis illustrations:
   a. What topics, topic limitations, and organizational approaches are indicated in each illustration? Be as specific as possible.
   b. Could the first and second topics and theses be broadened to make them more suitable for longer papers? How? Explain fully.

   c.   Could the third and fourth topics and theses be further limited to make them more suitable for shorter papers? Explain.

2.   Develop a topic from a general subject. Create a diagram similar to the previous four that we have provided by using the *what, how,* and *why* questions, and through your responses to these questions, evolve a thesis statement. Develop it into an essay of approximately 500 words.

THE VALUE OF AN EXACT THESIS

An exact thesis statement will give your essay *unity, precision,* and *coherence. Unity* means that all the elements in your essay stand in support of your thesis. If, for example, you write "Cigarette smoking endangers a person's health because it attacks both heart and lungs," you are clearly stating the essay's main point. You are also allowing yourself to concentrate on developing your main point and enabling your audience to follow the progression of ideas.

An exact thesis will also lend *precision* to your essay. Precision is exactness, the quality of avoiding ambiguity or vagueness. If, for example, your thesis is "My new roommate is a very strange person," you may confuse your audience because you give no indication of what makes the roommate strange. Ambiguous or vague words (such as *good, bad, nice, lovely, interesting, meaningful, exciting,* or *wonderful*) are only relative—they mean different things to different people. If you use vague words in your thesis, you risk confusing and misleading your audience; you also risk confusing yourself because such words cannot suggest specific ways you might develop the body of your essay. You should therefore select words and phrases for your thesis that can have only one meaning in the particular context. If you find that you absolutely must use a vague word, follow it immediately with an explanation: "My new roommate must be a very strange person *because* he paints himself a different color each night." An imprecise thesis can lead to an inexact, confusing essay. Precision, on the other hand, invites clarity.

Coherence, which literally means "sticking together," is the quality an essay has when its parts are presented in a *logical order.* Thus, if you are writing an essay that discusses how to live for a week on twenty dollars' worth of groceries, you might survey *first* what kinds of inexpensive foods could be bought for twenty dollars and *then* describe their nutritional value in various combinations. If, however, you reversed the order of these two aspects of the essay, you would make the essay less coherent. Similarly, if you were arguing why a certain history course should be required, you might *first* present a definition of a college education and *then* discuss how history is interrelated with various other subjects. Finally, you might show how a certain history course specifically applies to the needs raised in the first two parts of your essay. *Coherence,* in essence, is a means of ordering the parts that, taken together, bring *unity* to an essay.

By arriving at an exact thesis—one that provides unity, precision, and coherence—you will lend *emphasis* to your essay. An exact thesis announces to your audience that you have given careful thought to, and established control over, your topic. You therefore indicate to your audience that the rest of the essay is worthy of its attention. A generalized thesis such as "The battle of the sexes is one of the many problems that men and women face" fails to indicate careful thought, and its vagueness suggests a lack of control over the topic. But if you revised this thesis with attention to unity, precision, and coherence, you would give force to your entire essay. Such a thesis might be as follows: "Uncle Harry and Aunt Linda continually wage comic battles over his passion for smoking, her poker playing, his desire to hear Bach, and her love for Kenny Rogers."

An exact thesis lends unity, precision, and coherence to an essay.

- *Unity* is the quality of having all essay elements supporting the thesis.
- *Precision* is the quality of avoiding ambiguity or vagueness.
- *Coherence* is the quality of presenting an essay's parts in logical order.

EXERCISES

1. Take some time to evolve a thesis from the general subject "travel." After arriving at and writing your thesis, explain in a paragraph how the thesis reflects the qualities of unity, precision, and coherence.
2. The following essay is the work of a student. Examine the thesis for unity, precision, and coherence, and explain how those qualities are reflected throughout the essay. You may also wish to suggest ways that the thesis and the essay could be improved.

HO-HUM

My high school commencement speaker accomplished one thing: he persuaded me that high school commencement speakers should be abolished. His speech was too long and too dull, and he had distracting mannerisms.

The length of Mr. Beak's speech was exceeded only by its dullness. The speech began at nine o'clock in the evening and rambled on for one hour and forty-five minutes, during which time the audience could be observed yawning, coughing, and counting the bricks in the gymnasium wall. The worst thing about the talk, though, was its dullness. The topic was "The Need for Higher Education in a Changing World," which most of us had heard about in one form or another from assorted guidance counselors, progressive teachers, and parents. Naturally, the speech was peppered with countless trite expressions, such as "twenty years from now we shall all look back," "at this point in time," "the happiest days of your lives," "the challenge of the future," and "our responsibility as citizens." As Mr. Beak droned on, the class clown pretended to fall into a coma. It was the most exciting moment of the evening.

Because Mr. Beak's chief claim to fame was his position as state coordinator for humanistic advancement, it was assumed that he would be an effective speaker. Mr. Beak, however, was obviously used to committee meetings and seminars rather than crowds of 500. Thus, he seemed awestruck to find himself at the podium addressing a sea of faces. Unfortunately, after a couple of feeble jokes, he assumed that the crowd had warmed to him. In spite of a bad lisp, frequent stuttering, and wild gesturing with both hands and one eyebrow, Mr. Beak delivered what he obviously thought to be a timely message, and the time he wasted was ours.

If my commencement experience was typical—and many of my peers assure me that it was—perhaps our public institutions should begin to rethink having this yearly form of torture. Although some kind of commencement ceremony may be necessary to formalize the high school education experience, it seems ridiculous to end one's secondary education on such a weak note.

3. Like the student writer, the social historian Max Lerner in the following essay uses an exact thesis that gives his essay unity, precision, and coherence. Read Lerner's essay with care and describe how each of these qualities is reflected throughout the essay.

SPORTS IN AMERICA

The psychic basis of American mass sport is tribal and feudal. Baseball is a good example of the modern totem symbols (Cubs, Tigers, Indians, Pirates . . .) and of sustained tribal animosities. The spectator is not *on* the team, but he can be *for* the team; he identifies himself with one team, sometimes with one player who becomes a jousting champion wearing his colors in a medieval tournament. Hence the hero symbolism in American sports and the impassioned hero worship which makes gods of mortals mediocre in every other respect, and gives them the place among the "Immortals" that the French reserve for their Academy intellectuals.

There is a stylized relation of artist to mass audience in the sports, especially baseball. Each player develops a style of his own—the swagger as he steps to the plate, the unique windup a pitcher has, the clean-swinging and hard-driving hits, the precision quickness and grace of infield and outfield, the sense of surplus power behind whatever is done. There is the style of the spectator also: he becomes expert in the ritual of insult, provocation, and braggadocio; he boasts of the exaggerated prowess of his team and cries down the skill and courage of the other; he develops sustained feuds, carrying on a guerrilla war with the umpires and an organized badinage with the players, while he consumes mountains of ritual hot dogs and drinks oceans of ritual soda pop.

Each sport develops its own legendry, woven around the "stars" who become folk heroes. The figures in baseball's Hall of Fame have their sagas told and retold in newspapers and biographies, and the Plutarchs who recount exploits become themselves notable figures in the culture. Some of these sports writers later become political columnists, perhaps on the assumption that politics itself is only a sport riddled with greater hypocrisy and that it takes a salty and hard-hitting sports writer to expose the politicians. The sports heroes become national possessions, like the Grand Canyon and the gold in Fort Knox. It is hard for a people who in their childhood have treasured the sports legendry as a cherished illusion to surrender it when they grow up.

America as a Civilization

REVISION EXERCISES

Rewrite each of the following thesis statements to improve unity, precision, and coherence.

1. The essential challenge facing the contemporary student in a world of disorder is to find a career that offers stability, security, and financial reward.
2. My roommate is a good person. I recall an occasion when she proved this to me.
3. Lacrosse (or another game) is an exciting sport that offers a number of meaningful experiences to its participants.
4. The willingness of the United Nations to be controlled by the demands of the Third World countries undermines its purpose as stated in its charter. In addition, it has proven incapable of dealing with disorders in the world.

PART TWO

DEVELOPMENT

As the result of performing various tasks during the planning stage, you advance further into the writing process: you arrive at the *development* stage. Here the essay assumes a form as thoughts take further shape. Development follows closely on planning. Once planning yields a thesis statement, which in turn generates an organizational plan for the essay, the next step is one of expansion. You want to deliver what your thesis statement promises. As you develop your thesis, expect it to become clearer and expect to see new ideas arise that are related to your thesis. You will probably find that you must at least tinker with your thesis and with your topic sentences—and sometimes revise extensively—as your development unfolds. Do not hesitate to revise them—or to revise your development paragraphs as better examples come to mind or coherence problems become evident.

This part of the text discusses how to build the introduction, body, and conclusion of an essay in ways that develop your thesis intelligently. The development stage of the writing process involves constructing a network of paragraphs that present the main points of your thesis. The result is unified because each paragraph provides supporting information on one aspect of the thesis statement.

Part two discusses these aspects of development:

Constructing effective paragraphs
Creating special purpose paragraphs
Using methods of development

5

Constructing Effective Paragraphs

THE TOPIC SENTENCE

As its name implies, the topic sentence controls a paragraph by expressing one thought that other sentences in the paragraph develop and support. In turn, the topic sentences of the various paragraphs in an essay function together through their common relationship to the thesis statement. The following diagram of a student essay illustrates the relationship between the thesis statement and the topic sentences:

TOPIC SENTENCE

Some television commercials become boring because of their frequency and triteness.

THESIS

Many television commercials are disturbing because they are boring, insulting, or dangerous.

TOPIC SENTENCE

Commercials can also be insulting because of their blatantly illogical claims.

TOPIC SENTENCE

Occasionally, commercials are dangerous, especially to people who are impressionable.

Much of the power of the student's essay stems from the support structure in which every paragraph offers a topic sentence that advances the thesis statement in a particular way. Thus, when writing a topic sentence, keep in mind that it has three aims: (1) to indicate the purpose of the paragraph, (2) to focus the reader's attention on one central thought that controls all the other sentences in the paragraph, and (3) to establish the overall plan and purpose of the essay, because each topic sentence is related to the thesis statement.

Especially when you write your first draft, you will probably find your work easier if you place the topic sentence at the *beginning* of the paragraph. Such placement makes development of your essay easier, and you may wish to keep your topic sentence in that position through all your revisions. In the following example, notice how the topic sentence guides the content and development of the rest of the paragraph:

> (1) *There are roughly three New Yorks.* (2) There is, first, the New York of the man or woman who was born here, who takes the city for granted and accepts its size and its turbulence as natural and inevitable. (3) Second, there is the New York of the commuter—the city that is devoured by locusts each day and spat out each night. (4) Third, there is the New York in quest of something. (5) Of these three trembling cities the greatest is the last—the city of final destination, the city that is a goal. (6) It is this third city that accounts for New York's high-strung disposition, its poetical deportment, its dedication to the arts, and its incomparable achievements. (7) Commuters give the city its tidal restlessness; natives give it solidity and continuity; but the settlers give it passion. (8) And whether it is a farmer arriving from Italy to set up a small grocery store in a slum, or a young girl arriving from a small town in Mississippi to escape the indignity of being observed by her neighbors, or a boy arriving from the Cornbelt with a manuscript in his suitcase and a pain in his heart, it makes no difference: each embraces New York with the intense excitement of first love, each absorbs New York with the fresh eyes of an adventurer, each generates heat and light to dwarf the Consolidated Edison Company.
>
> E. B. White, "Here Is New York"

White announces his main idea—the complex aspects of New York that give the city its character—at the beginning of the paragraph: "There are roughly three New Yorks." From this, the topic sentence, we can assume that the remaining sentences in the paragraph relate to the main idea and that the substance of the entire paragraph reflects one specific thought unit. A close examination of White's paragraph reveals its unity, precision, and coherence:

TOPIC SENTENCE:	"There are roughly three New Yorks."
sentence 2:	the first city, of the native
sentence 3:	the second city, of the commuter
sentence 4:	the third city, "in quest of something"
sentence 5:	which city is the most important
sentence 6:	why it is important
sentence 7:	second, first, and third cities contrasted
sentence 8:	amplified detail on the third city

As you review your first draft, you may find that your topic sentence is more effective at the end of the paragraph. Such placement may be best when (1) the abstract nature of the topic requires a variety of explanations and definitions before you can pursue your point; (2) you desire to engage the reader's interest by asking a leading question or by citing a pertinent quotation; (3) you wish to establish a dominant mood or tone by offering a statistic, anecdote, or series of particular details before asserting your central point in the topic sentence. Whatever your reason for leading gradually into the topic sentence, remember that the basic function of any topic sentence is still to announce the purpose of the paragraph and the relationship between the sentences in the paragraph.

The following paragraph illustrates the principle of moving gradually into the topic sentence—in this case, the last sentence of the paragraph. (The opening sentence of the paragraph is transitional.)

> (1) It took some time but finally we were able to identify most of the contrasting features of the American and British problems that were in conflict in this case. (2) When the American wants to be alone he goes into a room and shuts the door—he depends on architectural features for screening. (3) For an American to refuse to talk to someone else present in the same room, to give him the "silent treatment," is the ultimate form of rejection and a sure sign of great displeasure. (4) The English, on the other hand, lacking rooms of their own since childhood, never developed the practice of using space as a refuge from others. (5) They have in effect internalized a set of barriers, which they erect and which others are supposed to recognize. (6) Therefore, the more the Englishman shuts himself off when he is with an American the more likely the American is to break in to assure himself that all is well. (7) Tension lasts until the two get to know each other. (8) The important point is that the spatial and architectural needs of each are not the same at all.
>
> Edward D. Hall, *The Hidden Dimension*

EXERCISES

1. Outline Hall's paragraph, showing and explaining the relation between the topic sentence and other sentences in the paragraph.
2. Why does Hall lead gradually into his topic sentence?
3. What topic do you think might logically follow in the next paragraph?

When dealing with complex issues, some writers may use *implied topic sentences*. Sometimes, instead of sandwiching four key points into one awkward sentence, a writer will split his or her points into two or three sentences. At other times, the major aim of the paragraph may be so obvious that a specific topic sentence is unnecessary. And at still other times, a paragraph may be devoted entirely to an example or anecdote when the reason is indicated in a previous paragraph. It is not always possible to find one topic sentence in every paragraph.

In the following paragraph from *A Layman's Guide to Psychiatry and Psychoanalysis,* Eric Berne gives an example of a personality type that he subsequently analyzes:

> Mr. Krone had a good income, but he was miserly and lived on crusts in a tiny room on Railroad Avenue. Every day he had the same meals at the same time in the same corner, and every day he put his dishes back in exactly the same place. His mornings he spent fussing about in the bathroom, his afternoons calculating his expenses for the previous day, and his evenings going over his old ledgers from former years and looking through his collection of magazines.

The implied topic sentence for the paragraph may be stated, "Miserliness and obsessive ordering of daily life characterize a certain type of immaturity." The specific details of the rather brief description serve to give the impression of someone who is compulsively meticulous.

Implied topic sentences are valuable writing tools, especially for complex issues and perspectives. However, writers should become comfortable using the *explicit* topic sentence before attempting the *implied* topic sentence.

EXERCISES

Examine the following paragraphs for topic sentences and identify each. Explain the relationship between the topic sentence and the supporting sentences in each paragraph.

1. (1) The dorm room presents a picture of last evening's celebration. (2) Twenty empty Budweiser cans are stacked in a precarious pyramid. (3) Three sweatshirts, a sweater, and my winter coat are piled onto the two coat pegs near the door. (4) Loud drips of water splatter into the crowded basin, which is clogged with half-submerged poptops, cigarette butts, a scarf, and someone's tube of lipstick. (5) Under the sink, a large, expended box of All detergent, which serves as a wastebasket, is stuffed to the top with crumpled beer cans and cigarette butts and ashes. (6) Heaped before the closet door is an assortment of dirty underwear, damp washcloths, and two pairs of jeans.

student essay

2. Some people, when asked about a particular gesture, retorted that only the inarticulate need to "wave their hands about." They felt it was unsophisticated to admit to gesturing themselves, although, ironically, they often gesticulated animatedly when making this point. Essentially, what they were saying is that *certain kinds* of gestures are class-restricted, and this is true enough. But to generalize, as they sometimes did, to include all gesturing, and to look upon the use of the hands as always indicative of a failure to find the right words, is a gross exaggeration. People who are inarticulate are often equally

limited in their gestural expressiveness, and people who are articulate are often extremely sensitive in their use of manual signals. But when it comes to certain types of symbolic gesture, then the class distinctions do begin to emerge. This is particularly true of insulting gestures. Joke insults are common among children, for example, and many symbolic gestures such as the popular nose-thumbing action are largely confined to the younger members of the population. More serious, obscene gestures are also class-restricted to a great extent and are rare among the more sophisticated sectors of society. By contrast, the more polite or complimentary gestures are used by almost all sectors of society, although even here, there is a tendency for men to employ them more often than women.

> Desmond Morris, Peter Collet, Peter
> Marsh, and Marie O'Shaughnessy, *Gestures*

3. (1) We are now in a position to see the wonder and terror of the human predicament: man is totally dependent on society. (2) Creature of dream, he has created an invisible world of ideas, beliefs, habits, and customs which buttress him about and replace for him the precise instincts of the lower creatures. (3) In this invisible universe he takes refuge, but just as instinct may fail an animal under some shift of environmental conditions, so man's cultural beliefs may prove inadequate to meet a new situation, or, on an individual level, the confused mind may substitute, by some terrible alchemy, cruelty for love.

> Loren Eisely, "The Real Secret of Piltdown"

4. (1) Axel once made a reasonably good living repairing televisions and installing antennas on houses. (2) Now, he has only the repair service because most homeowners in town have signed on with the cable company. (3) In fact, Axel himself had cable installed at his mobile home so that he could see the wrestling matches broadcast from Lincoln, several hundred miles away. (4) He made the mistake of subscribing to all the cable channels. (5) Now, while Axel sits in his shop hoping for customers, his young daughter sits in the trailer watching pornographic movies. (6) For some, the advent of cable television has been a curse.

> *student essay*

5. (1) My Uncle John read constantly. (2) It was not uncommon for him to sit through lunch and supper reading the Sunday paper. (3) I can recall one weekend many years ago when John sat down on Friday evening and read through Sunday afternoon. (4) He occasionally ceased for short intervals, during which he refilled his coffee mug and ate a Danish. (5) My mother grew increasingly worried. (6) She told him that he was losing his mind and that he should cease reading immediately. (7) "No," he said indifferently, "I think I shall read a while longer." (8) Mother sighed in disgust at this man seemingly out of touch with the world. (9) I saw a faint smile threaten John's stoic lips.

> *student essay*

6. (1) On any map of the screwing of the average man, the lawyer appears all over the landscape. (2) The lawyer is a member of a professional monopoly, and he is also the expert hired by the other experts. (3) Hardly a hustle worthy of the name can be conducted without a lawyer among the conspirators. (4) Mystifying the public by manufactured complexity, the essential strategy of the experts, is normally achieved by hiring a lawyer to write the fine print in which is hidden the barbed wire that protects the hustle from the citizenry. (5) In fact, whenever some new complexity is added to his world, the average man can be fairly sure of two things: first, a new way to hustle him has just been born, and, second, the lawyers will do more business—one lawyer representing the hustlers and another offering his services to the victims.

David Hapgood, *The Screwing of the Average Man*

7. (1) When Captain Frederick Marryat, the author of "Mr. Midshipman Easy," came to the United States in 1837, he got into trouble at Niagara Falls when a young woman acquaintance slipped and barked her shin. (2) As she limped home, he asked, "Did you hurt your *leg* much?" (3) She turned from him "evidently much shocked or much offended," but presently recovered her composure and told him gently that *leg* was never mentioned before ladies; the proper word was *limb*. (4) Even chickens ceased to have *legs*, and another British traveler, W. F. Goodmane, was "not a little confused on being requested by a lady, at a public dinner-table, to furnish her with the *first and second joint*."

H. L. Mencken, *The American Language*

8. Those who dig bomb shelters hope to survive by surrounding themselves with the latest products of modern technology. Communards in the country adhere to an opposite plan: to free themselves from dependence on technology and thus to outlive its destruction or collapse. A visitor to a commune in North Carolina writes: "Everyone seems to share this sense of imminent doomsday." Stewart Brand, editor of the *Whole Earth Catalog*, reports that "sales of the *Survival Book* are booming; it's one of our fastest moving items." Both strategies reflect the growing despair of changing society, even of understanding it, which also underlies the cult of expanded consciousness, health, and personal "growth" so prevalent today.

Christopher Lasch, *The Culture of Narcissism*

BUILDING TOPIC SENTENCES FROM THE THESIS STATEMENT

Topic sentences and the paragraphs they control are the means by which you deliver what you promise in your thesis statement. You will find that an exact thesis will enable you to build your topic sentences directly from that thesis, thus permitting you to unfold your major point gracefully and with precision and ensuring that your essay is unified and coherent. When, in the course of revising, you decide to alter your thesis or one of your topic sentences, be sure that the topic sentences remain consistent with the thesis. In other words, revision of the thesis usually requires revision of topic sentences, and vice versa.

Deriving topic sentences from the thesis statement involves three tasks: (1) isolating the most important aspects of your discussion as expressed in the thesis statement; (2) incorporating each of those aspects in a separate topic sentence; (3) stating the topic sentence with precision that can lend emphasis, clarity, and reinforcement to the thesis. Considering the following thesis statement and the topic sentences it will help generate, will enable you to understand this process:

> Bicycle riding through city traffic is a satisfying, though dangerous, means of transportation.

From this thesis statement you could logically build a topic sentence on each aspect of the central idea. Thus, your first paragraph after the thesis would focus attention on the "satisfying" aspect of bicycle riding, and you might therefore construct the following topic sentence to guide and control it:

> Commuting to work last summer, I found bicycle riding a satisfying way to exercise while saving parking fees and gasoline costs.

Your second paragraph would deal with the "dangerous" aspects noted in the thesis, and your topic sentence for this paragraph might be as follows:

> Despite its benefits, commuting by bicycle leaves the rider dangerously exposed to the rudeness and thoughtlessness of drivers.

Sometimes you may find it necessary to *combine* more than one aspect of the thesis into a single topic sentence. By way of illustration, let's say that from the subject "energy conservation" you have evolved the following thesis statement:

> Carpooling *benefits society by conserving energy and reducing pollution,* and it *saves me money;* however, I find it *inconvenient* and *frustrating.*

There are several separate aspects of this thesis on which to build topic sentences, but you may wish to combine certain aspects so that you deal with them all in two separate paragraphs in the body. Note that the thesis states positive and negative factors of carpooling. A topic sentence can be built on each:

Carpooling contributes to the social good while saving me money. (Support would consist of developing details about conserving energy and reducing pollution and details on transportation costs before and after the carpool was formed.)

Despite its benefits, carpooling takes much extra time and traps me with a boring person. (Support would consist of details on the extent and frequency of delays and the frustration of being confined with a bore.)

Whether you choose to give each aspect of the thesis a single topic sentence or to combine more than one aspect into a single topic sentence will depend on individual circumstances. Nevertheless, building topic sentences from your thesis and developing body paragraphs that reinforce each topic sentence will give any essay you write unity, precision, and coherence.

Deriving topic sentences from the thesis statement involves:

- *Isolating* the most important aspects of your discussion as expressed in the thesis statement.

- *Incorporating* each of those aspects in a separate topic sentence or combining more than one aspect in a single topic sentence.

- *Stating* the topic sentence with precision that can lend emphasis, clarity, and reinforcement to the thesis.

- *Remembering* that revising the topic sentences may require revising the thesis, and vice versa.

EXERCISES

Build topic sentences from each of the following thesis statements and construct a diagram for each like the one that appears at the beginning of this chapter. Feel free to revise the thesis statements as necessary.

1. Although there are many fast-food hamburger restaurants, McDonald's commands my loyalty because of its menu and its cleanliness. I am also impressed by McDonald's willingness to channel some of its profits into the Ronald McDonald Houses that accommodate the families of hospitalized children.

2. My high school study hall would have been more accurately named "daily chaos." Studying was impossible because of too much noise, too many discipline problems, and too few teachers.

3. Many television viewers find police dramas exciting and suspenseful, even though they most often are very repetitive. They seldom offer more than a romatic hero—usually unmarried—who represents "good" fighting someone who represents "evil," and the outcome is never in doubt.

REVISION EXERCISES

Revise the following paragraphs so that each has an effective topic sentence.

1. There are many ways to help yourself stop smoking. Keep your mouth busy by chewing gum. Chewing works off tension, and it makes you do something with your mouth. Gum puts a taste in your mouth that you will probably find incompatible with the taste of burning tobacco. You can also chew gum nearly anywhere, anytime you are awake, without offending others.

2. I used to laugh at my friends from the parochial school, who had to wear the same uniform every day: black shoes and socks, gray slacks, white shirt, and maroon tie. "Glad I'm not you," I'd sneer. "You must be hot in that tie and jacket." Later, when I thought myself more sophisticated, I was quick to point out that their uniforms undercut values of individuality and creativity, both of which I had recently discovered. But my parochial school friends had also become more sophisticated and deflated my newfound pride in individuality. "Nice uniform," one sneered at me, "just like everyone else's: loafers, jeans, and T-shirt. You all look like slobs, and you all wear the same uniform."

3. Steve is hot tempered, and his coffee mug reflects his personality. It says "No More Mr. Nice Guy." Other people in the office where I used to work have mugs that show their characters, too. Carl has a flowered mug with a bird on it. He is gentle and quiet. The boss has a gray mug. She is very quiet.

4. One of the customs that I find most offensive involves cremation, specifically the ostentatious way in which some people display the ashes of a loved one on a mantel or a coffee table. I encountered this custom for the first time only recently, when a friend whose husband had died invited me over for coffee a few months after the funeral. Having been in Camille's house hundreds of times, I was immediately struck by a recent addition—a pale blue urn on a walnut base. Trying to keep the conversation light, I remarked on the beautiful urn. She sobbed, "That's Vito."

5. The lead singer had a beautiful voice. Not one of the other performers, however, should have been allowed in the musical. The plot had potential, though the acting was bad. I could have stayed interested in the play if there had not been two noisy children behind me.

DEVELOPING PARAGRAPH UNITY

A paragraph is a visual device. Set off from other lines and columns of words by the white space provided by indentation, a paragraph signals that a new unit of thought is to begin. Paragraph breaks in the course of an essay let your reader pause to reflect momentarily and absorb or summarize what he or she has just read, before moving on to the next thought unit. These breaks also enable the reader to go through the mental processes of absorbing and connecting thoughts sentence by sentence. As a writer, you should shape your paragraphs to take advantage of the reader's brief period of mental rest and absorption. This task requires paying particular attention to how each paragraph begins, how it ends, and how it announces its thought to your audience.

It is sometimes practical to think of the paragraph as a miniature essay, containing components similar to those of a complete essay. An effective paragraph proceeds from a central, controlling idea, just as an essay does. It follows a definite organizational plan, as an essay does. And it displays unity, precision, and coherence, as any piece of writing should. Like an essay—but on a smaller scale—a paragraph is a single thought presented in an orderly manner.

A unified paragraph is one in which all sentences relate to and provide convincing support for the topic sentence. Extraneous sentences and elements in your paragraph may confuse your audience and detract from your point.

The following paragraph suffers from disunity. It is also underdeveloped, as its sparse detail fails to provide convincing support for the topic sentence:

> Many of the people who came to buy gasoline were rude to me. A couple of times I felt insulted by their personal remarks. Sometimes, the rudeness was a matter of their not saying "thanks" after I had done something extra for them, and when I told one lady she should be more polite, the boss threatened to fire me.

The topic sentence indicates that the *customers' rudeness* is the focus of the paragraph, but the last sentence goes into the *writer's reaction* to the rudeness and into his *supervisor's response* as well. Thus, the disunity is caused by material in the paragraph that goes beyond the limits stated in the topic sentence. The paragraph meanwhile remains unconvincing because the writer fails to develop even the few details he supplies.

Here is the paragraph after it has been revised for unity and development:

> Many of the people who came to buy gasoline were rude to me. Some apparently were unable to read my name as sewn onto my uniform and instead referred to me as "kid," "dude," "hey, Jack," "son," "boy," or "slowpoke." One man, after rolling down the window of his Cadillac and frowning at me from above his Christian Dior glasses, snarled as I approached to find out how many gallons he wanted, "Make sure ya don't get no oil on the fenda." Even some of my friends from school appeared to go out of their way to tell me—usually after I had been doing an oil change—what a "mess" I looked. I found the common failure to say "thanks," however, to be the most insulting and thoughtless, and I would estimate that only about half the customers I waited on were willing to extend this courtesy. Such rudeness was especially demeaning after I had performed an extra service. I still recall one winter day with the temperature below zero, the wind howling, and freezing rain

pelting down as a lady commanded that I check and inflate her tires. I thereupon crawled about on all fours, fumbled with the frozen valves, and finally got the pressure just right. As I stood up, she drove off without even looking at me.

EXERCISE

Examine the following two paragraphs for problems of disunity and underdevelopment, paying close attention to the topic sentences. Revise the paragraphs in order to eliminate these problems.

   1.   Life insurance agents make me uncomfortable. They remind me that I am mortal, and those thoughts always make me nervous. They use language I don't understand, tossing out terms like "fiduciary" and "prorated" and checking long tables and columns of figures. And they can be almost impossible to get rid of. Some of them spend lots of time talking about the good things their companies do with the premiums and how lots of donations to charity are made.

   2.   Some drivers present a greater threat to society when they are outside the car than when they are behind the wheel. In two recent cases in Montgomery County, infuriated drivers pulled off the road and began shooting at vehicles that had cut in front of them. Last week I saw a driver weaving on the interstate highway near here, and she nearly caused several accidents. The drunk driver is a great threat to our well-being, and we should all support tougher legislation against drunk drivers.

PRECISION

Paragraphs that have precision have an exactness of detail that provides convincing support for the topic sentence. As indicated in chapter one, details are particular examples, descriptions, reasons, and facts that *show* rather than tell. They must be specific and concrete.

Details are specific when they refer to only one thing. A statement such as "She makes a good living" is ambiguous because its meaning depends on what the writer intends by the word "good." No such ambiguity exists, however, in the more precise statement, "She earns $300,000 a year." Similarly, the sentence "He is ill" could suggest conditions ranging from the common cold to Parkinson's disease. A statement such as "He has a stuffy nose and a fever of 102 degrees" requires no interpretation.

Bear in mind that precise language is a matter of moving from the general to the specific. Applying this principle will help ensure that your paragraphs have sufficient support and that your details illustrate rather than tell. The following list shows the process of increasing precision; only the last item is a specific detail:

transportation
vehicle
automobile
General Motors automobile
Chevrolet
Chevrolet Nova
1987 Chevrolet Nova
Harold P. Johnson's 1987 Chevrolet Nova

REVISION EXERCISE

Examine the details in the following paragraphs. Revise to make the details more specific and the paragraphs more precise.

1.   Sometimes I have found major social engagements to be utterly uninteresting. I have been to many dances, for example, and liked neither the music nor the partners I danced with. On one formal occasion, the food was uninteresting and so was the drink. The music was terrible, and the two persons I danced with moved like steel robots.

2.   Our vacation was miserable. The weather was terrible most of the time, and when I was able to get some sun at the end of the week, I got too much. To top it all off, we had car trouble on the way home and had to spend the night in a really crummy motel.

Precision is not only one of your concerns within individual paragraphs, however, but also throughout the entire essay. To illustrate, recall the thesis statement on bicycle riding discussed earlier in this chapter: "Bicycle riding through city traffic is a satisfying, though dangerous, means of transportation." You will remember that two topic sentences were derived from this thesis, one involving the benefits of bicycle riding, the other involving its drawbacks. Though both topic sentences were more specific than the thesis statement, neither provided the detail necessary to convince readers. That would be the function of the bodies of the two paragraphs generated by these topic sentences. Thus, the paragraph generated by the first topic sentence would be developed through specific details about the rewards of exercise and the money that the bicycle rider saved; the paragraph generated by the second would provide specific details about the dangers caused by discourteous and ignorant drivers. By reinforcing both the "satisfying" and "dangerous" aspects of the thesis statement, these specific details help persuade an audience that each topic sentence is valid and, by extension, that the thesis is also valid.

The following diagram of a student essay illustrates the close relation between the thesis statement, topic sentences, and supporting detail in the body paragraphs.

THESIS

The college homecoming, although supposedly a festival designed to honor returning alumni, has degenerated into a mindless autumn ritual that is motivated by financial exploitation and characterized by reckless, lawless behavior.

TOPIC SENTENCE 1

The returning alumnus, in his desire to recapture "the best years of my life," is victimized by the collegiate and local wolves who appear to unite for purposes of financial gain.

SUPPORTING DETAIL FOR PARAGRAPH

The college hopes that allowing the alumnus to relive his youth will result in a contribution to the athletic fund. Local merchants, meanwhile, increase their prices exorbitantly.

The most obvious collusion takes place at the traditional football game, as is evidenced by the high ticket prices and advertisements in the program.

TOPIC SENTENCE 2

The alumnus is an easy mark, as he judges his fun by the amount of money spent and quickly gives himself over to unchecked emotions and extravagant behavior.

SUPPORTING DETAIL FOR PARAGRAPH

The alumnus judges his fun by the amount of money spent and seizes the opportunity to behave extravagantly by staying out late, drinking too much, behaving boisterously at the football game, and careening noisily through town in his car.

As you can see, the strength of this structure results from the student's exact thesis: her main point ("the college homecoming has degenerated into a mindless autumn ritual") is developed by specific topic sentences that, in turn, will require body paragraphs that are rich in supporting detail. Although there will be much more to say about the methods of developing body paragraphs in subsequent chapters, the student's finished essay is included here to illustrate the value of building topic sentences and precise, supporting detail from the thesis statement:

HOMECOMING—A SHAM

The college homecoming, although supposedly a festival designed to honor returning alumni, has degenerated into a mindless autumn ritual that is motivated by financial exploitation and characterized by reckless, lawless behavior.

The returning alumnus, in his desire to recapture "the best years of my life," becomes easy prey for the collegiate and local wolves who appear to unite for purposes of financial gain. In return for publicity and perhaps a tax-deductible contribution to the athletic fund, the college allows the alumnus to experience the nostalgia that comes with parades, beer blasts, wine parties, liquor on the quad, and, of course, the traditional football game against a "hated" rival. The local merchants, meanwhile, do a large business in everything from clothing and State U beer steins to loud pom-poms and dyed gardenias. In addition, the three-dollar "Sunrise Special" at the local greasy spoon suddenly becomes five dollars; the forty-dollar motel room jumps to seventy-five dollars; and a lukewarm dinner at any of the town restaurants costs the same as a lavish feast at the Ritz. The exploitation comes to a head with the Saturday afternoon ball game, as tickets—already high at twelve dollars for regular games—now go for twenty. The program, the most obvious collusion between the college and the town, is packed with advertisements for Doug's Drive-In, Hector's Hamburgers, Caspar's Clothing, and the Hayloft Hotel ("special home-coming luncheon on Sunday, seventy-five dollars per couple"). The advertisers are, of course, full of spirit: "Good Luck, State U," "Welcome Home, Alumni." And why not? As one local businessman candidly admits, "We figure that each out-of-towner will drop at least 200 dollars over the weekend. Some come close to spending a thousand."

The alumnus is an easy mark, however, as he judges his fun by the amount of money spent and quickly gives himself over to unchecked emotions and extravagant behavior. He expects to stagger to his bed no earlier than 4:00 A.M., and he is disappointed if he does not wake up the following morning with a hangover. It is, however, the football game that best epitomizes his drunken enthusiasm as, surrounded by other screaming, chanting businessmen, he tries to recall the old fight song while swilling bourbon or scotch from his none-too-carefully concealed flask. Growing progressively louder and more boisterous, the alumnus howls for the blood of the opponents, boos the officals, cheers banners that shriek "Kill the opposition!" and applauds every bone-jarring tackle made by State U. As he files out of the stadium after the game, his enthusiasm expands into the town itself as he honks his horn, screams from the car window, and heads for the local watering hole to replenish his liquor supply. As if fearing an invading motorcycle gang, some townspeople lock their doors and shutter their windows, finding relief only in knowing that the next homecoming is a year away.

The degeneration of homecoming thus becomes complete. In return for his money, the alumnus receives a weekend of mayhem encouraged by an institution of higher learning, and assisted by the local merchants. Ultimately, it is a well-struck bargain. The college and local businesses gain money and the alumnus recaptures his youth. If anyone suffers, it is only the serious undergraduate trying to study or the innocent townspeople seeking peace and quiet in their homes. But everyone else is well satisfied. And next year, the ritual honoring school spirit, good fellowship, and returning alumni will begin anew.

EXERCISES

1. Choose one of the thesis-topic sentence diagrams from the preceding text. From it, develop another diagram that includes details that support each topic sentence. You may first want to reexamine the diagram in the previous section.
2. Identify the thesis statement and each topic sentence in the following student essay. Also note how the precise details in each body paragraph support each topic sentence and the thesis statement. Then construct a diagram of the entire essay (similar to the one on page 57), showing the relationship among the thesis statement, topic sentences, and supporting detail in each body paragraph.

DETECTIVE STORY

A water moccasin hunt is not the mere seeking out and killing of a snake—it is an adventure similar to one in a detective story. You are the detective; you use specialized equipment to snare your quarry; and you participate in a number of scenes as you bring the villain to justice.

The setting is night—the dark swamps of the Atlantic coastal region from southeast Virginia to the tip of Florida. You will need at least one assistant because your challenge is difficult and your quarry is dangerous. A moccasin's venom is similar to that of a rattlesnake, and although fatalities are rare, a bite can cause excruciating pain and rapid swelling, and can possibly lead to amputations. The risks add to the excitement, however, for without them, snake hunting—like a detective's investigation—would not be as challenging.

As in a detective story, the first scene involves preparation. You collect your equipment, knowing that each piece has its own function. The gig is a spearlike pole with five metal barbs attached to one end used to guide the snake and to protect yourself. The loop stick is a pole with a string attached that goes around the snake's head. The fork stick is about five feet long with a V-shape at one end to hold the snake's head. You also check your flashlight, because the hunt will take place at night, and you make sure that your cage will adequately house the prisoner once it is apprehended.

By ten o'clock—the second scene—the frogs, crickets, and other creatures of the wild are adding to the eerie feeling of the night. You are in a boat in shallow water, pushing your way along with a pole, your flashlight at the ready. Your eyes look and your ears listen for the camouflaged serpents of the darkness. They lie among the swamp grass along the banks of creeks, waiting for unsuspecting prey. When they swim, their heads angle out of the water and their bodies wiggle like cross sections of waves. They often hit the water with a plop—a noise that will alert you to their presence. You shine the flashlight along the bank's edge, and suddenly, you see two glowing red-orange eyes at the end of something resembling a stick. You have found your quarry, and you keep the hypnotic light in its eyes.

Now the chase—the third scene—begins. Your assistant maneuvers the boat close enough to the snake so you can use your equipment, and you remember to keep the light directly in its eyes. You approach cautiously, avoiding any quick movements or loud sounds. After getting into position, you know that you must decide what tool to use. From experience, you know to use the loop stick if the snake is swimming, the fork stick if it is in the mud or on the bank, and the gig if your position is not good. This time the fork stick is the right tool, and with a thrust, you trap the snake's head against the bank. The snake is squirming, viciously trying to bite anything it can.

The last scene is the moment of decision, that point when you actually apprehend the quarry. With your assistant holding the boat and the flashlight steady, you reach out and grab the back of the snake's head. The animal's mouth opens, fangs bared, but it cannot reach your hand. Your assistant opens the cage, and you thrust the snake—still wriggling and writhing—headfirst through the opening. Your assistant looks scared, perspiration beading his forehead. But you have been here before, and you remain calm and collected— at least on the outside.

Like any good detective, you know that the rewards of the hunt can be lucrative. On a good night you might catch two or three of these criminals, whose skins may be worth fifty dollars each. But you also know—like any good detective—that the real reward is the chase itself.

COHERENCE

There are several patterns of coherence. When a paragraph is coherent, all the ideas in it are *logically connected,* that is, they are presented in an appropriate *order.*

General to Specific. The most common pattern in developing coherent paragraphs is to move from the general to the specific—usually from a topic sentence to supporting detail. Note how the following paragraph from a student essay exemplifies this type of coherence:

> The elementary school playground, which offers the only basketball court in the area, is crowded on weekends with kids doing many things other than playing basketball. Under one basket, a drug sale will be taking place; under the other, a couple of kids will be playing jacks. Half a dozen will be playing hopscotch on a grid they have chalked out in the center of the court. Two or three others will be throwing a softball over the heads of the rest of the people on the court, often coming dangerously near to causing head injuries to the hopscotchers.

Specific to General. Coherence may also be achieved by moving from the specific to the general, as in the following discussion of farm employment in England and Wales:

> 183,200 of England and Wales's farms employ no workers at all; they are cultivated entirely by the farmer and his family. 24,600 employ only part-

time help. And of the 116,000 which employ whole-time workers, over ninety per cent employ less than five. With the methods of culture having undergone complicated technological changes which involve heavy fertilizer and machine bills, nearly all the young workers are bound to have lives of swiftly increasing responsibility.

Ronald Blythe, *Akenfield, Portrait of an English Village*

Order of Importance. Another pattern in developing coherence is to arrange supporting details according to their order of importance, moving from the least important to the most, or from the most important to the least. In the following paragraph from a student essay, note the ascending order—the most important detail is saved for last.

Meredith bought and sold stock in a different company each year. Though her investments produced mixed success for years, Meredith has done well on the whole. In 1981 she lost over $1,000 on airline stocks. In 1982 she lost $2,000 on investments in a pipeline company. In other years, she broke almost even. In 1986, however, she made nearly $20,000 in a satellite communications stock issue.

In the following paragraph from a student essay, the details are arranged in descending order of importance:

We tried several methods of getting Bart to move out of the room. What finally worked was to bring in a friend who was studying electrical engineering. He fixed the wiring so that the current going to Bart's room was insufficient to power Bart's stereo much above a hum and to leave his lights too dim to read by. Earlier methods that we tried in vain included using up all the hot water each morning by getting up before Bart and taking long showers. We tried that after short-sheeting his bed did not discourage him; he just short-sheeted ours in return. We also had friends call late at night several times. (The phone was in Bart's room.) He just pulled the phone plug when he went to bed. Over and over we asked him, at first politely and later rudely, to move out.

Spatial Order. The spatial arrangement of details can also achieve coherence in a paragraph. Such an arrangement may be linear (such as a description of the towns along a highway as one drives from east to west), or vertical (such as a description of a mountain that begins at the top and moves to the base, or that begins at the base and moves to the top). Descriptions of the exterior of a house, the interior of a room, or of the physical characteristics of a person all lend themselves to spatial order. The following example from a student essay is a spatially ordered description of a teacher:

Professor Cuthbert was eccentric. Before Thanksgiving vacation, he climbed atop his desk and gave the class a benediction, and I was able to view him from a new perspective. Planted on his blotter, his Gucci tassel-topped shoes were glossy black, showing that they had recently been polished. Cresting their tops was a pair of faded jeans, with a tiny patch above the right knee. A well-tailored tweed jacket next loomed into my view, held apart by his hands to reveal bright red suspenders over a white silk shirt and bow tie. His benevolent smile was framed by long, curly brown hair, and on the top of his head was a red felt fez he had purchased on his sabbatical year in Turkey.

Chronological Order. Placing details in a logical time sequence is another method of giving coherence to paragraph development. In the following passage, the social historian Kellow Chesney describes a system of using stolen bank checks in Victorian England:

> There were several variations on the system but they were all based on the same principle. A good start was to put a notice in a newspaper offering a vacancy for a junior clerk at an attractive salary, applications to be addressed to a box number or accommodation address. A candidate whose letter suggested he would make a suitable dupe got an answer instructing him to present himself punctually for interview, perhaps at an office in a building shared by several businesses, perhaps at a coffee room—a reasonable rendezvous if the job was supposed to be out of town. If the interview was to be at an office, the applicant's entry into the building was probably forestalled by a bustling man who appeared in the doorway as he arrived and announced himself as the prospective employer, called out on unexpected business. In any event, if the lad seemed up to expectation he was handed a paper and told to take it to a bank not far away, collect so much cash, and return directly by the same route. After walking a little way the stooge was likely to notice that he was being followed—possibly by the bustling businessman himself—and conclude that he was being subjected to a test. Shortly after coming out of the bank he was stopped by his smiling employer, who took over the cash, congratulated him on having got the job, wished him goodbye till Monday week, and vanished.

> *The Victorian Underworld*

You should now realize that coherence is more than a matter of ordering material. Note that in each of the paragraphs above you find words and phrases that affect your understanding of how or why one sentence follows another. Words and phrases that provide transitions and improve coherence may generally be broken down into time signals and contrast words. Time signals include terms such as "after," "shortly," "first," "later," "previously," "subsequently," and "meanwhile." Contrast words include terms such as "however," "nevertheless," "but," and "on the other hand." Both time signals and contrast words help to show connections and provide coherence to the sentences of a paragraph. (You will find further discussions of sentence coherence, as well as of time signals and other transitions, in chapter 12.)

EXERCISES

1. Write a coherent paragraph for each of the following topic sentences according to the pattern of development stipulated for each:
   a. The modern art exhibit not only displayed pictures notable for their bright splotches of color but also patrons dressed as if to outdo the pictures themselves. (general to specific)
   b. As much as I had looked forward to supervising the six-year-olds' party, the cumulative effect of each disaster during the festivities caused me repeatedly to sigh "Never again!" (specific to general)
   c. A series of incidents soon convinced me that keeping a Great Dane in my one-bedroom apartment was impractical. (ascending order of importance)
   d. I enjoy living in a climate where all the seasons, especially spring, have at least one distinctive quality. (descending order of importance)
   e. My room often mirrors the chaos of my mind. (spatial order, with both linear and vertical arrangement)
   f. Making the perfect hamburger begins with. . . . (chronological order)
2. Review your completed paragraphs "a" through "f" above. In each, identify the words and phrases that help one sentence flow smoothly into the next. Make a list of all the time signals and contrast words and phrases that you have used. Examine each paragraph to see where additional transitions would improve coherence.

PROPORTION

Paragraph breaks to some extent are influenced by considerations of length as well as content. As you reread your essay in an early draft, you may find that an unduly long paragraph, though unified and coherent, should be broken into two paragraphs so as not to tax your reader's attention. During revision, consider the length of each paragraph in relation to the length of other paragraphs in your essay.

If you were writing a book of 200 pages, you could reasonably ask an audience to read a 15-page introduction. In a two- or three-page essay, however, you may often achieve maximum impact with an introductory paragraph consisting of your thesis statement alone. In proportion to the other, longer paragraphs that follow, such an introduction thrusts the thesis forward for special notice. You might also use a fuller introductory paragraph containing a vivid example or quotation that engages the reader's attention and leads up to the thesis statement. The thesis statement would then appear at the end of the introduction, thereby achieving visual emphasis from the paragraph break that immediately follows it.

In the body of your essay, you should develop paragraphs that are long enough and provide sufficient information to convince the audience of the validity of your points. Normally, this would mean no fewer than four or five supporting sentences. But if you have a statement that deserves special attention and it comes in the body of the essay, you may want to use a *paragraph fragment* for emphasis. For example, if you were writing directions for using a bottle of ammonia, you would want your audience to know that the fluid is highly poisonous and that it gives off a deadly gas if mixed with chlorine bleach. Because this warning deserves all the emphasis you can give it, a separate, one-sentence paragraph would be appropriate—as would large red capital letters if your format permitted.

Remember that relatively brief introductory and concluding paragraphs usually help to emphasize your main point, but a series of relatively brief paragraphs in the body of the essay can distract your audience. If you write a 500-word essay with a body that has half a dozen or more paragraphs, the effect may be like that of a series of choppy sentences in a first-grade reader: emphasis gets lost.

Paragraph proportion is a matter of length as well as content. As you reread and revise your essay, consider the following:

- An unduly long paragraph, just as a series of brief paragraphs, can dull the audience's attention.

- Body paragraphs should be developed sufficiently to convince the audience that the point of each paragraph is valid and believable.

- A paragraph fragment can be used in order to emphasize a crucial point.

EXERCISES

Examine the following student essay for proper paragraph proportion and respond to the following questions:

1. Should any paragraph be divided or subdivided? Why?
2. Should some paragraphs be combined to make a longer paragraph? Why?
3. Is there a single statement that might be placed as a paragraph fragment to give it special emphasis? Explain fully.

HOW FIREMEN STAY PREPARED

Volunteer firemen have to have lifestyles that let them stay prepared to leave in an instant both from home and from the firehouse. Preparations to get quickly to a fire fall into three stages: home preparations, considerations while driving to the firehouse, and firehouse preparations before hopping on the engine to go to the fire.

Since most fires occur at night, a volunteer has to make several careful preparations at home that will permit a fast getaway, with a minimum of confusion and unnecessary delay. The first is to point the car out the driveway and to be certain that no other cars, bikes, or toys are blocking it. Next, the volunteer should turn the volume control on the radio scanner up to be loud enough to awaken him or her if a call comes. The most crucial step is the placement of clothes and car keys. Pants should be on a chair under a light switch, next to unfolded socks and untied shoes, with a shirt hanging on the doorknob of the exit. The ignition key, separate from other keys on the chain, should be in the pants pocket. Then the volunteer fireman can retire. When the call comes, the fireman quickly gets dressed and runs out to the car. A fast drive to the firehouse also takes special considerations. The first step, of course, is to attach the magnetic, revolving red light to the car roof. This merely requires pulling it from under the front seat and slapping it on the car roof—just like Kojak used to do. The siren is turned on. But the fireman can't drive at ninety miles per hour. It is crucial to slow at major intersections, especially if the red signal is on, because other drivers may not see the approaching car or hear the siren.

When the volunteer arrives at the firehouse, there is another preparation ritual. First, the fireman pulls on boots and pulls up a pair of fireproof pants, which are attached to the boots by straps. The next step is to don a fireproof, insulated coat and snap every hook, knowing that the coat also provides crucial protection.

Then the volunteer grabs a helmet and gloves from the locker and puts them on. They also provide essential protection.

Next the volunteer races to the truck and jumps on board.

Sometimes the volunteer finds that he or she has responded to a false alarm—then all the excitement has been in getting to the scene. At other times, the excitement as well as the danger will continue for many hours. And at these times, the property and lives of the victims—and the volunteer's own life, too—will depend on how well he or she prepared.

6
Creating Special Purpose Paragraphs

A paragraph break, like a period ending a sentence, gives mind and eye a rest. Even as sentences can question, exclaim, or declare, so do paragraphs have different uses. Once you have completed a draft of your essay, you will want to give special attention to special purpose paragraphs. There are three types of special purpose paragraphs. The *introductory paragraph* is used to present your topic and thesis and to stimulate the reader's interest. The *transitional paragraph* helps the audience see connections and relationships between one part of your essay and another. The *concluding paragraph* reasserts your main point and leaves the audience with the major impression you wish to convey. Your first draft probably has tentative forms of these special paragraphs, but particular attention to their individual purposes can strengthen your writing.

WRITING THE INTRODUCTORY PARAGRAPH

Were you writing a book, you could legitimately devote a few pages and perhaps even a hefty chapter to the introduction. In an essay, however, you are constrained by matters of length and proportion, and your introduction will therefore usually consist of a single paragraph. Despite variances of length, the purposes of any introduction are essentially the same: to provide an interesting presentation of your thesis statement; to stimulate the reader's interest in your topic; to indicate clearly what the topic is so that the reader will understand the point you are pursuing as well as how you will approach it.

You will want to avoid using openings that have become timeworn. A commonly overused introduction is to state a dictionary definition ("Webster defines 'greed' as . . ."). If you wish to begin with a definition, state what the word means to *you*. (For example, "I don't find someone's working for his or her own self-interest objectionable, but self-interest pushed too far is 'greed.' ") Another opening that is worn out—and wordy as well—is "The purpose of this paper is. . . ." For example, instead of writing, "The purpose of my paper is to show that Atlanta needs improved public transportation," you can simply state your purpose: "Atlanta needs improved public transportation." A third kind of opening that is both trite and uninformative is the assertion about all humankind or all history. For example, you risk dullness with such assertions as "From the beginning of time, man has shown greed," or "Since the start of history, man has sought ways to fly," or "From the time of Adam and Eve, the battle of the sexes has raged."

Like all other aspects of the writing process, writing the introductory paragraph should reflect conscious decisions that you have made in relation to your purpose, audience, and topic. In addition, bear in mind that the introduction is the audience's first view of you and your topic; therefore, you want to use it to create a sound initial impression. Within this framework, you have a number of options open to you, which are explained below. Many writers, having decided on a thesis statement, then write the introductory paragraph *last*. Having written a draft of the entire paper, they have a better idea of the kind of opening strategy that will fit the paper.

Opening with the Thesis Statement

If your essay is brief, you may decide to limit your introduction to a particularly emphatic thesis statement, such as the following:

> Soviet and American policymakers have so politicized the Olympic Games that the purpose of international sports competition has been completely lost.

This thesis-introduction gains strong emphasis because it stands as an isolated paragraph. Moreover, it clearly suggests a three-part division of the essay (one on Soviet policy, one on American policy, and one on the purpose of international sports competition) that is to follow. A word of caution here: if you use only the thesis as your introduction, keep it uncluttered. Notice how the following thesis-introduction has been weakened by extraneous modifiers and details:

> Soviet and American policymakers have previously, for different reasons, decided to keep their athletes home from the Olympic Games, even though the games are not supposed to be subjected to political decisions, and regardless

of the fact that many of the athletes have trained for years in an effort to be judged the best in the world.

Similarly, notice how the potential impact of a sound thesis-introduction has been diluted by extraneous elements that serve only to confuse the audience:

WEAK	REVISED
Hitler's murder of eight million Jews—one more chapter in the long history of man's inhumanity to man—has given modern West Germany, like some other nations, a legacy of guilt that is evident in some of its major foreign policies.	Hitler's murder of eight million Jews has given West Germany a legacy of guilt evident in some of its major foreign policies.

Opening with a Broad Statement

One means of introducing your topic is to move from a broad statement on the nature of a general subject to a specific limitation of the topic in your thesis statement. The broad statement should be perceptive and thought provoking, thus enabling you to make a favorable impression on the audience. If your broad statement is self-evident, however, the audience might rightly resent your wasting its time. Notice the difference in the following introductions:

WEAK	REVISED
Practically since the beginning of time, people have loved to have parties. Sometimes a party can get out of hand, though. The New Year's Eve party I went to turned into an orgy.	Sometimes unwelcome guests are just what a party needs. A New Year's Eve party really began to be fun when the dean and our faculty adviser showed up a few minutes before midnight, just as the Mongolian mating call contest was getting underway.
Some persons really have a sense of charity. My roommate, George, showed a sense of charity on two occasions.	Some persons find it harder to receive than to give. My roommate, George Funderbeeck, becomes quite embarrassed at any offer of aid to himself, but he is exceptionally generous to others.

Opening with a Scene-Setter

Depending on the length of your essay and your topic, you may decide to lead gradually into your thesis by depicting a scene that will appeal to your audience's senses and help it to grasp your point readily. Notice how this technique enhances the following introductions:

WEAK	REVISED
Gypsy moths are destroying many of our nation's hardwood forests, and only strong action by both the government and the private landowner can slow the spread of this pest.	Mile upon mile of brown Pennsylvania hills unfolded as I drove in and out of the curves and over the crests of Interstate 70. The world's worst forest fire could not have caused more destruction—and all because of the gypsy moth. If this pest is to be stopped, it will only be through the strong action of the government and the private landowner.
I have always enjoyed a fireplace and would not want to live in a house without one. There are three steps to building a fire: preparing the fireplace, arranging the materials before igniting, and tending the fire.	For anyone fortunate enough to have a wood-burning fireplace, sitting in front of a healthy fire on a frosty winter afternoon provides a sense of comfort and luxury. Unfortunately, many fireplace owners do not understand the three essential steps for achieving a successful fire: preparing the fireplace, arranging the materials before igniting, and tending the fire.

Opening with a Quotation

Beginning your essay with a quotation that is pertinent to your topic is another means of introduction. This method can often stimulate the audience's interest through humor or other devices, while also suggesting that you have thought about—and researched—your topic. Be aware, though, that you can offset the benefits of this method by selecting a lengthy, complex quotation to introduce a short essay. As a general rule, use quotations whose length and complexity are appropriate to the length and complexity of your essay. Freshness is also important. Avoid opening with a quotation from a dictionary, as such openings have been overworked, and avoid quotations that your reader may find trite.

In the following examples, notice how dull thesis statements have been improved by the use of quotations:

WEAK	REVISED
According to my dictionary, "frustration" means "the condition of being kept from fulfillment." That's what I feel at registration time.	H. L. Mencken defined "Puritanism" as "the haunting fear that someone, somewhere, may be happy." The clerks in the registrar's office must be Puritans. They do their best to see that each student receives a totally frustrating schedule—and has to wait a long time to get even that.
The last time that I tried to fix a leaking toilet ended in disaster.	"Never do yourself what you can afford to pay someone else to do." That is a motto my brother lives by. Had I lived by it, too, I could have saved myself a large expense, much griminess, and a painful injury to my hand the last time I tried to fix a leaking toilet.

Opening with an Anecdote

One of the best techniques for generating audience interest in your topic is to begin your essay with an anecdote, a brief account of an amusing or otherwise attention-getting incident. But make sure that the anecdote is short and to the point.

In the following examples, notice how the student writers have used anecdotes to improve otherwise bland theses:

WEAK	REVISED
Many retired persons die within six months after retirement, apparently because of boredom. Psychologists suggest that there are three ways to prevent the boredom from becoming terminal.	In *Lake Wobegone Days,* humorist Garrison Keillor tells of a retired dentist in a little Minnesota town. He sits in a fishing boat much of the day. "Open wide," Dr. Nute says to the fish. "This may sting a little bit. Okay. Now bite down." Unfortunately, not all

WEAK	REVISED
	retired persons are so easily able to continue their once interesting professions in some form, as Dr. Nute has. Retirees have a high death rate within the first six months after retirement, apparently because of boredom, and psychologists suggest two ways to prevent it.
Both of the science professors I have had were too involved with their research to bother with students. I think the university should enforce three requirements for all professors, but especially those in science. They should be required to have an interest in students as well as expertise and curiosity.	When Jonathan Swift described Gulliver's trip to the land of Laputa in *Guilliver's Travels,* Swift depicted scientists who had one eye turned inward and the other aimed at the stars. In the case of two science professors I have had at this school, life imitates Swift's art. The university should require all professors, especially those in science, to have an interest in students as well as expertise and curiosity.

Opening with a Statistic or a Fact

Sometimes a statistic or fact will add emphasis or interest to your essay, and simultaneously help you to assert an authoritative voice. It may be wise to include the source of your information.

Notice how the following weak introductions have been strengthened by this technique:

WEAK	REVISED
Many drunk drivers cause car accidents.	Fully half the fatal automobile accidents in Maryland involve a drunk driver, according to the State Division of Motor Vehicles. We should support concerned citizens who are now demanding that three strict laws be passed to alleviate this problem.

WEAK	REVISED
The shape of a car is a factor in its safety, as I can testify from personal experience.	A study at the University of North Carolina indicates that persons riding in a passenger van are twice as likely as other riders to suffer serious or fatal injuries. Recently I learned from personal experience that the shape of a vehicle is a major factor in how safely it handles.

Ways to develop an introduction:

- Open with the thesis statement.

- Open with a broad statement.

- Open with a scene-setter.

- Open with a quotation.

- Open with an anecdote.

- Open with a statistic or a fact.

EXERCISES

1. Identify the technique used in developing each of the following introductions and explain why each is or is not effective.

   a. "Let my skin wither, my hands grow numb, my bones dissolve; until I have attained understanding I will not rise from here." Dusk had come, and the resolute prince—the day was his 35th birthday—sat down cross-legged beneath a leafy pipal tree. He touched his right hand to the ground so Earth could bear witness and began to meditate. Through the watches of the night, under a full moon, he sat. And when he finally rose, there arose with him a new religion. For he was Siddharth Gautama and the understanding he attained in a night of transcending revelations made him Buddha, "awakened"—the Enlightened One. Out of the mission he then set for himself—to impart the secret of enlightenment to all who desire salvation—came the faith we call Buddhism.

   Joseph M. Kitagawa, *"The Eightfold Path to Nirvana,"*
   in Great Religions of the World

b.   Once tax advantages are figured in, the oil companies make an average profit of twenty-five cents on each gallon of gasoline sold, according to David Hapgood in a recently released study. Such wildly skewed profiteering is one of several good reasons for urging a revision of the tax laws.

student essay

c.   One day twelve years ago an outraged cartoonist, four of whose drawings had been rejected in a clump by *The New Yorker,* stormed into the office of Harold Ross, editor of the magazine. "Why is it," demanded the cartoonist, "that you reject my work and publish drawings by a fifth-rate artist like Thurber?" Ross came quickly to my defense like the true friend and devoted employer he is. "You mean third-rate," he said quietly, but there was a warning glint in his steady gray eyes that caused the discomfited cartoonist to beat a hasty retreat.

With the exception of Ross, the interest of editors in what I draw has been rather more journalistic than critical.

James Thurber, "The Lady on the Bookcase"

d.   It was the best of times, it was the worst of times—it was Manhattan's afternoon rush hour. For most of the 800,000 drivers who were braking and honking toward the bridges and tunnels leading off the island, it was the nadir of their day, the teeth-grinding hour of creep and stop, of bumper banging, of dyspepsia. But for Samuel Schwartz, it was a golden time: it was his chance to confront the enemy, grille to grille.

Richard Wolkomir, *"Untying the Knots of Metropolitan*
Traffic," Smithsonian, April 1986

e.   Nobody likes to get ripped off, and so I find it puzzling that the airline industry is able to get away with pricing that appears whimsical at best and downright unfair at worst. A good case in point involves the fare from West Palm Beach, Florida to Washington, D.C. One company, for instance, charges $89, another $149, and still another $279. Each imposes restrictions, but the mind is boggled by the dramatic differences in price for exactly the same service between exactly the same cities.

student essay

2.   Choose a topic and from it evolve a thesis statement that will function also as an effective introduction to an essay.

3.   Now write separate introductions to the same essay, employing each of the following types of openings:
   a.   broad statement
   b.   scene-setter
   c.   quotation
   d.   anecdote
   e.   statistic or fact

REVISION EXERCISES

Expand all of the following statements into effective introductions for essays:

1. There are several ways to deal with the frustration I feel just before I start filling out my income tax forms.
2. My aunt has given me many art objects as gifts over the years. There are several reasons why I don't display any of them.
3. I had an interesting time at the beach.
4. The toys on the shelves of the nation's department stores this year appear reminiscent of traditional sexual stereotyping, with dolls dominating for girls and robots and other adventure-oriented creations being aimed at boys.
5. The funeral industry exploits emotions and guilt in order to make a profit.

WRITING TRANSITIONAL PARAGRAPHS

The term "transition" literally means to change, to move from one state or position to another. In writing, transitions have two major purposes, both of which are designed to aid an audience: (1) they signal that the writer is moving from one thought to another; (2) like bridges, they connect one thought with another, thereby enabling the audience to see relationships as the writer sees them and strengthening a piece's coherence. You will use transitions most often to link sentences or parts of sentences and to establish relationships between paragraphs. Most transitions require only a single word or phrase.

On occasion, you may find that a word, phrase, or even a sentence transition is insufficient to signal your intent clearly or to move your audience gracefully from one thought to another. Your option in such an instance is to include a brief transitional paragraph of one or two sentences. As a general rule, however, you should exercise this option only with longer essays of, say, a thousand words or more. Despite their uses—explained below—transitional paragraphs in relatively short essays can result in a halting, choppy structure that may distract your audience.

To Separate

Some essays involve broad, complex topics that for the sake of clarity must be broken down into specific divisions. A short transitional paragraph will therefore enable you to signal your audience that you have completed one aspect of your discussion and are about to move to another:

> Such are the mating habits of the Siamese fighting fish. We now turn to its aggressive nature.

> These, then, are the liabilities faced by the realtor in a poor housing market. Fortunately, there are ways to offset them.

In some instances, you may use a transitional paragraph to signal that you have completed your explanation of one aspect of the topic and are ready to illustrate it through examples:

This, then, is the theory. Let us see how it works in practice.

A few examples will further illustrate the process.

On occasion, a transitional paragraph may function not only to separate explanation from illustration but also to signal a movement from the abstract to the concrete, or vice versa. In "Appomattox," the American historian Bruce Catton spends a number of paragraphs contrasting the physical appearances and styles of Robert E. Lee and Ulysses S. Grant during their meeting at Appomattox Courthouse at the end of the Civil War. Catton then uses a transitional paragraph to move his audience away from physical description toward an analysis of the symbolism of the meeting—the death of the old, gracious way of life embodied in the South and exemplified by Lee:

> . . . No two Americans could have been in greater contrast. . . . Lee was legend incarnate—tall, gray, one of the handsomest and most imposing men who ever lived, dressed today in his best uniform, with a sword belted at his waist. Grant was . . . rather scrubby and undersized, wearing his working clothes, with mud-spattered boots and trousers and a private's rumpled blue coat with his lieutenant general's stars tacked to the shoulders. He wore no sword. . . .
>
> Yet the contrast went far beyond the matter of personal appearance. Two separate versions of America met in this room, each perfectly embodied by its chosen representative.
>
> There was an American aristocracy, and it had had a great day. It came from the past and it looked to the past; it seemed almost deliberately archaic, with an air of knee breeches and buckled shoes and powdered wigs, with a leisured dignity and a rigid code in which privilege and duty were closely joined. It had brought the country to its birth and it had provided many of its beliefs; it had given courage and leadership, a sense of order and learning, and. . . .
>
> *This Hallowed Ground*

To Summarize

In a lengthy or complex discussion, you can provide an effective transition by restating in a paragraph the principal point or points you have established before going on to treat the next one. This gives you the opportunity to summarize for the benefit of the audience, and gives the audience an additional opportunity to digest what you have already said. Suppose, for example, you were writing an essay on the process of assembling a fertilizer spreader. If there are four major steps, some of them complicated, you might summarize after discussing the first three:

> You have now completed three of the four basic steps: (1) connecting the wheels to the spreader frame, (2) attaching the fertilizer container to the frame, and (3) affixing the distribution regulator to the container base.

Another option would be to summarize after discussing the first three steps, and then go on to describe the fourth:

> Once you have completed the steps of (1) connecting the wheels to the spreader frame, (2) attaching the fertilizer container to the frame, and (3) affixing the distribution regulator to the container base, one more step remains: attaching the hand control to the regulator.

In the above and following examples, combining a summary with the topic sentence or topic idea of the main paragraph to follow provides an effective transition for the audience and strengthens the coherence of the entire essay:

> Thus, current television censorship guidelines reflect prudery, dated mores, and logical inconsistencies. The strongest reason for dumping those guidelines, however, is that they distort reality and thereby diminish the credibility of both serious drama and comedy.

To Compare and Contrast

A comparison of the ideas of two or more topics in the body of an essay may provide a useful transition between main paragraphs. For example, if you are writing an analysis of a certain actor's ability and discussing his performances in several movies—two of which are treated in separate paragraphs in the body of your essay—a statement comparing performances might serve as a useful link or transition in your discussion:

> Sterling Hawkbarf's ability to witness murder with a perplexed expression delighted audiences in *Attack of the Hammertoe* as well as in *Night of the Gerbil*.

Similarly, a transition paragraph contrasting performances might be equally effective:

> Although Sterling Hawkbarf delighted audiences with his bewildered expressions in *From Albania with Love*, he reached the height of bemusement only in his starring role in *Piers the Plowman*.

To Emphasize

Because it is set off from the other columns of words by an indentation, any paragraph beginning has a natural emphasis. You may sometimes decide to use the inherent emphasis of a paragraph opening by writing a brief transition paragraph to announce to your audience that what follows is especially important.

You can also use the inherently emphatic qualities of a brief transition paragraph in setting a particularly important scene. In the following excerpt from *The Year of the Whale,* Victor B. Scheffer makes use of a one-sentence transitional paragraph to set a scene that will be central to his argument against the senseless exploitation of the whale:

> . . . This humid strip is the habitat or native haunt of a peculiar race of men who see in any new event . . . a potential source of dollar revenue. They speak of the "fast buck," though only to members of their own kind. To others they speak of "opportunity," "advancement," "progress," or "improvement." Each member of the race has an angle. His delight is to guess the other's angle while concealing his own.
>
> All of this sets the stage for a certain July event.
>
> During the night, a dead sperm whale floats on a flood tide to a beach north of the Golden Gate. It is a small whale, only twenty-two feet long. It comes to rest in a fog. No one knows it is there until a beachcomber . . .

A brief transitional paragraph also allows you to call the audience's attention to a particularly important question, the answer to which will constitute a new aspect of your essay. In the following example, a student uses a transitional paragraph to establish the essay's central question:

> When my friend Robert found a slightly injured squirrel beside the road, he scooped it into a box and took it to the veterinary hospital. Later—sixty-two dollars later—he carried the animal out in the same box and let it loose among the trees in his backyard. His vet bill for his cat last year amounted to eighty-five dollars for treatment of its sinus infection. Shots for his dog cost thirty-five dollars. Robert is very compassionate about animals. When I sought a contribution from him for the American Cancer Society, he came up with ten dollars. To put it another way, he contributed about six percent of the amount he spent on animals. And I don't think the proportion of his charity for humans versus animals is unusual, particularly in the prosperous suburbs of America.
>
> What do the values of people such as Robert tell us about the need to publicize worthy causes that will benefit mankind?
>
> Three approaches to publicize human needs are required. . . .

Use transitional paragraphs to:

• Separate.

• Summarize.

• Compare or contrast.

• Emphasize.

EXERCISE

Choose an essay you have already written and write at least two of the following kinds of transition paragraphs in the body of the paper: separation, summary, comparison/contrast, emphasis.

WRITING THE CONCLUDING PARAGRAPH

The conclusion is your last opportunity to put across your thesis. An effective conclusion offers the audience a way of viewing your essay as a whole. In addition, it eases the audience out of the piece and enables you to offer final affirmation of your thesis. Each word of the conclusion should therefore contribute to the impression you wish to leave with your audience.

If your thesis has been well sustained by the body in a relatively short essay, you may not need to provide a separate conclusion. Do, however, use a conclusion with longer essays and with short ones that are complex—such as a discussion of a process involving many steps. Like an introduction, a conclusion should be of suitable length in proportion to the rest of the essay. Usually a conclusion is written as a separate paragraph, though it can also be effective when introduced in the middle of the final paragraph.

There are a number of options open to you in writing the conclusion, and your choice should reflect the purpose of your essay as well as the thesis you set out to establish. There are six methods you may find useful to explore as ways of concluding. They include the *summary*, the *prediction*, the *question, recommendations*, the *quotation*, and various *combined methods* from among the preceding, which often overlap.

Concluding with a Summary

Summary is the simplest—and potentially the most effective—means of concluding. If your essay is primarily argumentative, a summary conclusion enables your audience to recall your main points. Summary also works effectively with expository writing. You might, for example, list the steps in a process you have just explained in order to reinforce the audience's memory of them. And if your essay is relatively long, a summary conclusion can effectively reemphasize points you established earlier in the text.

As the following examples illustrate, summarizing places the points of an essay in a simple, coherent perspective for the audience. Writing a summary involves (1) drawing out the topic sentences from the previous paragraphs and (2) restating them with appropriate transitions and subordination of the less important ideas. Note, for instance, the coherence with which the sociologists Nena and George O'Neill summarize a complex discussion of "trust" in their chapter on that subject:

> Trust, then, open trust, has nothing to do with expecting or doing specific, predetermined things in marriage, but rather with sharing the knowledge of your immediate desires and needs with your mate, living for now and not for yesterday or tomorrow, living not the life that somebody else has laid out for you in terms of role expectations, living instead for your own self through shared communication and growth with your mate's self. Trust then is freedom . . . to assume responsibility for your own self first and then to share that human self in love with your partner in a marriage that places no restrictions upon growth or limits on fulfillment.
>
> *Open Marriage*

An audience reading through the O'Neills' chapter will find its memory refreshed by the conclusion because the generalities carry with them the associations of the supporting detail that preceded. Notice the transitions from thought to thought consist of contrasts: "nothing to do with . . . but rather with . . . ," "for now . . . not for yesterday . . . ," and so on.

The summary of a shorter piece of writing may be correspondingly briefer. Here, for example, is a conclusion summary of a 500-word narration concerning a student's frustrating trip to see a legislator, in which the student simply restates the main impressions she wishes to convey:

> The frustration I felt after waiting three hours to see Senator Powell resulted not so much from the boredom of having nothing to read but seven-month-old *Newsweek* magazines but more from seeing him slip out the side door of his office after his secretary had told me he was not in. He had been there the whole time.
>
> *student essay*

Concluding with a Prediction

Prediction is an effective means of concluding, particularly in a narrative or in a discussion that emphasizes cause and effect. If the body of your essay is primarily a statement of events or conditions, your conclusion may suggest or predict what the results may or will be in the situation discussed or in similar situations. For example, "If these conditions are allowed to continue, then . . ." or "If you follow the above three steps, you will find that . . ." Thus, if you are writing a brief essay on some aspect of exercise, you might conclude as follows:

> The recent proliferation of health spas and exercise groups will indeed produce a healthier America, according to the American Osteopathic Academy. However, if you do exercise regularly—especially if you practice aerobics three hours a week or jog more than ten miles a week—the odds are high that you are going to injure yourself.

In "Tracking the Elusive Snow Leopard," authors Rodney Jackson and Darla Hillard detail the threat to that endangered species of Nepal. Note how they use prediction to conclude:

> The children of Dolphu and Wangri are learning that the *sabu*—snow leopard—is worth more to them alive than as a pelt for barter. As they come of age and take their places in village concerns, they could become the most effective guardians of their national treasure, keeping the snow leopards of the Langu a safe distance from the edge of extinction.
>
> *National Geographic*, June 1986

Concluding with a Question

Closing with a question lets your audience make its own prediction, draw its own conclusion. For example:

> It is clear from the examples above that the state is spending far more on highways than it is on education. Most residents will be glad to have efficient road systems for getting to and from work as well as for easy access to recreation areas. However, if current spending trends continue, the question that voters will have to answer is, "Do I want to be on the same highway with functionally illiterate drivers?"

Or

> Those who wish to lower the legal drinking age to eighteen have thus far given no good basis for their argument: they have argued by a loose analogy equating subjection to the military draft with the right to drink. If a person can be drafted, they say, then he or she should have the right to buy liquor. I have argued that judgment and maturity are required for drinking responsibly. Look again at the statistics I have cited on highway slaughter, driving while intoxicated, and driver age. Do these statistics bear out my position or not? Won't you vote to keep the age limit at twenty-one?

The question conclusion involves the reader in the logical process of your argument, which, if it has been laid out properly, may bring the reader to believe that your position is the obviously just conclusion. If you are addressing readers who probably already agree with your position, you can include a negative in your question (as in the second example), and the question will presuppose a positive answer.

By use of the question conclusion, you can hope to affect your readers in one of these ways: (1) those strongly opposed to your views have at least allowed themselves to reconsider the issue; (2) those who were unsure can now make the decision to agree with your views; (3) those who already agreed with you will hold their views more strongly.

Concluding with Recommendations

A recommendations closing is one that stresses the actions or remedies that should be taken. For example, if you are writing an argument opposing Ace Oil Corporation's plan to use its high profits to purchase Buffalo Brothers' Circus, you might conclude with a call for a letter campaign to Senator Basketsweat, whose committee oversees policies of energy development. Similarly, your discussion of the failure of the school board to appropriate adequate money for the education of retarded children might conclude with a request that the board follow the principles of the State Education Act.

The noted British author George Orwell provides near the closing of his "Politics and the English Language" six specific recommendations for improving the use of the language. We include this excerpt because it illustrates an effective use of recommendation—and because Orwell's advice with regard to writing is especially sound:

Afterwards one can choose—not simply *accept*—the phrases that will best cover the meaning, and then switch round and decide what impressions one's words are likely to make on another person. This last effort of the mind cuts out all stale or mixed images, all prefabricated phrases, needless repetitions, and humbug and vagueness generally. But one can often be in doubt about the effect of a word or a phrase, and one needs rules that one can rely on when instinct fails. I think the following rules will cover most cases:

(i) Never use a metaphor, simile or other figure of speech which you are used to seeing in print.

(ii) Never use a long word where a short one will do.

(iii) If it is possible to cut a word out, always cut it out.

(iv) Never use the passive where you can use the active.

(v) Never use a foreign phrase, a scientific word or a jargon word if you can think of an everyday English equivalent.

(vi) Break any of these rules sooner than say anything barbarous.

These rules sound elementary, and so they are, but they demand a deep change of attitude in anyone who has grown used to writing in the style now fashionable.

Shooting an Elephant and Other Essays

Concluding with a Quotation

Since a quotation may summarize, predict, question, or recommend, you may use a quotation within a conclusion, or as the entire conclusion, for nearly any kind of essay, from narrative to argument. Suppose, for example, you were writing an essay on the philosophy of Horatio Alger. You might end the essay effectively by quoting Tom Nelson, Alger's hero in *The Young Adventurer,* since Nelson's words typify the author's philosophy. Tempted to keep a money-filled wallet he has found, Tom thinks, "It wouldn't be honest . . . and if I began in that way I could not expect that God would prosper me."

A concluding quotation can also enable you to cite the views of an expert in the field that your essay discusses. If clear and not too technical, the direct words of the expert may make a stronger impression on the audience than your own summary of the expert's views. For instance, in the following conclusion (which is largely summary), the psychologist Thomas Harris uses a quotation by the philosopher Will Durant to give authority to Harris's own philosophy:

> We cannot produce responsible persons until we help them uncover the I'M NOT OK—YOU'RE OK position which underlies the complicated and destructive games they play. Once we understand positions and games, freedom of response begins to emerge as a real possibility. As long as people are bound by the past, they are not free to respond to the needs and aspirations of others in the present; and "to say that we are free," says Will Durant, "is merely to mean that we know what we are doing."
>
> *I'm OK—You're OK*

A student essay that discusses the poor qualifications of certain modern political leaders and the attitudes of party bosses concludes as follows:

> In *Plunkitt of Tammany Hall,* William L. Riordan records the thoughts of the corrupt politician George Washington Plunkitt on the subject of education and political leadership: "Most of the leaders are plain American citizens, of the people and near to the people, and they have all the education they need to whip the dudes who part their name in the middle and to run the City Government. We got bookworms, too, in the organization. But we don't make them district leaders. We keep them for ornaments on parade days."

Concluding with Combined Methods

Combinations of the above kinds of conclusions provide you with a variety of additional choices. For example, if you have discussed a problem, you may end your essay with *recommendations,* suggestions of ways to improve conditions. If the problem you have discussed is capital punishment, you may conclude with a *quotation* of recommendations by an authority on criminology or sociology. If you are writing on the need for environmental protection, you may use *prediction, recommendations,* and perhaps also *quotation* or *question.*

When considering the various choices open to you, remember that devising an effective conclusion is best determined by your answer to two fundamental questions: "Who is my audience?" and "What type of conclusion will best lead my audience to my way of thinking?"

Among the ways to conclude your essay are:

- Summary.
- Prediction.
- Question.
- Recommendations.
- Quotation.
- Combined methods.

REVISION EXERCISES

1. Choose an essay you have already written and now write separate conclusions employing at least two of the following methods:
   a. summary
   b. prediction
   c. question
   d. recommendations
   e. quotation
   f. combination of two of the above methods
2. Revise the following conclusions to make them more effective:
   a. For all these reasons, I am against any kind of United States involvement in South Africa. Again, I think Washington should break relations with Pretoria.

b. If the arms race is allowed to continue unchecked, we will eventually blow ourselves up—whether by accident or design. And then where will we be?

c. As a friend once remarked, "If we don't all hang together, we'll all hang separately." As consumers against ripoffs by unscrupulous merchants, we must maintain a unified front, coordinate our actions, and demand our rights.

7

Using Narration

Narration is story telling. Whenever you explain what you did last night, recount an interesting experience, or detail the plot of a movie, you are informing your audience of an event or series of events. Your purpose generally is to enable the audience to relive the event as you discovered it. At a minimum, therefore, you provide specific information regarding what happened, where, to whom, when, and why. Answering these questions gives a narrative a particularly concrete quality, as in historian Frederick Lewis Allen's account of the flooding of the Ohio River in 1937. Having cited figures on the numbers of drowned and homeless, Allen continues:

> But these figures give no impression whatever of what men and women experienced in each town during the latter days of January as the swirling waters rose till the Ohio seemed a great rushing muddy lake full of floating wreckage, and the cold rain drizzled inexorably down, and every stream added its swollen contribution to the torrent. Railroad tracks and roads washed away. Towns darkened as the electric-light plants were submerged. Business halted, food supplies stopped, fires raging out of control, disease threatening. The city of Portsmouth, Ohio, opening six great sewer valves and letting seven feet of water rush into its business district, lest its famous concrete flood wall be destroyed. Cincinnati giving City Manager Dykstra dictatorial powers. The radio being used to direct rescue work and issue warnings and instructions to the population as other means of communication failed: a calm voice at the microphone telling rescuers to row to such-and-such an address and take a family off the roof, to row somewhere else and help an old woman out of a second-story window.

> *Since Yesterday: The 1930s in America*

Sometimes a writer's purpose in narration goes beyond the strictly informational. Historians, for example, generally seek to portray the reasons for social change and indirectly prompt their readers to reflect on the values in their own society. Like description, narration is often used in support of exposition or argumentation. Thus, narration is a method for developing both individual paragraphs and entire essays.

NARRATIVE PATTERNS

The emphasis in any story is on *what happened*. By establishing that *A* happened and then *B* happened and then *C* happened, you create a narrative sequence grounded in time. When using the narrative method of development, you will probably choose to unfold actions chronologically, moving from past to present. The following excerpt, by author and cartoonist Walt Kelly, shows chronological narrative:

> Moodily I set about catching two grasshoppers in the back yard and hitching them to a matchbox with thread. The grasshoppers were pretty unruly, but every once in a while they would pull together and the team and cart would go flying through the air in a highly satisfactory fashion. Chance, a black dog who was living with us at the time, thought this was all pretty exciting and barked wildly enough to scare the chickens, which set up a clatter of their own. Mother came to the door to discover the cause of the uproar. I pointed out the charms of having trained grasshoppers and she was enchanted for about three minutes while we watched the matchbox go soaring over the grass. Then she decided that the enterprise was too cruel and ordered me to cut the insects loose. This I did with a heavy heart, having envisioned myself as ringmaster in a grasshopper circus, and world famous.
>
> *Five Boyhoods*

You may sometimes choose to rearrange the chronology to emphasize a special episode, as the narrator does at one point in F. Scott Fitzgerald's novel *The Great Gatsby:*

> For a while I lost sight of Jordan Baker, and then in midsummer I found her again. At first I was flattered to go places with her, because she was a golf champion, and everyone knew her name. Then it was something more. I wasn't actually in love, but I felt a sort of tender curiosity. The bored haughty face that she turned to the world concealed something—most affectations conceal something eventually, even though they don't in the beginning—and one day I found what it was. When we were on a house-party together up in Warwick, she left a borrowed car out in the rain with the top down, and then lied about it—and suddenly I remembered the story about her that had eluded me. . . . At her first big golf tournament there was a row that nearly reached the newspapers—a suggestion that she had moved her ball from a bad lie in the semi-final round. The thing approached the proportions of a scandal—then died away. A caddy retracted his statement, and the only other witness admitted that he might have been mistaken. The incident and the name had remained together in my mind.

The contrast between the Kelly and Fitzgerald narratives illustrates the different purposes that narration can accommodate. Kelly was interested in a recollection that revealed his feelings during a minor conflict of views with his mother. Apart from "Moodily" in the first sentence, Kelly's emphasis is on the chronological and concrete until the final two sentences, which contrast his and his mother's feelings. On the other hand, the narrator in the Fitzgerald account is primarily interested in understanding why he is curious about Jordan Baker. Thus, he recounts a series of incidents not in chronological order but in order of psychological importance.

The following excerpt from a student essay shows a combination of narrative patterns: a strictly chronological account comes first, followed by a paragraph of reflection, as the recollection of experience on an assembly line triggers an insight about the writer and the education process.

> Throughout the summer, I got up at 6:00 A.M., washed, groped for my clothes, grabbed some coffee, and drove to the plant. At 7:00, I was at my job on the assembly line. First, I would put the bolt into the casing, then fit a screw to the bolt, and finally insert the casing into the cylinder. Then I would begin again, praying for the lunch break and after that, for the quitting bell at 3:30. This was mindless work, I knew, and by the time I got home, I was fit only for sitting in front of the television set watching mindless programs.
>
> My God, I thought. Imagine thirty years of doing this. Thirty years of casings and bolts and lunch breaks and bad TV. I had often felt victimized by the routine of college, but this was a routine that was completely beyond comprehension. Yet this was what many people did. They must be crazy, I thought. Or maybe they had no choice. But I did, and I decided that the assembly line made my gripes about college seem petty—and made college seem like heaven.

NARRATIVE VOCABULARY AND PERSPECTIVE

The appeal of narration is partly a product of its dynamic sense. You undoubtedly realize that most aspects of experience are constantly changing. Through its emphasis on time passing and events unfolding, narration is uniquely suited to capture the sense of change. To convey this sense, narration uses a vocabulary of prepositions, adverbs, adverb phrases, *-ing* verbs, and the active voice to suggest temporal or physical movement. Here is a random—by no means complete—list of such words and phrases:

once	during	last week (year)
then	while	by (midnight)
now	as	on (Sunday)
meanwhile	began	at that point
before	starting	going
after	expecting	having gone
previously	today	early
next	tomorrow	presently
soon	yesterday	currently

Examine the movement and the narrative vocabulary in the following excerpt from a student's journal:

> My father left home yesterday, after two kids and twenty-four years of marriage. Last year, while my brother and I waited and anticipated, he returned after a two-month separation from my mother. She had previously left him in 1980 but returned just before Christmas for "the sake of the children." I woke up this morning hoping that she'd call to say Dad was back, and if she doesn't call later today, I know that tomorrow I'll continue to hope.

Notice that in just four sentences, the writer unfolds four closely related events linked by "movement" words and phrases. Notice, too, that part of the action takes place in the writer's mind as she attempts to deal with changes in her family structure.

As suggested by this and previous examples, the appeal of the narrative method of development can be enhanced by the use of the first person "I." Because the first person helps form an intimate, personal bond between writer and audience, it is especially useful in presenting autobiographical material or in describing situations in which you were a participant or an observer. In using the first person in your essay, you invite your audience to see an event through your eyes, thus narrowing the distance between you, as writer, and your audience. For the same reason, when referring to yourself, use "I" rather than "the writer of this essay," which is both wordy and pretentious.

Of course, you may on occasion decide to use the third person (he, she, they). The third person is effective in historical narratives. Depending on your purpose, the third person can be useful in writing case studies and reports, that is, in highly objective writing where the emphasis is on the event itself rather than on its interpretation.

NARRATIVE EMPHASIS

The effectiveness of your narrative writing reflects your clarity of purpose. Understanding exactly what you want a narrative to accomplish will enable you to select and emphasize details that will strengthen the idea or impression you wish to convey. As a writer, you should realize that while some narratives are intended to operate exclusively on the "what happened" level, others reflect the author's desire to probe deeply into what has been gained or lost during the passage of time and events.

In the following narrative, a young army deserter describes his feelings while on a train in Italy during World War I:

> In civilian clothes I felt a masquerader. I had been in uniform a long time and I missed the feeling of being held by your clothes. The trousers felt very floppy. I had bought a ticket at Milan for Stresa. I had also bought a new

hat. I could not wear Sim's hat but his clothes were fine. They smelled of tobacco and as I sat in the compartment and looked out the window the new hat felt very new and the clothes very old. I myself felt as sad as the wet Lombard country that was outside through the window. There were some aviators in the compartment who did not think much of me. They avoided looking at me and were very scornful of a civilian my age. I did not feel insulted. In the old days I would have insulted them and picked a fight. They got off at Gallarate and I was glad to be alone. I had the paper but I did not read it because I did not want to read about the war. I was going to forget the war. I had made a separate peace. I felt damned lonely and was glad when the train got to Stresa.

Ernest Hemingway, *A Farewell to Arms*

The effectiveness of this short narrative underscores Hemingway's careful attention to his purpose: indicating the change that has come over the narrator between the present—the time of his "separate peace"—and "the old days." Notice that Hemingway chooses to include only details that reinforce his purpose and gives special emphasis to the contrast between the narrator's new hat and the old clothes. This contrast mirrors the conflicting loyalties that the narrator feels toward himself on the one hand and the army on the other.

The process of writing a narrative begins with identifying the idea or feeling you wish to present. Next, you should sketch out roughly the events of the incident or episode you wish to relate in chronological order. Finally, arrange the events in an order that will strengthen the idea or impression, and include only those details that are necessary to give your account credibility. You can usually decide best what to cut or amplify once you are revising. Particularly when you begin your revision, determine if your impression would be strengthened by the use of details involving all the senses, not just sight. In revising for a particularly emphatic impression, you may decide to hold the single most significant detail until the end.

Within a narrative paragraph, the topic sentence—which openly states the impression you intend to make—may logically be presented at either the beginning or the end. If you place it at the end, the topic sentence should forcefully summarize and reemphasize the impression you were aiming at. With narration, the absence of a topic sentence can be highly effective if you present convincing details that are carefully selected to support the topic sentence you wish to imply.

In the following narrative paragraph, note how the writer has chosen details to emphasize the impression of brutality:

That autumn, late every afternoon, I watched the middle-aged woman across the street march into her front yard, leading a large, black, reluctant dog out for an obedience lesson. Dragging him by the collar into the grass strewn with dead leaves, she would first take five steps; the dog, sometimes dragged and sometimes following voluntarily, stayed a pace behind. Then the woman executed a quick turn, shouted "Heel!" and, jerking the leash, brought the dog in step behind her. Back and forth. Back and forth. I watched as the sun, tinting the October sky with red, cast its fading light on the woman, the dog, and the dead leaves.

student essay

Though the overall impression is left unstated, the narrator's selection of detail and choice of words (or *diction*) suggest that he senses death and a military authoritarianism in the scene. The narrator chooses to omit certain details: we learn nothing of the physical appearance of the woman; we know only her approximate age, which parallels the time of year (autumn) and time of day (sunset). Sunset, autumn, and middle age all suggest approaching death; the dead leaves, the blood color of the sunlight, even the color of the dog (we get no other physical details about it other than its relative size) reinforce that impression.

You should also notice that the writer omits other details. For example, he indicates nothing of the appearance of the house before which the scene takes place, the length of the training session, the breed of the dog, the size of the yard, or the location (geographically) of the event. Note also the care with which he has chosen words that enhance the feeling of destructive authoritarianism ("dragging," "march," "executed," "shouted," "jerking"). Again, the writer creates an impression without directly stating it.

EXERCISES

Respond to the following questions with specific reference to the above narrative:
1. Which senses does the author appeal to? Could the paragraph be more effective if other senses were employed?
2. Would some arrangement other than the strictly chronological be more effective?
3. Rewrite the narrative on dog training to establish an impression of *warmth* and *love* instead of *approaching death* and *brutality*.

The following is a full-length narrative essay written by a student. The thesis statement, the last sentence of the introductory paragraph, indicates the dominant impression, the most significant effect, feeling, or image the writer wants to establish:

RAILROAD DAYS

Although my summer job on the railroad maintenance crew was a sort of physical torture, I regretted its coming to an end because I knew I would miss my coworkers. My last day at work was physically difficult, but it had a charming conclusion.

The three of us, Dave, Larry, and I, had spent the morning removing rotten railroad ties from the track bed, and in the afternoon we put in the new ties. As the afternoon sun beat down on my back and bare head, perspiration dripped from my forehead onto the air hammer I was using to pound in new rail spikes. Then the racket from the hammer and air compressor combined with the heat to give me a headache. Soon, the pain was jumping with the vibrations of the hammer. While I was driving the final spike late that afternoon, the air hammer twice slipped from the silver head of the spike and struck the top of my shoe, bruising my toes painfully. At 4:00 P.M., we left the work area to clock out. I felt dirty and tired. My shoulders ached from the strain of moving the ninety-pound air hammer from spike to spike.

From the office, after we punched out, we went across the street to the Oasis Bar, where they sold beer to us even though we were under age. Before we sat down at our regular table, Dave put a quarter in the juke box. As he had done each afternoon of the summer, Dave punched the set of buttons that brought the soothing sounds of Tammy Wynette. All of us were tired; all of us ached. Soon, all of us were mildly drunk. But the beer was cold and the air conditioning felt good, and soon each of us began to speak of plans for going to college the following week. Slightly drunk and weary as we were, we each made a sentimental testimonial to the friendship we had enjoyed for three months and vowed to get together for a drink during Thanksgiving vacation.

I thought then that I would never see them again, and I haven't. But they did leave me with mellow memories of a time when I did the most physically tiring and demanding work I likely ever shall do.

EXERCISES

1. Respond to the following questions on the previous essay:
   a. How do certain details in the third paragraph parallel details in the second? Why may the writer have chosen to use parallel details?
   b. Would further detail in either the second or third paragraph make the impression (as stated in the introduction and in the conclusion) more convincing?
   c. Are there any details that do not reinforce the impression that the writer is attempting to convey?
   d. From which senses does the writer draw his detail?
2. Narrate an incident in your experience, establishing one of the following as the dominant impression:

   irritation   surprise
   fatigue   disappointment
   happiness   relief

REVISION EXERCISE

Revise the following paragraph to bring out the impression of relief more clearly. Cut irrelevant details and supply pertinent ones if necessary.

> "Relief" is more than an antacid tablet. The bus ride from campus to my home takes forty-five minutes during rush hour, and I have always found the crowds to be rude and pushy, and the drivers to be surly. Last Tuesday the ride began as usual, with the driver snarling and the other passengers pushing and elbowing me. I arrived home tired and irritated. I had lasagna for supper and watched the news on television. I usually don't watch the local news because I can't stand the announcer. Anyway, about eight o'clock that evening I looked for my purse so I could find my homework schedule. It was only then that I realized I had left my purse on the bus. My heart sank into my stomach. I slumped into a chair and stared blankly for several minutes. Then the doorbell rang. When I opened the door, a young man stood before me. He handed me my purse and said he had found it on the bus and got my address from my driver's license. He wouldn't accept any reward. I was so surprised and delighted that I felt relief that was real exhilaration.
>
> *student essay*

NARRATIVE ORDER

You will generally use a chronological order of development in presenting a narrative, and you therefore need to ask "In what order did (or do) these events actually take place?" Your developmental order, then, will be the sequence in which the event, or the steps in a process, occurred in time.

The following example is an account of a natural disaster in a rural African village as recalled by a man who witnessed it. The author allows the unfolding of events in their natural sequence to shape his narrative:

> When I was a schoolboy a locust invasion came to my home area. An elderly man who was a neighbor and relative of ours, burnt a "medicine" in his field, to keep away the locusts. Within a few hours the locusts had eaten up virtually everything green including crops, trees and grass, and then flown off in their large swarms. Everybody was grieved and horrified by the great tragedy which had struck us, for locust invasions always mean that all the food is destroyed and people face famine. Word went round our community, however, that the locusts had not touched any crops in the field of our neighbour who had used "medicine." I went there to see it for myself, and sure enough his crops remained intact while those of other people next door were completely devastated. I had heard that a few people possessed anti-locust "medicines,"

but this was the first person I knew who had actually used such medicine and with positive results.

John S. Mbiti, *African Religions and Philosophy*

The chronology established in Mbiti's account simply follows the events as they unfold: (1) the precautions that the elderly man takes against the locusts; (2) the locust attack; (3) the results of that attack; (4) the effect of the attack on the villagers; (5) the report that the elderly man's fields have been spared; (6) the narrator's visiting the man's fields and confirming that the reports are true.

Chronological progression may be used in a variety of ways. For example, instead of arranging events strictly in time sequence, you might emphasize the most important point by presenting it first, then provide the chronological background events, and finally discuss the outcome or conclusion of the incident. The following paragraph is taken from a student essay arguing that riding a motorcycle may be safer than driving a car; notice that conclusions and statements of analysis precede and follow the narrative itself:

> The exposed position of the cyclist seems to make him more vulnerable to injury and accidents, but his extra alertness and his protective clothing allow the skilled bike rider to walk away from otherwise disastrous incidents. I was riding in my neighborhood at thirty-five miles per hour when, unexpectedly, a driver pulled out in front of me and blocked the entire street. I slammed on my brakes, causing the bike to skid, stood up for better control, avoided the car but smashed into the curb. To save my bike I thrust myself toward the street, forcing the bike to land on the grass. I rolled the entire width of the street, yet, protected by my helmet and clothing, I got up immediately to turn off my cycle—a thirty-five-mile-per-hour spill with no injury. The maneuverability and small size of the bike enabled it to avoid a collision that could well have been fatal if I had been driving a car. I concluded that bikes can execute seemingly minor miracles that enable them to avoid accidents. Furthermore, the apparently vulnerable situation of a cyclist actually gives him greater visibility since, unlike the motorist, he has no blind spots, no obstructions, and a much higher line of vision.

Notice that the writer *begins* his account with a conclusion about the experience that he has yet to unfold: the motorcycle rider's "extra alertness and his protective clothing allow [him] to walk away from otherwise disastrous incidents." He then provides the chronology of events that form the basis of his conclusion. Finally, he ends the paragraph by elaborating on the meaning of the first sentence.

Using narration effectively requires that you carry out the following tasks:

- *Identify* the feeling or idea you wish to convey through your narrative.

- *Arrange* the narrative events chronologically, selecting the details that will reinforce that feeling or idea.

- *Include* only those other details that you need to make the narrative credible.

- *Determine* whether you can gain greater impact by rearranging the chronology, perhaps placing the most important or interesting episode at the beginning or at the end.

- *Revise* to cut irrelevant detail, select the most appropriate detail, and arrive at the most effective order.

EXERCISES

1. The following narratives deal with a common subject: awakening. Examine these narratives and respond to the questions that follow:

   a. At first, opening his eyes in the blackness of the curtains about his bed, he could not think why the dawn seemed different from any other. The house was still except for the faint, gasping cough of his old father, whose room was opposite to his own across the middle room. Every morning the old man's cough was the first sound to be heard. Wang Lung usually lay listening to it and moved only when he heard it approaching nearer and when he heard the door of his father's room squeak upon its wooden hinges.

   But this morning he did not wait. He sprang up and pushed aside the curtains of his bed. It was a dark, ruddy dawn, and through a small square hole of a window, where the tattered paper fluttered, a glimpse of bronze sky gleamed. He went to the hole and tore the paper away.

   "It is spring and I do not need this," he muttered.

   Pearl Buck, *The Good Earth*

   b. It was dark when I awakened—or when I came to, if it was that. I was aware at once that there was something wrong. There was no sound, not even the honk of a frog or the chirp of a cricket. There was smell, a fire very different from ours, pungent, painful as thistles to the nose. I opened my eyes and everything was blurry, as though underwater. There were lights all around me, like some weird creature's eyes. They jerked back as I looked. The voices, speaking words. The sounds foreign at first, but when I calmed myself, concentrating, I found I understood them: it was my own language, but spoken in a strange way, as if the sounds were made by brittle sticks, dried spindles, flaking bits of shale. My vision cleared and I saw them, mounted on horses, holding torches up.

John Gardner, *Grendel*

c. This time he woke up with the real thing. Somebody was tapping his skull as if it were a breakfast egg. When he moved loose flints rattled inside it. His mouth seemed full of corrosive sublimate. He had a breath like an old tyre on a smoking dump. He lay on a wooden bench in a dark, dusty room. There was very little furniture—a table, two wooden chairs, a basin, and a bed. Rascasse was painting by the window on an easel. Naylor closed his eyes, opened them, and was sick. For some time after he lay like a crushed snail on a garden path. Rascasse gave him a towel soaked in water and a tumbler of brandy. The sunbeams danced in the window. The flies whirled above him, he felt their damp suckers on his eyelids whenever they were closed. He was through. He would go home. He thought of the office in the city, the regular hours. 'Hullo, Naylor, had a good holiday?' He thought of the London library, the beginnings of autumn in the parks, the mists, the lights being lit, the curtains drawn for tea.

Cyril Connolly, *The Rock Pool*

1. Is the pattern in each narrative chronological?
2. Identify elements of the narrative vocabulary in each.
3. Write a statement of "what happened" for each of the narratives.
4. What idea or feeling is emphasized in each of the narratives?
5. What understanding does the narrator or main character reach in each narrative?
6. Write a short narrative of how you awoke (a) on a morning you eagerly awaited or (b) on a morning of a day you knew you would hate.
7. Develop a narrative paragraph or full-length essay on one of the following. Use more than the sense of sight for your developing detail, and place the most dramatic detail at the end. Keep your dominant impression in mind.
    a. a trip during a severe winter or summer storm
    b. a visit to a hospital
    c. a bitter argument
    d. a time you were cheated
    e. an occasion in which a driver lost his or her temper

REVISION EXERCISE

Revise the following narrative so that it has a clear dominant impression, makes use of more than a single sense in the developing detail, and makes the most effective use of chronology.

I worried about the interview for almost a week. When I finally had to get ready to go to it, my stomach had a nervous feeling. I wore my blue suit, so that I would look like a conservative, reliable, solid-citizen. When I got into the car, my hands were perspiring so much I thought it might be dangerous to drive. I didn't know if I would be able to grip the steering wheel tightly if I had to. It was 9:00 A.M., so rush hour was almost over. I drove into the city easily and got to the office by 9:35. My appointment wasn't until 10:00. I made the mistake of getting a cup of coffee before going to the office for the interview, and that just made me more nervous. When I went to the office promptly at 10:00, I was told that Ms. Sharp, who was to interview me, had gone home ill that morning and that the office had tried to call me to tell me not to come. ~~It seems~~ *since* I had already left for the interview. I was really disappointed.

student essay

8

Using Description

Description is portraiture with words. Whenever you describe a person, place, or object, you impart the way it looked or sounded or felt or tasted or smelled to you. You therefore lend your audience your senses, and the effectiveness of your description depends on the exactness with which you capture and present a sensory impression. You may have participated in a conversation in which someone said that something was "too beautiful (or ugly or horrible) for words," or "so lovely (or whatever) that I can't describe it." You probably realized the intensity of the speaker's feelings from these comments, but given such scant information you were forced to probe further by saying, "Well, go on. Describe it. Tell me about it." As a writer, you should realize that *your* audience does not have the luxury of questioning, and that your description must therefore have the exactness necessary to accomplish your purpose.

Description serves many purposes. In some writing it is a vehicle for enhancing an audience's understanding and appreciation of a person or a scene. In others, its major objective may be to help an audience identify something by providing specific information about what to look for, or to persuade the audience to buy a certain item. On occasion, the purpose of description may simply be to share a feeling, establish a mood, or create an atmosphere necessary to achieve another objective within argumentation, exposition, or narration. Whatever your purpose, remember that description serves to involve an audience through sensory experience, and that without description, most writing would be colorless and dull.

PURPOSE AND EMPHASIS

Like other types of prose, a description should have a purpose, clearly understood if not openly stated. If you have ever lost a pet and decided to put up a notice on a bulletin board at a neighborhood supermarket, you probably wrote a simple description that relied heavily or perhaps exclusively on the visual sense:

> LOST: two-yr.-old mongrel. Small, black, with white feet and white face. Short hair. Friendly. Answers to "Heathcliff." If found, please call 555-0922. Reward.

This description presents the bare essentials for recognition and identification of the dog, indicates that the finder need not fear the dog, and offers convenience and inducements for the pet's return. The notice serves its simple purpose. As a piece of writing, however, its appeal is limited to the narrow audience of those who may have information on the pet.

To be worthwhile reading for a general audience, a description should have a broader purpose as revealed in a *dominant impression*. A dominant impression is an attitude, image, or feeling that you, the writer, have about the topic of your description and one that you want the audience to share. As with narration, you provide exactness and bring out the dominant impression by relying on details that convey sense impressions: details of sight, sound, touch, taste, and smell. "Axel has an orange wart on his nose" is a visual image, an image relying on sight. "The train whistle hooted faintly in the distance" is an auditory image, an image relying on sound. "The coat felt soft" is a tactile image, one relying on touch. "The aroma of frying grease wafted from behind the restaurant" is an olfactory image, one relying on smell. "The water is sweet" is an image of taste. Relying almost exclusively on the visual sense can weaken a description when details involving other senses would add precision and emphasis. "She swallowed the wine" is, for example, a simple visual description. Notice how a combination of images can lend interest and exactness: "The warm, musty red wine bit sharply on her throat" uses sight, touch, taste, and smell.

Any description may convey several impressions, but as the following description illustrates, one should be dominant:

> The most striking characteristic of the university's indoor stadium is its visual beauty. The artificial grass sparkles like a new carpet. Though soft to the eye, it is prickly to the touch, and if a runner slides on it, the grass burns and scrapes the skin. This man-made football field is 100 yards long, with an additional 20 yards for end zones. Large white numerals mark each 10 yards from goal to goal. Encircling the field is a track, one-sixth of a mile long. When the huge, bright lights directly overhead blaze down on the artificial grass at night, the turf resembles a large, flat, luminous piece of jade.
>
> *student essay*

Notice that the writer clearly indicates the dominant impression ("visual beauty") and that most, though not all, the details support the sense of sight. Notice also, however, that the writer is relatively objective in his description insofar as he does not show a strong feeling for or against his subject since he mentions both positive and negative features (the artificial turf is luxuriant, but it is "prickly"). Similarly, a description of a city district may convey impressions of both fear and excitement. A description of a grandparent may be governed by the attitudes of strict authority and a contrasting gentleness. You may, in the first draft of your essay, find yourself combining seemingly contradictory attitudes, since different feelings—unlike different objects—can exist in the same place at the same time, and often do when you feel close to a particular person or place. In revising your essay, sort through the supporting detail as you sort through these attitudes. It may be that in your final draft you will choose to present an ambiguous attitude. If so, do it consciously—and with well-chosen detail.

An impression may be one of beauty, fear, serenity, ruggedness, hopelessness, or any other characteristic or feeling by itself or in combination with others. Identifying the characteristic or feeling that predominates will give your description unity and assist you in determining the details you want to include or exclude. The following description proceeds from a dominant impression stated explicitly and reinforced by detail designed to support the impression:

> He was not at all like the teachers at school, but David had seen rabbis before and knew he wouldn't be. He appeared old and was certainly untidy. He wore soft leather shoes like house-slippers, that had no place for either laces or buttons. His trousers were baggy and stained, a great area of striped and crumpled shirt intervened between his belt and his bulging vest. The knot of his tie, which was nearer one ear than the other, hung away from his soiled collar. What features were visible were large and had an oily gleam. Beneath his skull cap, his black hair was closely cropped.
>
> Henry Roth, *Call It Sleep*

The dominant impression, one of untidiness, is reinforced by the various details of the man's dress. Notice that Roth gives us no details of the rabbi's face—the shape of his nose, the color of his eyes, the expression on the face. All we know is that the visible features "were large and had an oily gleam."

Many written descriptions do not state openly the dominant impression, relying instead on the audience's ability to respond to sensory details that individually and together imply a certain mood, quality, or atmosphere. As the following passage illustrates, however, any well-written description does have a dominant impression that can be stated in a single sentence:

> A thin man who looked as if he never ate regularly, Professor Lawrence would sit in the classroom windowsill, speaking softly to the small group. With dark circles under his eyes that made me think he had been up all night reading, he would speak in a soft, rich voice of Kant and slowly exhale great clouds of cigarette smoke through his nose and mouth. The soft gray cloud

would stand eerily in the shaft of afternoon sunlight coming through the window. As the quantities of smoke puffed gently from his mouth with each soft syllable he spoke, his dark eyes would glint in the one beam of sunlight in the dusky room. He seemed dreamily unaware of the presence of students, like an ancient seer, an abstract, disembodied voice of wisdom coming through mystic vapors.

student essay

Simply stated, this is a description of a presence rather than a man, and the writer emphasizes the qualities of quietness and dreaminess. Notice also that the audience's vision of Professor Lawrence is obscured by the clouds of smoke, and that the only physical attribute stressed is his eyes, as befitting "an ancient seer."

You may sometimes find that certain topics involve more than one impression. You may therefore choose to employ a combination of dominant impressions, as in the following example:

From both sides of the valley little streams slipped out of the hill canyons and fell into the bed of the Salinas River. In the winter or wet years the streams ran full-freshet, and they swelled the river until sometimes it raged and boiled, bank full, and then it was a destroyer. The river tore the edges of the farm lands and washed whole acres down; it toppled barns and houses into itself, to go floating and bobbing away. It trapped cows and pigs and sheep and drowned them in its muddy brown water and carried them to the sea. Then when the late spring came, the river drew in from its edges and the sand banks appeared. And in the summer the river didn't run at all above ground. Some pools would be left in the deep swirl places under a high bank. The tules and grasses grew back, and willows straightened up with the flood debris in their upper branches. The Salinas was only a part-time river. The summer sun drove it underground. It was not a fine river at all, but it was the only one we had and so we boasted about it—how dangerous it was in a wet winter and how dry it was in a dry summer. You can boast about anything if it's all you have. Maybe the less you have, the more you are required to boast.

John Steinbeck, *East of Eden*

Notice that Steinbeck captures two distinct attitudes about the river: the dominant impression in the winter is that of danger, with the river characterized by harsh, action verbs ("tore," "toppled," "trapped"); the dominant impression in the summer is one of dryness, a river transformed to an underground stream that was no longer "fine."

EXERCISES

1. Write a descriptive sentence conveying the sense of sight. Repeat the exercise for each of the other four senses.

2. Write a paragraph describing a person, and appeal to more than one sense.
3. Write a paragraph describing a memorable meal you have enjoyed, and appeal to three or four senses.
4. Write a paragraph describing a scene, and appeal to three or four senses.
5. Write a descriptive paragraph in which you clearly announce the dominant impression you wish to convey. Underline the details that reinforce the impression.
6. Repeat exercise five, but this time imply the dominant impression.
7. Write a descriptive paragraph in which you combine contradictory attitudes such as love and hate, attraction and repulsion, or fear and admiration.
8. Examine the following descriptive paragraphs. Identify the dominant impression in each, explain how the details reinforce that impression, and note which senses are appealed to.

a. She passed the church, and went down the lane till she came to a high wall by the wayside. Under this she went slowly, stopping at length by an open doorway, which shone like a picture of light in the dark wall. There in the magic beyond the doorway, patterns of shadow lay on the sunny court, on the blue and white sea-pebbles of its paving, while a green lawn glowed beyond, where a bay tree glittered at the edges. She tiptoed nervously into the courtyard, glancing at the house that stood in shadow. The uncurtained windows looked black and soulless, the kitchen door stood open. Irresolutely she took a step forwards, and again forward, leaning, yearning, towards the garden beyond.

D. H. Lawrence,
"The Shadow in the Rose Garden"

b. I was surrounded by hills. They weren't mountains like you see in calendar pictures, topped with evergreens smiling down on a blue, sparkling lake. These were rolling, brooding hills, barren except for some brown scrub grass. As I looked up at the gray sky, I heard the whine of the wind and felt its sharp fingers pierce my thick, black coat. A driving rain soon began to beat me. Large drops smacked my face and ran into my mouth. They tasted sour. The hills continued to look down at me, making me small and afraid. I felt completely alone.

student essay

c. It was beautiful, with alternating bright bands of orange, green, and black. When it moved, it glided slowly and effortlessly, producing the faintest of slithers as its skin proceeded across the glass case. To touch it was to touch parchment. But when the snake reared up, I was held by the blankness of its unblinking eyes. And when the mouth unhinged, exposing two rounded fangs, shivers went up my spine.

student essay

d. Above all, it was the head [of the elephant man] which created such an amazing impression. This did indeed seem huge . . . a misshapen mass of bony lumps and cauliflower-like growths of skin. It had the circumference of a man's waist, and the forehead was disfigured by bosses of bony material which bulged forward in great mounds, giving it an appearance something like that of a cottage loaf laid on its side. The greater mound pressed down upon the right eyebrow so that the eye on that side of the skull was almost hidden.

Michael Howell and Peter Ford,
The True History of the Elephant Man

e. Her eyes were what first caught my attention, violet eyes, Elizabeth Taylor eyes. They looked right at me and commanded me to respond, to like her because they were sincere eyes, unafraid to bore right through me. Her mouth was generous, with small, even teeth. She laughed easily, a deep whiskey laugh that I soon began to listen for. In time, I could sense when she approached. Her movements were graceful, fluid, and promising, and she gave off a scent of wildflowers that remained throughout the day.

student essay

9. Examine the following description, explain its purpose, and identify the details that reinforce that purpose.

The Great Quadrangle washed this feeling [of resentment] away in an instant. It was a composing place, particularly at night. And this was a frosty mid-October night in which a clear sky was powdered with stars. The most brilliant of them appeared to have congregated together in the west; they might have been suspended from the scaffolding round the tower as lamps on a Christmas tree. The central fountain was still playing . . . , and its gentle plash was the only sound to be heard. The Great Quadrangle is given over in the main to senior persons of a sober habit. One would not have expected from it any sharp impression that after summer slumbers the college had filled up again, was murmurous and pulsating like a vast and intricate honeycomb of caverns into which there had once more flowed some codling-crowded sea. Yet the impression did hold, and fairly enough. Of the several hundred young men who had been dining in [the] hall a couple of hours before, the majority were still within bow-shot of me now.

J. I. M. Stewart, *Full Term*

10. Follow the same directions as in exercise nine above.

Everything in the restaurant smacked of old England: heavy beamed ceiling, dancing fires in all three fireplaces, dark brown creaking tables with ages-old initials carved in their tops. One had only to look about, sink back into one of the sumptuous green leather easy chairs that surrounded the tables, and feel an overwhelming sense of mellow contentment. This would soon be replaced with anticipation, however, as the smells of the kitchen pervaded the atmosphere. Few would fail to be stirred by the rich earthiness of the roast haunch of venison with red-currant jelly and chestnut puree, let alone the chicken cooked in red wine with mushrooms or the trout poached in white wine with shrimp and mussels. And as waiter after waiter moves from kitchen to table, the easy anticipation is replaced by impatience. Taste buds at attention, knife and fork at the ready, the cozy room seeming to be getting too warm, a little voice—inside—begins to murmur, "Where's mine?"

student essay

11. Write a descriptive paragraph designed to explicate or reinforce a point you wish to argue for or against. Be ready to explain how the dominant impression and your selection of detail help to achieve your objective.

REVISION EXERCISE

Revise the following descriptive paragraph so that it makes use of senses other than just the visual.

The open market had a large variety of fruits: apples, oranges, watermelons, peaches, and pears—all colorfully arranged. Sunshine poured over the square, brightening the copper pots, pans, and utensils as well as the red, green, orange, and yellow bolts of cloth. People dressed in their native ethnic costumes crowded between the tables that displayed the wares. The square on International Day is a glorious sight.

student essay

PERSPECTIVE AND ORDER

An effective description is often presented from a particular *vantage point*. For example, you may present a view of a city by starting from the tops of the buildings and progressing downward to the street, cataloging detail after detail. Or you may begin at the street and move upward to the tops of the buildings. Similarly, if you are rendering a view of a person, you may decide to begin with a description of how she appears from half a block away and then describe her changing appearance as she walks nearer and nearer. In other instances, you may choose to begin with a close-up view and describe the person as she walks farther and farther away.

Developing detail from a particular vantage point is known as *spatial* order. As with chronological development, spatial development allows emphasis of the significant aspects of a person, object, or scene as it appears to you. Spatial development is an additional tool for achieving emphasis that will serve your purpose in description.

The following example of the spatial order of development is from Frank Norris's *McTeague,* the story of a dull, brutish dentist at the turn of the century:

> When he opened his Dental Parlors, he felt that his life was a success, that he could hope for nothing better. In spite of the name, there was but one room. . . . There was a washstand behind the screen in the corner where he manufactured his moulds. In the round bay window were his operating chair, his dental engine, and the movable rack on which he laid out his instruments. Three chairs, a bargain at the secondhand store, ranged themselves against the wall with military precision underneath a steel engraving of the court of Lorenzo de'Medici, which he had bought because there were a great many figures in it for the money. Over the bed-lounge hung a rifle manufacturer's advertisement calendar which he never used. The other ornaments were a small marble-topped center table covered with back numbers of *The American System of Dentistry,* a stone pug dog sitting before the little stove, and a thermometer. A stand of shelves occupied one corner, filled with the seven volumes of *Allen's Practical Dentist.* On the top shelf McTeague kept his concertina and a bag of bird seed for the canary. The whole place exhaled a mingled odor of bedding, creosote, and ether.

Note that Norris presents the room exactly as it would appear to someone opening the door. The view begins with the "washstand behind the screen in the corner" and proceeds in a circular fashion around the room. The description of the room then has a vertical order, beginning with the steel engraving and concluding with the various objects on McTeague's stand of shelves. By emphasizing the careful arrangement of the room and the objects it contains, Norris is able to suggest much about McTeague's nature, personality, and taste. Notice also that Norris, even in a physical description, appeals to more than the visual sense.

One of the most famous passages in American literature is Herman Melville's description of Captain Ahab in *Moby-Dick.* Viewed through the eyes of Ishmael, the narrator, Ahab takes on a frightening aspect:

> There seemed no sign of common bodily illness about him, nor of the recovery from any. He looked like a man cut away from the stake, when the fire has overrunningly wasted all the limbs without consuming them, or taking away one particle from their compacted aged robustness. His whole high, broad form, seemed made of solid bronze. . . . Threading its way out from among his grey hairs, and continuing right down one side of his tawny scorched face and neck, till it disappeared in his clothing, you saw a slender rod-like mark, lividly whitish. It resembled that perpendicular seam sometimes made in the straight, lofty trunk of a great tree, when the upper lightning tearingly darts down it, and without wrenching a single twig, peels and grooves out

the bark from top to bottom, ere running off into the soil, leaving the tree still greenly alive, but branded. . . .

So powerfully did the whole grim aspect of Ahab affect me, and the livid brand which streaked it, that for the first few moments I hardly noted that not a little of this overbearing grimness was owing to the barbaric white leg upon which he partly stood. It had previously come to me that this ivory leg had at sea been fashioned from the polished bone of the sperm whale's jaw.

Melville employs spatial development. Ishmael begins with Ahab's general aspect—"a man cut away from the stake"—and then supports his impression by directing the audience's attention to Ahab's head where he notices "a rod-like mark." The development moves vertically, from top to bottom, and concludes with a description of Ahab's leg, "fashioned from the polished bone of the sperm whale's jaw." The spatial order of development aids Melville in comparing Ahab to a tree that has been struck by lightning. Just as Ahab has been branded by the mark that runs the length of his frame, lightning darts down the tree trunk and "grooves out the bark from top to bottom . . . leaving the tree still greenly alive, but branded."

You may sometimes decide to employ a combination of spatial and chronological development, thus enabling you to stress the perspective of the narrator in relation to the unfolding of events. You therefore alternate description and narration, proceeding first spatially, then chronologically, then spatially, and so on.

In the following example from a student essay, the writer uses a combination of the spatial and chronological methods of development:

> The Greeb estate took on a new look after Euclid Greeb, the banker, died last winter and his daughter Hilda became responsible for maintaining the property. Hilda spent most of her time delivering her philosophical views to the beauticians at the nearby Hair Pantry, and her neglect of the old house and grounds was apparent by late spring. "Uky," as most of the townspeople knew him, had always taken great pains to keep up the property, probably because he thought it reflected on how well he managed the bank. Hired workers seemed to be always painting the gables on the lovely old Victorian home or replacing shingles or working in the yard. And Uky himself carefully tended a splendid rose garden. But now it was different.
>
> One evening last May I happened to pass by and look up at the Greeb estate. The sky behind the house was a pale orange, but it left enough light for me to see that the paint was peeling on the gables, the hedge was becoming tangled and overgrown, and the rose bushes, many of which had lost their leaves to disease and insects, were growing in a bed of weeds. I could see Hilda through the parlor window, sitting in a rocker near a reading lamp, and studying, no doubt, her favorite volume of John S. Mill. When I returned from my errand twenty minutes later and passed by the Greeb estate again, it looked even more decrepit. The sky was now a dark violet, and the house was a black silhouette of straight lines and sharp angles, slowly becoming

unrecognizable as a house. The grounds—the hedge and rose garden—now looked dark and ragged. Hilda still sat reading in the window, drapes undrawn, now more clearly visible than before because of the lit interior and the outer darkness. Her clothes were old and faded, and her hair was, like the rose garden, a tangled mass. But there seemed to be a light in her eyes as she studied her volume of philosophy, her presence like the Greeb estate itself—a well-lit soul in an untended body.

Notice how the narrator uses vertical progression, twice moving from the sky to the house and grounds. Similarly, there are two chronologies: from winter to spring as well as from early evening to late evening. Note how the estate presents two sets of contrast: (1) the general neatness and orderliness during the time Euclid Greeb was in charge compared to the disorder and neglect under the hand of his daughter; (2) the untended appearance early in the evening compared to the unrecognizable mass of angles in the late evening. All the while, the narrator leads up to a characterization of Hilda Greeb: the entire description becomes a metaphor equating the estate with the physical person and the light with her love of philosophy.

Developing a description involves the following tasks:

- Determining the purpose of the description.

- Determining the dominant impression you want to create, and selecting details that will reinforce that impression. (You may wish to establish two or three impressions, but be clear about which is most important.)

- Drawing details from the other senses—hearing, smell, taste, and touch—in addition to sight.

EXERCISES

1. Examine the paragraph by Roth that appears earlier in this chapter. By what principle does the writer order the details?
2. Write a paragraph from a distant vantage point in which you describe the way someone walks.
3. Write two paragraphs, the first describing the way a building looks from 300 feet and the second from 10 feet.
4. Write a paragraph describing a favorite room; use the spatial order of development.
5. Combine the spatial and chronological ordering schemes to develop a paragraph describing your first meeting with a person who became important to you. Use narration, if you like, as well as description.

6. Write a description of one of the following. Be sure to identify a dominant impression.
   a. the crowd at a sports event
   b. a subway station
   c. a road or trail
   d. a cafeteria at noon
   e. a concert

REVISION EXERCISE

The following paragraph relies on spatial development, and its images are exclusively visual. Revise the paragraph to include chronological as well as spatial order, and appeal to at least three senses.

The first day of boot camp, and, at its conclusion, my first meal in a mess hall. I seemed propelled by the line of the other recruits in front of and behind me. A voice from behind the steam table ordered me to hold my plate up. A gray mass supposed to be mashed potatoes fell on the plate; next came creamed corn, dirty-looking water seeping from the mound at its center; next came bits of brown meat bobbing in a greasy sea of gravy. "Dessert?" a voice said. I said I'd pass.

student essay

9

Using Exposition

Exposition is clarifying and explaining. The last time you gave someone directions to your house, you used exposition. If you explained to a friend how to play chess, you used exposition. If you informed your parents of the reasons for your decision to major in economics rather than history, you used exposition.

Exposition often takes a supporting role in a narration, description, or argument. Whenever you pause to define, give an example, use an analogy, or otherwise clarify or explain what you are writing about, you are using exposition to strengthen the point you are making. In a narrative about a soccer match, for instance, you may find it useful to compare and contrast the skills of two players. In a description of a city, you may find it effective to offer an analogy to a garden or perhaps a swamp. In an argument for public health care, you may find it necessary to define social responsibility.

Used by itself, not in a supporting role for other types of prose, exposition is the method of development that tells *how* something is done, explains *what* something is, or explains *why* something happens or is brought about. Forms of exposition are *exemplification, process analysis, comparison/contrast, analogy, classification, definition,* and *causal analysis*. One or more of these forms of exposition would be used in essays addressing topics drawn from the following questions:

> What is a Marxist?
> What are the main differences between the IBM
>   and Apple personal computers?
> How does one choose a career?
> What careers are open to a college graduate
>   with an economics major?
> What marketing communications systems are
>   available?
> How can I save on utility costs?
> What is software?
> What should I see during a weekend visit to
>   Colorado?

128

What are the characteristics of Gothic
  architecture?
What are the drawbacks (or benefits) of
  compulsory military service?
How do I plan a track meet?
How do I repair a rust spot on the hood of
  my car?

Combining types of exposition is often necessary and useful. For example, addressing an issue such as "What is a Marxist?" would probably require both definition and exemplification, since an abstract definition would best be clarified by examples. "What careers are open to a college graduate with an economics major?" would probably involve classification as well as definition and exemplification. Definition, exemplification, and comparison/contrast would likely be involved in addressing "What are the main differences between the IBM and Apple personal computers?"

EXEMPLIFICATION

Exemplification explains or clarifies by providing illustrations, examples, and supporting details. A marketing analysis, a chemistry lab report, an analysis of the causes of industrial pollution, an explication of the process of caring for tropical fish—all require a certain amount of exemplification.

A common method of exemplification involves presenting a variety of illustrations that together strengthen and give emphasis to a particular idea. The following is an excerpt from *Less Than Words Can Say,* by educator Richard Mitchell, discussing the failure of American schools and the results for society:

> Nevertheless, there are signs of trouble. Somebody keeps losing enriched plutonium and even gold bullion. . . . In some cars somebody has been putting the wrong engine, and other cars are cunningly designed to explode on impact. If your car doesn't explode, maybe your tires will. Deadly substances seep from the earth under the swing sets in the backyards of innocent homeowners. A keypunch operator punches the wrong key and sends you 436 subscriptions to *Poultry Gazette,* and another keypunch operator deposits an extra $30,000 in your checking account, which seems grand until the IRS starts asking you to account for it. You discover that it is no longer humanly possible to change an erroneous bill from the gas company. A Christmas card from your great-aunt arrives three and a half years late, and the freight car bringing your new trash compacter has disappeared somewhere on a siding in Nebraska. It looks as though things are beginning to fall apart.

In the following paragraph examples are used to assist the reader in understanding the difficulties of producing stage effects in nineteenth-century theatrical productions:

Volcanoes, waterfalls, battle scenes, rescues on horseback, amazing transformations—all were done often on the stages of the nineteenth century. But the questions of how—and of how well—are more difficult to answer. Certainly the handling of scenic effects was often crude and blundering. A Philadelphia manager famous for his dramatic spectacles almost failed once when a gauze representing rain fell properly on the stage, but had to be removed by drawing it up again. The sight of rain rising offended the audience's sense of reality, but, impressed with the other scenery, they chose to be amused rather than angered. The failure of Vesuvius to erupt on cue, however, totally ruined a lavish production of *The Last Days of Pompeii*. The stage manager ordered the curtain down and managed to get the eruption going, but by the time the curtain was reopened the disappointed audience, already leaving the theater, saw only the last sputters of the cataclysm.

David Grimstead, *Melodrama Unveiled*

Sometimes a single, thoroughly developed illustration will effectively substantiate a general observation, as in the following paragraph written by a student:

The restaurants that prosper near the turnpike have fast service, mediocre food, moderate prices, and tacky decor. Typical of them is Alf's, where for $1.75 and a five-minute wait, a diner receives a greasy hamburger patty on a day-old bun, served with a squirt of mustard, a translucent pickle slice, and a hard white leaf of lettuce speckled with brown. Included in the cost is an eight-ounce, watery Coke. The diner consumes this fare while sitting on a brown vinyl bench at a formica table covered with crumbs, coffee stains, and the gray swirled residue of a damp dish cloth. Beside each booth is a dusty plastic potted palm, and if the diner has been lucky enough to sit facing the foyer, the view is of a cracked, gray plastic fountain with a jungle and a tiger on the wallpaper behind it. The tiger does not appear to look with interest on either the hamburger or the diner.

Whether you weave together examples or illustrations, or elaborate on a single one, the most effective support for your point comes from the use of *specific details*. Note that in the student paragraph on turnpike restaurants, the writer did not just say that the restaurants have "fast service, mediocre food, moderate prices, and tacky decor." He makes these assertions convincing and interesting by using specific details: "a greasy hamburger patty on a day-old bun, served with a squirt of mustard, a translucent pickle slice, and a hard white leaf of lettuce speckled with brown." These details effectively illustrate the mediocre food. And similar details exemplify the "tacky decor."

In the following paragraph from an essay, a student offers an analysis of why a date was embarrassing. Although she provides some exemplification, she does not make use of specific details:

My first and only date with Harvey was embarrassing from the start. He said several stupid, thoughtless things that made me uncomfortable. He also arrived early, and I was embarrassed because I wasn't ready and did not look my best. Harvey hadn't dressed very appropriately either, and we were going out to a nice restaurant for dinner. He also had some personal habits that made me uncomfortable.

Here is the paragraph revised by the student to provide specific supporting detail:

My first and only date with Harvey was embarrassing from the start. Harvey arrived thirty minutes early, and my mother let him in without telling me. Unsuspecting, I walked into the living room where he was sitting—with my hair in curlers. Before I could leave, my father came into the room, and I introduced Harvey to him. Harvey's first remark was, "This is the first time my parents let me take the car by myself. I sure hope I don't have an accident." Then he said: "Don't worry about your daughter. My intentions are honorable." I felt mortified. Then I noticed that Harvey was chewing a large piece of sickening green Bubble-Yum. Great! I could hardly wait to see what the waiter at the Glass Oyster would think of Harvey's dirty sneakers, bright yellow jeans, and faded Mickey Mouse sweatshirt.

Exemplification involves the following tasks:

- Giving your readers enough evidence to convince them of the reasonableness of your general observation or main idea.
- Using specific details.

EXERCISES

1. In the revised paragraph above, identify the details added by the revision. What do the details accomplish?
2. List specific details that could substitute for each of the following general activities:
   a. preparing a meal
   b. driving a car
   c. going shopping
   d. growing flowers
   e. taking a walk
3. Write a paragraph containing a single, well-developed illustration to support an observation about a recreation spot or a city or town you have recently visited.

4. Write a paragraph that presents several illustrations to exemplify the difficult life of a student.

REVISION EXERCISES

1. Revise a paragraph you have written to improve the use of specific details.
2. Revise the following paragraph to improve the use of specific detail:

> A lot of people in my art class dress oddly. One guy wears sloppy clothes and another guy looks very formal. One of the women comes to class looking like a hooker, another like a star athlete, and another like a stately matron.

PROCESS ANALYSIS

Process analysis concentrates on *how* something is done. When you develop an essay or a paragraph by process analysis, you enumerate the major and perhaps the minor steps involved. If a particular order of steps is essential, provide proper warnings. You may, for example, describe a process of copperplating that involves four main steps and warn the reader that if step four is done before step three, a cloud of poisonous gas will develop. Above all, a process analysis presents steps in a clear *order,* indicating when a particular order is essential.

How much your audience knows about your subject is another important consideration with process analysis. If your audience is not well-informed on the subject, your discussion will have to be detailed. In the following paragraph, for example, travel writer Stewart Edward White tells how to set up a tent in a forested area:

> In a wooded country you will not take the time to fool with tent-poles. A stout line run through the eyelets and along the apex will string it successfully between your two trees. Draw the line as tight as possible, but do not be too unhappy if, after your best efforts, it still sags a little. That is what your long crotched stick is for. Stake out your four corners. If you get them in a good rectangle and in such relation to the apex as to form two isosceles triangles of the ends, your tent will stand smoothly. Therefore, be an artist and do it right. Once the four corners are well placed, the rest follows naturally. Occasionally in the North Country it will be found that the soil is too thin, over the rocks, to grip the tent-pegs. In that case drive them at a sharp angle as deep as they will go, and then lay a large flat stone across the slant of them. Thus anchored, you will ride out a gale. Finally, wedge your long sapling crotch under the line—outside the tent, of course—to tighten it. Your shelter is up. If you are a woodsman, ten or fifteen minutes has sufficed to accomplish all this.

The Forest

With a well-informed audience, you may employ technical terms that use less explanatory detail than might otherwise be necessary. Most of us have had the unfortunate experience of trying to assemble a kit or a toy that came with poorly written directions and wound up with bleeding knuckles, an object that did not do what it was supposed to, or a strangely puzzling heap of leftover screws and parts. While such an experience may seem humorous in retrospect, ask yourself what the result would be if a delegate to a nuclear arms limitation conference received equally confusing instructions.

Some processes are fundamentally the same under any circumstances. When explaining such processes, you may effectively use the second-person point of view, which suggests an active or *participating* audience ("These are the steps *you* follow"). Other processes, however, vary according to the individual circumstances of members of your audience, and thus would not be presented as a single set of steps to follow. For example, in explaining how to organize a political campaign, you would have to allow for varying circumstances from town to town, city to city, election to election. Such a process could most effectively be presented as a case history, written from a first-person point of view ("These are the steps *I* followed to organize the local campaign for reelecting Senator Dunning"). Thus, you would be writing for an *observing* audience.

Grouping a series of many small steps into two or three major ones will simplify your audience's job. A discussion of how to raise a healthy Saint Bernard, for instance, could present the following main steps: (1) provide adequate space for the dog; (2) be certain the animal has a proper diet; (3) see that the dog receives preventive medical care. Each of the three main steps involves a series of smaller steps, and a knowledgeable writer could easily devote a full paragraph to each of the three items.

Let us say you decide to write a brief process essay entitled "How To Find a Summer Job" for an audience of high school students. The thesis (addressed to a participating audience) could begin with some words of encouragement and suggest the paragraph divisions to come:

> By starting your search early in the spring, you have a good chance of finding a summer job that will provide you with spending money and give you some useful experience. You will need to (1) choose where to apply and (2) be persistent in your application.

You could then develop the material into paragraphs that deal with the two major steps: (1) how to decide where to apply and (2) how to be persistent in applying. The first main paragraph might read as follows:

> Planning your search for a summer job begins with your decision on where to work. An early start will give you a jump on other applicants. Location should be your first consideration because if you cannot get to and from work easily, you will use up too much of your time and earnings on transportation. Your next step will be to decide which of the businesses at the appropriate

location would be likely to hire you. Although opportunities vary from summer to summer, stores and restaurants are most likely to have openings for summer workers for two reasons: they normally must be open more than the eight hours that comprise a regular workday (so part-time positions are available), and they usually have a high turnover rate of employees because of minimum wages and irregular hours. If you would prefer to look into some other kind of establishment, such as a factory, look for a company that has to operate more than eight hours a day. Your next step, if possible, is to find a friend or acquaintance who has worked at the place where you plan to apply. Ask that person to recommend you to the manager a few days before you go in to apply.

This paragraph establishes the aspect of the process analysis on deciding where to apply. Several smaller steps are included in the main step, and the writer thoughtfully includes warnings or reasons for the steps so that the audience can follow the instructions with a minimum of difficulty ("Stores and restaurants are most likely to have openings for summer workers for two reasons. . . ."). A subsequent paragraph, dealing with how to be persistent in applying, could describe the various steps involved in talking with the manager, filling out the application, and following up on the application.

The following full-length essay also shows the combining of smaller steps into larger ones. Notice, however, that this essay is written for an observing, rather than a participating, audience.

PROTECTING THE ELDERLY

When my grandfather was beaten and robbed after opening his door to a stranger one night, I decided to look into ways to help him minimize the chances that he would be victimized again. By talking with the local police, I learned that there are several forms of protection against crime available to the elderly. I helped my grandfather by (1) providing him with better physical security and (2) educating him on how he could help protect himself.

The physical security measures, which were simple and inexpensive, involved improving locks, lighting, visibility, and telephone access, and placing some valuables in a safe location. First, I took the obvious measures to keep out an intruder: I installed window locks and dead bolts. Grandfather had been relying on a doorknob latch lock and a security chain to secure his doors, and they could have been forced easily or opened by someone using a plastic credit card and a pencil. Next, I put the lights and a radio on an automatic timer, so they would go on and off at the same time every day, to make the house seem occupied whether or not it was. To improve visibility, I installed a spotlight to illuminate the small backyard and put a 100-watt bulb in the front porch light outlet. I also put a peephole in the front door and cut back the shrubbery next to the house so that it would be difficult for anyone to hide in it. To improve communications, I installed an extension telephone and extra long phone cords so that Grandfather would have easier access to his telephone if he needed to call 911. Finally, I persuaded Grandfather to rely less on cash and more on his checkbook when paying for purchases, and I arranged for him to have his Social Security check sent directly to the bank for deposit.

The police told me that con games are usually directed at elderly citizens, so my next step in increasing protection for my grandfather was to educate him as the police had educated me. According to the police, the basic step in helping the elderly avoid being victimized in a con game is to teach them wariness of strangers, whether in person or on the telephone. When a stranger asks for money for any reason—insurance coverage, dancing lessons, home repair—thievery may well be the object. A con game currently popular in our city, the police said, was for someone to call an elderly person, say that he or she should make a withdrawal from a bank account, and bring the money home, where a bank examiner would arrive and take the money for redeposit in a few days. The caller claimed that by making the withdrawal, the elderly person would be helping the bank to determine which teller was falsifying accounts. I do not know if I saved my grandfather from that particular scam, but I did succeed in making him more leery of strangers.

Perhaps the only real protection against crime comes from having expensive alarm systems and hiring bodyguards for escorts. Perhaps my grandfather will again be a victim of crime despite all my efforts to increase his security. But even if my grandfather is never again the victim of crime and even if all the new security measures should turn out to have been unnecessary, they will still have achieved one important thing: they have greatly improved his peace of mind, which I thought had been forever destroyed after he was mugged.

student essay

The following tasks apply to writing developed by process analysis:

- Presenting steps in a clear order, indicating when a particular order is essential.

- To make the process simple to follow, organizing the many small steps involved in the process into a few main steps.

- If the process is one that your audience can participate in, using the second person ("you"); if the circumstances of the process vary from situation to situation, give a case history of your own performing of the process, using the first person ("I").

- Defining any technical terminology that may be unfamiliar to your audience.

- Being sure to provide all essential information.

EXERCISE

Use process analysis to develop a paragraph or an essay on one of the following:
1. How to select the college that is best for you (for an observing audience).
2. How to pass the time while waiting two hours in a doctor's or dentist's office (for a participating audience).
3. How to evaluate a piece of sports (or other type of) equipment (for a participating audience).
4. How to operate a modem or other piece of computer equipment (for a participating or observing audience).
5. How to detect a shoplifter (for a participating or observing audience).

REVISION EXERCISE

Revise the following paragraph. See that the steps are properly and clearly ordered, that steps are not repeated unnecessarily, and that the audience is consistently treated as either participating or observing:

Maybe you would like to grow a rose bush but you've heard that involves a lot of work. Well, it isn't too bad so long as you follow a few easy steps. First, buy your rose from a nursery and you'll probably get a healthy one with a guarantee. Next, you must have a piece of ground that is sunny most of the day and that has good drainage. The ground should be fertile. I had to get my soil built up by applying plant food regularly. I bought it at a nearby hardware. You can usually find it anyplace that sells seeds. Anyway, I had to build up my ground. You need to have good soil, lots of sunshine, and good drainage, because a rose needs lots of water but can't live if its roots are always soaked. Remember that right after you get the rose planted, you should water it thoroughly. So, first, to grow a rose you need a good piece of ground. Next you go to a nursery and select a rose. At a nursery you're likely to get a healthy plant. I have sometimes bought a rose at a grocery store or department store. Roses bought at those places tend to be unhealthy and unguaranteed. Then you dig a hole about eighteen inches across, chop up the clods so that they're no bigger than pea-size, set your rose in the hole, and pack earth up to the "crown" (the knobby part at the base of the plant), about where the roots start. Then sit back and watch it grow. Finally, I fertilize it once a week and see that the plant gets lots of water about every five days.

COMPARISON/CONTRAST

Comparison/contrast is the identifying of similarities and differences. It is one of the simplest yet most effective expository forms. If your topic is suited to this method, you must first determine the points of comparison and of contrast and then decide which points you wish to emphasize. You then have two alternatives. You might first discuss qualities of Subject A, and then discuss qualities of Subject B, taking care to treat the strikingly similar or distinctively different qualities of A and B in the same order. You might, however, wish to make alternate statements (again carefully arranged so as to be parallel) on A, then on B; A again, then B again; and so on. The comparison/contrast method of development is usually used in combination with other expository forms such as exemplification, analogy, or classification. Whatever combination you use, as you revise, arrange the material to highlight the most significant similarities and differences at either the beginning or the end of your essay.

In the following excerpt from a student essay, comparison/contrast helps to convey the desire for escape that some children feel when they attend church. Notice that the writer uses the first comparison/contrast method, that of discussing A, then B:

> The seat next to Mom and Dad was a dreaded position. Here I was forced to do all the things in a church that, as a child, I hated to do. I had to pay attention to the mass, I had to sing, and I had to recite all the prayers throughout the entire service. No talking, sleeping, or daydreaming was permitted. I not only had to sing, but I had to listen to Dad sing as well. That was real torture. Trips to the bathroom were positively prohibited. "You'll just have to hold it!" Mom would say.
>
> Sitting away from my parents—in the rear pew and near the aisle—was a much more desirable position. I was far enough away from my parents so that I could daydream all I wanted without being bothered. I didn't have to worry about singing, or praying, or paying attention. I could even fall asleep. The end seat was a place in a world all my own. I didn't have to hear Dad sing, and I could dart out anytime I wanted to go to the bathroom. Most important, I could be the first person to leave when the service ended, and leaving was my favorite part of church.

In the following paragraph from a student essay, the writer uses the method of alternating statements on A and B:

> The advantages of cable television over commercial television are illustrated by last Saturday's schedule: in sports, one cable network offered live coverage of two baseball games involving teams vying for first place in the National League, while the commercial networks showed only a wrestling match. In movies, cable featured a new and popular film that was still playing at local theaters; the commercial networks offered two older movies, a Doris Day film from 1966 and a 1975 western starring no one I'd ever heard of. In addition, cable had no commercial interruptions, but the commercial channels had dozens. The one disadvantage to cable is its cost (from twenty-two dollars to thirty-three dollars a month), whereas the commercial networks are free.

In the following example of comparison/contrast, civil rights activist Dick Gregory uses alternating statements of ironic contrast to introduce the subject of racial discrimination in the North:

> To me there's no difference in the North and the South. Down South they don't care how close I get as long as I don't get too big; and up North they don't care how big I get as long as I don't get too close. Yep, we have the same problems up North; 'course, up North we're more clever with it. Take my home town, Chicago. When the Negroes move into one large area, and it looks like we might control the votes, they don't say anything to us—they have a slum clearance.

> Dick Gregory, *The Back of the Bus*

The comparison/contrast method of development involves the following tasks:

- Identifying points of comparison (the similarities).

- Identifying points of contrast (the differences).

- Determining the points you wish to emphasize.

- Choosing an order of discussion (treat all of topic A, then all of topic B, or use alternating treatments of A and B).

- Arranging the material to highlight the most significant similarities or differences at the beginning or at the end of your discussion.

EXERCISE

Use comparison/contrast to develop a paragraph or an essay on one of the following:
1. an ethnic or racial stereotype and a member of the ethnic or racial group
2. a professional and an amateur practitioner of the same sport or activity
3. two musical groups

REVISION EXERCISE

Revise the following paragraph, rearranging or adding details as necessary to sharpen the points of comparison and contrast:

I hope that Peahen Airlines and Mudlark Air both go bankrupt. Peahen has poor service. Its employees are often slow, rude, and sloppy. On my last trip, I had to wait an hour in line (I was behind only three other customers) just to buy my ticket. A Peahen stewardess spilled coffee on my shoulder and never even apologized. What I remember most about my last flight on Mudlark is that Mudlark lost my luggage, and I've heard other travelers complain that Mudlark usually loses a large portion of the luggage it carries on each flight. At least Peahen doesn't lose luggage often. Mudlark's employees are like Peahen's. Mudlark must save money by not giving training to its stewards and stewardesses, who chat with each other until the last few minutes of a flight, then rush around trying to serve drinks at the last, never allowing time to pick up the bottles, cans, and plastic cups. Moreover, Mudlark employees' uniforms usually look wrinkled and soiled, often by food stains that result from carelessness and rough weather. It's hard to tell which airline is worse.

ANALOGY

Analogy is a type of comparison. Its main function is to clarify something unfamiliar by comparing it to something familiar or easily understood. By employing analogy, you offer an audience a simple means of understanding complex subjects or processes, and you will find that it is particularly effective when used in combination with comparison/contrast. Bear in mind that there usually are differences, as well as similarities, between the items being compared, and because of the differences, analogy is not valid for proving a point. But it is very useful for clarifying one.

A fundamental task in developing an analogy is to determine the impression you, as the writer, wish to create about your subject. Suppose, for example, that you were writing a flier on behalf of a candidate for political office and you decide to characterize your candidate's opponent as "invidious"—someone who unjustly creates ill will. After selecting a subject (such as a form of sport) that offers some parallel to the political campaign, you would select an aspect of the sport that illustrates "invidiousness"—a detail that depicts colorfully, in terms that a wide audience can understand, the characteristic that you want to depict in the opponent. Thus you might draw an analogy from a baseball game and argue that stealing a political point is like stealing a base:

> Though it is legal to steal a base, it is unsportsmanlike to spike the shortstop. When my opponent refers to me as "a man who would rather breathe fresh air than see his neighbor have a job," then he is spiking me and stealing the political issue. He is trying to draw off the support of union members who should be able to have both clean air and a job.

The following analogy, which was made by a member of the Federal Trade Commission, effectively illustrates how the shorthand of this expository form aids in clarifying a complex subject:

> Overregulation benefits no one. . . . Government cannot protect everybody from everything. There will be bears in the woods. It is wiser to accept that fact and proceed with appropriate caution than to employ a scorched-earth regulatory policy which gets rid of the bears by getting rid of the woods and leaving everybody with a serious erosion problem.

Though the analogy presents a concrete picture of the problem facing the government agency, its usefulness ends at pointing to the problem. It is not an argument supported by logic—at least, as it stands here. No facts, figures, or case histories are presented to convince the audience that does not agree with the writer at the outset. Nevertheless, the analogy is useful and may be analyzed thus: the woods are equivalent to the marketplace in which consumers walk; the bears are the persons or products that threaten the well-being of the consumers. Government regulations, applied too widely, bring "scorched earth" (the ruining of the marketplace or economic system). The "serious erosion problem" is equivalent to the destruction of opportunities to develop the economy and the marketplace (the "woods"). Such destruction, however, would rid the consumers of the "bears" (the threats to their well-being).

As a general rule, it is best to keep analogies concise and self-contained, and, because an analogy clarifies rather than proves a point, you should never allow it to dominate an essay. On occasion, however, you may be writing a very long essay in which you are dealing with a particularly abstract or complex subject. In such instances, you may weave into your essay a lengthy analogy, as illustrated in the following excerpt from the novel *The Andromeda Strain* by Michael Crichton:

> The great advantage of the electron microscope was that it could magnify objects far more than the light microscope. The reason for this had to do with quantum mechanics and the waveform theory of radiation. The best simple explanation had come from the electron microscopist Sidney Polton, also a racing enthusiast.
>
> "Assume," Polton said, "that you have a road, with a sharp corner. Now assume that you have two automobiles, a sports car and a large truck. When the truck tries to go around the corner, it slips off the road; but the sports car manages it easily. Why? The sports car is lighter, and smaller, and faster; it is better suited to tight, sharp curves. On large, gentle curves, the automobiles will perform equally, but on sharp curves, the sports car will do better."
>
> "In the same way, an electron microscope will 'hold the road' better than a light microscope. All objects are made of corners, and edges. The electron wavelength is smaller than the quantum of light. It cuts the corners closer, follows the road better, and outlines it more precisely. With a light microscope— like a truck—you can follow only a large road. In microscopic terms this means only a large object, with large edges and gentle curve: cells, and nuclei. But an electron microscope can follow all the minor routes, the byroads, and can outline very small structures within the cell—micochondria, ribosomes, membranes, reticula."

> **Using analogy involves these tasks:**
>
> - Deciding on the impression you wish to give your audience about your subject.
>
> - Thinking of another subject that lends itself to comparison with your subject.
>
> - Finding areas of likeness between the two subjects.
>
> - Drawing the comparison between the subjects.

EXERCISES

1. Develop an analogy for two of the following:
   a. McDonald's and a church building
   b. a photographer and a novelist
   c. a car and a monster
2. Create the basis for an analogy for each of the following:
   a. a textbook and _____
   b. a professor and _____
   c. a politician and _____
3. Develop a paragraph for each of the analogies in exercise two.

REVISION EXERCISE

Revise the following paragraph to develop areas of likeness indicated in the analogy:

> The four people who were vying for the office of senior class president last year reminded me of Dorothy, the Cowardly Lion, the Tin Woodsman, and the Scarecrow in *The Wizard of Oz*. Louise was like Dorothy, and Howard was like the Cowardly Lion. Phil reminded me of the Tin Woodsman, who was looking for a heart, and Rae reminded me of the Scarecrow, who wanted to find a brain.

CLASSIFICATION

Classification is used to arrange or group—and thereby make understandable—a complex set of ideas or items that share some common feature. Whether you are trying to arrange library books, types of insulation, antiques, sales methods, desserts, or breeds of cat, your first step is to choose the *basis* for the classification. Because the basis will help you determine the categories into which you will group the items being classified, you must choose it with an eye to the quality or element that is likely to be most useful or relevant to your audience.

You must be careful not to pick categories that overlap. For example, you might decide to classify works of art by period, or by genre, or by subject matter, or by medium. In each case, you would have a consistent basis for classification. If, however, you chose as your categories Renaissance art, landscape painting, oil painting, and sculpture, you would have a problem. For instance, what would happen when an oil painting depicted a landscape? If a piece of art fits into more than one category, the classification becomes confused. A logical set of categories could be based on the single concept of period, and the works of art might then be classified as Romanesque, Gothic, Renaissance, neoclassical, Romantic, and modern. In addition to providing mutually exclusive categories, the basis of the classification should be such that it can be applied to *all* items in the set. Every item should fit into a category; there should be no leftovers.

You should also try to select the basis of classification that will be of the greatest use to your audience. For example, if you classify teachers for the benefit of other students, you might base your classification on *ability to dispense information,* or you might base your classification on *ability to entertain.* These are useful classifications. It would also be possible to classify teachers on several other bases, such as height, color of hair, age, or weight, but for your particular audience these classifications would be far less useful. A commodity such as supermarket meat might be usefully classified according to the type of animal from which it derives, the amount of fat it contains, the amount of sodium it contains, the price per pound, the amount of bone or waste per pound, and so on. If you are writing for dieters or heart disease victims, the category of sodium content would be more appropriate than the others. If, on the other hand, you are writing for buyers on tight budgets, the price per pound would be the most useful category.

The following student essay employs classification to help distinguish the various types of dairy science students. Notice that the writer explains the basis of the classification in the opening paragraph, the thesis statement:

OPTIONS IN DAIRY SCIENCE

On the basis of curriculum, dairy science students may be classified as (1) production management majors, (2) prevet majors, or (3) science majors.

One curriculum option, production management, is for students who are interested in the various aspects of dairy production, allied agribusiness industries, extension, and various other positions. Students who graduate from this option of study find a wide variety of jobs open to them. Some of these jobs are managing herds and dairy farms, working with feed and artificial insemination, operating equipment companies, and working as county agents and breed fieldmen. This option is the most flexible of the three because it allows seventy credits of electives. Students are able to choose the electives best suited to their needs and interests. More dairy science students choose this option, and about 75 percent of those students who graduate from this option go on to farm-related jobs.

Another course of study that dairy science students can choose is the prevet option. This is for those students who wish to become veterinarians. The prevet option does not have the flexibility that production management does because students in prevet have more required courses to take. They must take a number of courses in organic chemistry and physics, and they must take almost all of the courses given by the veterinary and animal-veterinary science departments. Since there is no veterinary school in this state, these students are restricted in where they can go to finish their study in order to become veterinarians. Only a certain percentage of prevet students are accepted into veterinary school, and the grade requirements for these schools are very high. This fact alone discourages many students from entering this course of study. However, with the anticipation of this university's getting a veterinary school, more and more students are choosing the prevet option.

Some dairy science students prefer the science option. This course of study is for those who plan to go to graduate school or who plan a career in quality control, laboratory work, or product development. The science option is very restrictive, too. Students must take many courses in chemistry, mathematics, physics, microbiology, and zoology. These courses give students a wide background for further study in many areas. And because of its wide variety of study, students in this option can change to one of the other options during their third or fourth year more easily than can students in one of the other options. Science students would not have to pick up courses they had missed, as students in one of the other options would. Only a few students choose the science option, however.

Dairy science students have, then, three options of study to choose from: production management, prevet, and science. Production management is the option most students choose because of its flexibility and because of the job opportunities it offers. Students in prevet, of course, plan to go on to veterinary school. And the science option is for students who want to go on to graduate school or who plan to pursue a career in research. Students in the science option can change most easily to one of the other two options because of the variety of courses they are required to take.

Notice in this essay that the basis of classification is logical and the classification is complete—all the options of study are covered. Each main paragraph is then developed by means of definition and comparison/contrast.

You can also develop a single paragraph by classification. The following, for example, is a paragraph from an essay on board games:

Board games may be classified on the basis of the element of chance each involves: (1) those that are almost entirely matters of luck, (2) those that are largely based on skill, and (3) those in which chance and skill play approximately equal roles. In the first group are such games as Ludo, Candyland, and Chutes and Ladders. In the second group are such games as chess, checkers, and Trivial Pursuit. The third group, those in which chance and skill operate equally, includes Chinese checkers, Monopoly, and Clue.

student essay

Classification involves the following tasks:

- Determining the group of items to be classified.
- Choosing the classification basis most useful to your audience.
- Being certain that the categories of the classification system are mutually exclusive.
- Being certain all items in the group can fit into the classification system.

EXERCISES

1. Think of three or four means of classifying students in the curriculum you have chosen or may choose. On what basis could you classify students who have not yet chosen a curriculum? In each case, consider your audience to be your fellow students. What basis of classification would be most useful for such an audience?

2. Think of three or four means of classifying automobiles. What basis would be most useful for a wealthy businessman living in a large city? What basis would be most useful for a young person who has lots of time and money for recreation? What basis would be most useful for a city manager faced with the problem of buying a fleet of police cars? For students just graduating from college?

REVISION EXERCISE

Revise the following paragraph of classification so that it is complete, useful, and logical:

Choosing a gift for a graduating high school senior requires knowing whether the student is planning to attend college and what the student needs. Judging from what I and my friends received, I would classify graduation gifts for the college-bound as highly practical, moderately practical, barely practical, and impractical. In the first category, highly practical, were cash, towels, sheets, a fan, an alarm clock, a new desk dictionary, a study lamp, a typewriter, and other such study accessories as stationery and pens, and a small refrigerator.

Moderately practical gifts included reference books, wall posters to prevent visually boring walls, and recreation things like music tapes for a radio-tape player. Also in this category is a small television set, which one of my friends got. Barely useful things included things like chess and Scrabble games, because so few college students have time for them. A basketball and frisbee are much more useful, because many students like to get exercise when they take breaks from studying. In the last category, the impractical, were such gifts as new ties and clothing for formal occasions, a tropical fish tank, and novels unlikely to be assigned reading in any course.

student essay

DEFINITION

Definition presents the meaning of a term. You use definition to show the specific characteristics that give something its identity, that set it apart from things that are similar to it. In defining, your first step is to identify the *class* (a set or group having at least one common characteristic) to which the term belongs. Your next step is to identify the *differentia,* the particular attributes or characteristics that the term possesses. The differentia distinguishes the term from other terms that fall into the same class that you have designated. Consider, for example, this definition: "An ear is an organ of hearing." The *term* is "ear"; the *class* is "organ"; the *differentia* is "of hearing." You develop the definition by amplifying the differentia, that is, by carefully describing the details that separate the term from the other terms that fall into the same class.

Definition often is combined with one of the other methods of development, such as narration, which may give an example of how the concept is illustrated or applied. For instance, a definition of "puritanism" may begin with the *term-class-differentia* formula: *"Puritanism is a belief in strict moral or religious conduct."* The definition could then be developed by a brief narrative of biographical episodes from the lives of two Puritanlike persons you know, or from recounting an event from the biography of the Puritan preacher Jonathan Edwards. Other useful means of defining are by using analogy or comparison/contrast with another similar term in the same class. For example, you could develop a definition of "liberty" by using an analogy with plane geometry, describing an optical illusion that parallels one person's idea of freedom with another's view of restraint— the opposite of freedom. Sometimes you will find that a one-sentence definition is useful in a technical paper for a general audience, as in the following:

> Indispensable to the computer setup is the *CRT.* (The "CRT" is a "cathode-ray tube," a television screen that gives you a visual display of the information you are dealing with.)

Dictionaries provide definitions using the *term-class-differentia* format. *The American Heritage Dictionary,* for instance, defines "gargoyle" as "a roof spout carved to represent a grotesque human or animal figure, and projected from a gutter to carry rainwater clear of the wall." The *term* is "gargoyle"; the *class* is "roof spout"; a gargoyle is distinguished from all other roof spouts by its being "carved to represent a grotesque human or animal figure, and projected from a gutter to carry rainwater clear of the wall" (the *differentia*). Further development of the subject may logically follow. If you have a 500-word limit, you might specify the restrictions on the subject as follows: "Gothic gargoyles are of special interest to readers of horror fiction"; or, "Gargoyles have practical uses, such as frightening children from the grounds of the mansion." In the first case, development by exemplification or analogy could be combined with definition. In the second, you could employ narration.

The following paragraph from a student essay employs definition. Notice how the writer has stated the *term, class,* and *differentia,* and then elaborated upon the *differentia* in order to make her definition clear and emphatic:

> Pretentiousness is a form of self-aggrandizement based on claims to a special dignity that has not been earned. Unlike pride, which may be based on real achievement, pretentiousness usually is offensive, showing itself in an attempt to belittle others. An acquaintance of mine, Bill, is pretentious. At a recent dinner gathering, Bill tried to give the impression that he knew a great deal about wine and lectured the group on the special merits of obscure brands of claret and burgundy. He judged the dinner wine, which was served in an unlabeled decanter, to be an expensive import, but I knew it was a cheap domestic. Later, I poured some inexpensive Scotch into his glass and told him it was a thirty-dollars-a-bottle brand. He extolled it as the best Scotch available, never knowing that he was drinking from a bottle that cost eight dollars. Bill told about a restaurant he claimed to own, but I had heard from a friend that he was really a cook in a diner and earned the minimum wage. Bill's pretentiousness also shows itself in his claims of purchasing expensive clothes and of holding a graduate degree he never earned. At first, the pretense seems offensive, but it soon becomes simply pathetic. Bill is an unhappy person who is afraid to let others judge him on the basis of what he really has achieved— accomplishments that make him as ordinary as the rest of us.

When employing definition, keep the following in mind:

- Whether you use narration, analogy, or any other means of development in conjunction with definition, you must at some point state *term, class,* and *differentia.*

- See that your definition is sufficiently elaborate, that the term you are defining is clearly distinguished from other terms in the same class.

EXERCISES

1. Respond to the following questions about the preceding paragraph:
   a. Identify the term, class, and differentia in the definition.
   b. What method of development has been combined with the definition?
2. Write a definition paragraph or essay on one of the following subjects:
   a. eccentricity
   b. a miser
   c. a virtue
   d. electrical (or some other kind of) engineering
   e. poverty
   f. carelessness

REVISION EXERCISE

Revise the following so that the opening sentence clearly defines the term and the paragraph sufficiently distinguishes it from similar terms:

> Satire usually shows skepticism or lack of respect. Like a sardonic remark, a satiric comment shows up weakness. A satiric remark may bite sometimes, but a sardonic remark always bites and always shows up doubts about values. Satire pokes fun at something by magnifying or diminishing it, and the result must be that people laugh. Jonathan Swift, for example, made people laugh at the vanity of man by first making Gulliver so much bigger than the Lilliputians that Gulliver looked ridiculous. Next, Swift put Gulliver on an island with giants, so that Gulliver was so trivial he seemed ridiculous. Satire is also present in my roommate's exaggeration of the accent of his math teacher. It remains satire as long as he does the imitation in front of people who like the math teacher. But it would get nasty and cross the bounds of satire if the imitation were done in front of people who didn't like the math teacher, because then it would not just be for fun but would be to hurt.

student essay

CAUSAL ANALYSIS

Causal analysis is a method of development that reveals and discusses the reason for an occurrence and for the consequences of it. Consider this statement, for example: "Continual interference by adults in children's squabbles may result in the children's being unable to solve their own problems." This statement points up first a cause and then its effect, as does the following: "Exposing your skin to smoke from burning poison ivy can bring on a rash." You could develop either of these cause-effect statements by citing examples, statistics, or case histories.

In the following essay, the journalist Carl T. Rowen uses causal analysis to explore some of the reasons why the use of alcohol is on the rise among young people. As you read the essay and note the cause-effect relationships propounded by Rowen, note also his use of examples and statistics to strengthen his assertions.

TEENAGERS AND BOOZE

America's young people have found a potent, sometimes addictive, and legal drug. It's called alcohol.

Drinking is nothing new for teenagers. In fact, it's a kind of ritual of youth. In recent years, however, a great many youngsters from all walks of life have turned to drugs like marijuana, heroin, and barbiturates. Reports coming in now from schools and national studies tell us that there's a change occurring. The newest way for kids to turn on is an old way—with alcohol.

Listen to these words of a high school senior in Brooklyn as told to a reporter from *Newsweek* magazine: "A lot of us used to smoke pot, but we gave that up a year or two ago. Now my friends and I drink a lot . . . and in my book, a high is a high."

Why are youngsters rediscovering booze? One reason is pressure from other kids to be one of the gang. Another is the ever-present urge to act grown-up. For some, it eases the burden of problems at home or at school. And it's cheaper. . . .

Perhaps the main reason is that parents don't seem to mind. They tolerate drinking—sometimes almost seem to encourage it. In part this may be due to the fact that parents themselves drink; in part it's because they're relieved to find that their children are *"only"* drinking, and are not involved with pot, LSD, or other drugs.

What these parents may not realize is that alcohol is also a drug, and a potentially dangerous one. Furthermore, few are aware just how young the drinkers are these days. The National Council on Alcoholism reports that . . . the age of the youngest alcoholics brought to its attention dropped from fourteen to twelve. Other studies have found that three fourths of senior-high students have used alcohol—an increase of 90 percent in three years. And 56 percent of junior-high students have tried alcohol.

The Medical Council on Alcoholism warns: The potential teen-age drinking problem should give far more cause for alarm than drug addiction. Many schools have reacted to teen-age drinking. They've started alcohol-education programs. But a lot of experts feel that teen-agers are not going to stop drinking until adults do.

Carl T. Rowen, *Just Between Us Blacks*

When you are using causal analysis to develop an essay, you must first be sure that a cause-effect relation indeed exists. Having assured yourself, you must then assure your audience by providing evidence. Your evidence may be narration, description, or some other appropriate means of development, but you may not use analogy to support your claim. Analogy may be used only for clarification.

There are different types of causes, and sometimes you may have to qualify cause-effect assertions. For example, the declaration that "cigarette smoking causes lung cancer" is not true in the case of all smokers, since many never contract lung cancer. But the assertion that "cigarette smoking *can cause* lung cancer" is supported by clinical evidence; thus, it is a statement of *sufficient* cause. Other sorts of causes are termed *contributing*. For instance, the assertion that "Mary's poor vision caused her to stumble" may point to only one of several contributing causes, such as icy sidewalks and poor coordination.

The following paragraph from a student essay presents a series of contributing causes for a particular problem in making tape recordings:

> A humming noise on a tape can result from a variety of recording errors. A common mistake in recording that will result in humming is to forget to change the amplifier dial to the recording source position: phonograph, radio, or microphone. Placing the microphone too close to the speaker or having the amplifier volume set too high will also produce a hum or even a howl. Another kind of interference that may result in tape hum comes from stacking the recorder and amplifier on top of each other.

Here is an example of a cause-effect paragraph in which the writers also use exposition in presenting the reasons for the development of tornadoes:

> Rising air, like air flowing toward a *low,* moves spirally in a counterclockwise manner, thereby causing extremely low pressure in the center of the rising column. The lower the pressure, the stronger the winds, the greater the gyratory action in the updraft and the more intense the low pressure becomes. The lowering pressure cools the air rapidly to below the dew point; as a result, a cloud develops in conformity with this chimney of low pressure; hence, the characteristic funnel-shaped cloud. . . . The very low pressure (as low as 23 inches recorded at Minneapolis in August, 1904) causes buildings to explode when the funnel cloud reaches the ground, and the terrific velocities of the wind—perhaps as great as 500 miles per hour—usually prostrate every standing object in the tornadoe's path.
>
> Clarence E. Koeppe and George C. De Long,
> *Weather and Climate*

Development by causal analysis involves these tasks:

- Being certain the cause-effect relationship indeed exists.
- Identifying the cause as contributing or sufficient.
- Providing supporting evidence by using narration, description, or another appropriate means of development.
- If using an analogy for clarification, not mistaking it for supporting evidence.

EXERCISES

1. Discuss each of the following as a *sufficient* or as a *contributing* cause:
    a. Charlie wore blue jeans to church because he wanted to irritate his mother.
    b. The president allowed 100,000 refugees into our country because of his humanitarian principles.
    c. This kitchen is hot because thirty people are packed into it.
    d. Coach Smith produces winning basketball teams because he has ten years of major league experience.
    e. Radial tires improve gas mileage.
    f. Doctors usually charge high fees to recoup the high cost of their education.
    g. The haystack burned because lightning struck it.
    h. Alcoholism causes marriages to fail.
2. Develop a paragraph on one of the above by combining causal analysis with narration, analogy, description, comparison/contrast, or exemplification.

10

Using
Argumentation

The word "argument" normally calls to mind two persons shouting at each other in disagreement, or else someone setting forth a controversial position, perhaps with barely controlled emotions. Shouting "arguments" usually involve judgments rather than courses of reasoning: "Cats are disgusting!" "The movie is superb!" "The clerk is an idiot!" An argument, however, need not convey emotional intensity or even deal with a controversial issue. In fact, there may not even be any opposition to the point made in an argument. An argument is simply the setting forth of reasons along with the conclusion drawn from them. A sound argument is fair—it tries to avoid offending needlessly or arousing a response based solely on emotion, and it attempts to examine all relevant aspects of the subject under scrutiny. Because it appears to be the rational product of an impartial mind, a sound argument is usually convincing.

ARGUING EFFECTIVELY

An argumentation essay usually employs *inductive reasoning*—the presentation of observations, experience, facts, and statistics that make up the evidence for drawing a *likely conclusion*. A likely conclusion is one that is probably correct but is not demonstrable beyond all doubt. As a writer, your main task in forming an argument is to present sufficient evidence while avoiding reliance on common but illogical methods of persuasion. The effectiveness of the following essay by a student writer is the result of sufficient evidence being presented to support the likely conclusion. As you read the essay, note those points that make the writer's argument especially convincing to you.

UNNATURAL ACTS

We are in danger of losing one of our most impressive national symbols—the giant redwood tree—because of the unscrupulous cutting practices of some California loggers. The redwood has survived all sorts of floods and other natural disasters for over 150 million years, but the method of harvesting the tree that has been in use since the beginning of this century is posing a much more serious challenge. Significantly, this situation is continuing even in the face of federal legislation designed to protect the redwood.

Logging companies harvest the trees by a method called clear-cutting, which involves selecting an area of between ten and forty acres and then leveling every tree in sight. Cuttings of this type create large areas of barren land within a larger stand of trees. The effectiveness of the method is reflected in the reduction of redwood acres from an estimated five million before the twentieth century to only a few hundred thousand today.

Congressional concern for the devastation of the environment and the damage to the forest ecosystem resulted in passage of the Redwood National Park Act of 1968, which was drafted to protect nationally owned areas of redwoods. The law was designed to reduce and control logging operations around the park. It authorized the Interior Department to: (1) enlarge the boundaries of the park by adding buffers of 2,000 acres at strategic locations; (2) create a scenic route along portions of the Redwood Highway; and (3) protect the timber, soil, and streams inside the park. Enforcement of the law has been lax, however, with the result that the logging companies have kept on cutting, and the reduction of redwood acres has continued at the rate of about 3,000 acres each year.

Beyond the obvious destruction of trees, clear-cutting has other more damaging effects on the surrounding forest areas. A major effect involves the elimination of cover for the forests' watersheds, essential to the redwoods because of the enormous amount of water they need to survive. Without the cover that the trees provide, the watersheds and their surrounding areas lose much of their absorption ability. They also suffer significant water loss owing to evaporation.

Perhaps the most devastating effect of clear-cutting is soil erosion. Following cutting, nothing remains on the ground to trap and absorb rain. Thus, rain becomes destructive, as it hits bare ground, loosens soil, forms puddles and gullies, and finally transports topsoil into nearby streams. This soil, called silt, accumulates at the bottom of streams and on the forest floor. The result is frequent flooding, a phenomenon that further destroys the ecosystem.

Hope remains for the redwood, however. The government is showing itself increasingly sensitive to the threat posed by clear-cutting, and environmentalist groups are continuing to bring suit to force tougher measures. Nevertheless, greater efforts at enforcement—particularly at the local levels—are now required, especially in terms of protecting the watersheds. This means that clear-cutting will have to be abandoned for the present, or else the redwoods will have no future at all.

While we recognize the strength of a logical argument such as the one in the preceding essay, each of us is also bombarded daily with illogical—though effective—forms of argument. Much of this is in the form of advertising urging viewers, readers, and listeners to buy something, try something, or support something. Think, for example, of a television commercial linking love and happiness to instant coffee, or one of a football player endorsing a truck he probably has not even sat in. Such arguments do not stand up to logic. As a writer, bear in mind that any sound inductive argument must provide sufficient support in the form of evidence drawn from observation and experience. To be fair, an argument should take into account exceptions (evidence that at first may appear to contradict or shed doubt on the conclusion). In addition, the more likely the conclusion, the stronger the argument.

Arguing effectively requires learning not only how to present a course of reasoning in a convincing manner but also how to spot and avoid illogic. Thus, before discussing the process of writing an argumentation essay, an examination of the principles and techniques of argument will help you both in presenting your conclusions and in ensuring that you do not commit logical fallacies.

Using Generalizations

The same principle of providing supporting evidence that applies in other major forms of nonfiction writing applies also in argumentation. When you state that something is true in a specific case and is therefore true for other, similar cases, you are drawing a conclusion in the form of a *generalization*. A generalization is a concept you have formed using inductive reasoning, examining particulars to conclude what is true in general or for similar particulars. Induction, then, involves asserting that what is true for A is probably true for B, and B may be another, similar case or a set of many such cases. If you expect a reader to consider your point believable, then you must supply convincing evidence consisting of facts and appropriate examples. Here, for instance, is a generalization and its basis:

> Americans are more likely to be influenced by quality than price when buying a compact car. (Reason: A nationwide survey of 10,000 people who recently bought compacts showed that 73 percent listed quality as the major determining factor in their decision.)

In the course of your presentation, you would illustrate your objectivity by considering exceptions to the generalization you have made and explaining why they exist.

Arriving at a conclusion on the basis of an isolated or exceptional case is called *hasty generalization*. Here are some examples of hasty generalizations:

> I met a helpful clerk in Mobile, Alabama. People in the South are always hospitable.

> The rude bus driver in New York did not surprise me, because city people are never helpful.

> After I heard the Bulgarian delegate speak on the evening news, I realized that all Communists want to overthrow the American government.

These statements are invalid—their cause-effect relationships are not logical—because they assume that what is true under a particular condition is true in all conditions. You have to think of only one contradictory example—an unfriendly gas station attendant you met in Georgia, a Philadelphia hotel clerk who stood in the rain to hail a taxi for you, a Communist peasant, depicted in a TV documentary you saw, who cares about little more than eking out an existence on a farm—and the conclusion in each case becomes false. You can identify hasty generalizations by thinking of exceptions to statements with such open or implied absolutes as "never," "always," "no one," and "everyone."

At the other extreme is the *sweeping generalization,* one that considers ample evidence but still fails to allow for possible exceptions. Examine the following statement:

> I have tested thirty Ace photocopiers, and each one gave clear reproductions. This thirty-first one, therefore, will make clear reproductions.

The writer has tested a sufficient number of machines so that the conclusion ought to be a valid one. However, it will not be valid if a workman dropped the thirty-first copier while loading it onto the truck, and each reproduction the copier makes looks like a butterfly. The conclusion should have a degree of qualification: "This thirty-first one, therefore, *probably* will make clear reproductions."

Using Authority for Support

An authority is an expert, a person with extensive knowledge (usually professionally acquired) in a particular field. You can use an expert's opinion to reinforce a point you are making as long as you cite the expert's views *in the area of his or her expertise.* If you were arguing, for example, that your school should install an artificial surface football field as opposed to a natural grass field, the opinion of a professional football or soccer player would legitimately reinforce your argument. If you were arguing in favor of a bond issue to improve an intersection of major highways in your community, citing the opinion of the county traffic control chief would lend valid support. Should your topic be more controversial—say, you were arguing in favor of a nuclear weapons freeze—you could legitimately cite the opinion of a chief arms negotiator as expressed in a newspaper editorial or a book. The more controversial the issue, the more you may want to make use of expert opinion.

Experts' opinions are persuasive. But an expert's status has no legitimate bearing on topics that are not relevant to his or her area of expertise. Consequently, if you use an expert's opinion on an irrelevant topic, the appeal is invalid. The football player whose comments on artificial surfaces are valid is not a suitable authority on the best brand of house paint. And an arms negotiator's opinions on a new tax to fund arms purchases have no more merit than the opinions of a kennel operator. Still, the public is prone to accept the word of an expert on a variety of subjects. Consider the use that advertising makes of film and rock stars whom the public instantly recognizes. Similarly, people who are used to taking a doctor's advice on matters of health may unconsciously transfer their respect for his or her medical expertise to the area of political issues. Here, the illogical *appeal to authority* is unstated. Of course, a doctor can make a good mayor. But to make a convincing case that he or she will probably be a good mayor, the doctor must provide evidence of ability and knowledge with regard to political issues as well as to medicine.

Using Positive, Not Negative, Support

Convincing evidence is positive evidence. If you are applying for a position as a computer programmer, you will want to show the potential employer that you have the qualifications for the job. You will want to show what training, experience, and course work you have had; you will want to provide examples of programs you have worked with and developed. Were you to say, "I will be a good programmer because no one has ever said that I would not," you would give no evidence at all of your ability or potential effectiveness. Similarly, if you are arguing in favor of secondary schools requiring art courses, you will want to give examples of the applicability of the principles of art to everyday decisions such as choosing clothes, enriching leisure hours, and designing the layout for an efficient yet attractive office. However, if you argue that art courses should be required because there is no reason that they should not be, you have given no support for your argument. To argue that something is true because it has not been shown to be false is fully irrational. Just because the Better Business Bureau has received no complaints about Dick's Used Cars does not mean that Dick always deals honestly. To argue that Dick is always honest would be an *argument from ignorance*. Buyers Dick cheated may have suffered in silence or complained to an organization other than the Better Business Bureau.

Using Specific Evidence

If you are conscious of the need to provide specific supporting observations and experience for any argument you make, you will avoid the trap of presenting the *reason* as the *conclusion,* and thus leaving the conclusion without a base to stand on. The error of stating the conclusion as the reason (though the word choice is different) is called *begging the question* or *circular argument.* If you argue that the United States has the strongest defense of any country, then you will need to give information as to what the defense consists of and compare/contrast it with the specific military capabilities of other nations. Were you to say, however, that "the United States has the strongest defense of any country because it has the mightiest nuclear arsenal," you would be presenting an argument that, instead of offering proof for its conclusion, simply states the conclusion in another form. This argument contains no information that the audience can use as grounds for agreement with you. Such circular reasoning can be deceptive, because the restated conclusion normally appears in wording quite different from the originally stated conclusion.

Incomplete comparisons are a form of begging the question:

> Buy Whizz because it gets clothes cleaner. (Cleaner than _____?)

> Bergblatt stereos give you better sound because they have superior tonal quality. (Better than _____?)

"Better sound" is just another way of saying "superior tonal quality." Note the restatement in the following:

> A landfill would *ruin the environment* of Potter City because it would *pollute the air and water.*

There may be good reasons for buying Whizz, such as its low price for cleaning power as compared to the prices of other detergents. Maybe Bergblatt stereos give a good sound for half the price of competing brands. And there may well be enough hard evidence to show that a landfill would indeed pollute the air and water of Potter City and that incineration would provide an acceptable alternative. The important thing to be aware of is that the arguments as stated contain no evidence beyond that provided in their conclusions.

Using Cause and Effect

When you draw a conclusion, be certain to keep the real issue in sight. Shifting the issue can lead you to an *irrelevant conclusion.* Suppose your argument deals with the issue of how to meet the nation's growing energy needs. To deal with the issue requires analyzing the various kinds of energy resources available and setting up guidelines (such as safety, efficiency, and cost) for finding the best answer to the problem; then the argument should be constructed on how best to follow the guidelines. Another approach would be to examine the practicality of reducing energy needs. However, were you simply to argue that "More nuclear power plants should be built because the nation has growing energy needs," you would be sidestepping the real issue of what is the best way, and why, to meet those needs. Similarly, to argue that eighteen-year-olds should have the right to buy liquor because they have the right to vote is to shift the issue. Appropriate support for the argument would lie in an examination of the desirable and undesirable results of eighteen-year-olds having the right to buy liquor. Voting is a separate issue that has little in common with drinking.

The error of *false cause* occurs in statements that suggest that events are causally connected when in fact no such connection may exist. The problem of false cause usually comes about through coincidence: the assumption is made that because two events occur at about the same time, one event is caused by the other. Actually, there may be no causal connection whatsoever. Here are some examples:

> Compared to the year before, traffic deaths in the state declined last year. The new safety campaign in our public schools is working.

> Unemployment has risen by 7 percent since the Independent party took power. Thus, you should vote for the opposition if you want to see more jobs available.

> As more women have joined the work force, juvenile crime has increased. If mothers would stay home where they belong, the crime rate would drop.

Although the safety campaign may be a contributing cause to the drop in traffic deaths, evidence other than timing is necessary. As for the Independent party, only time links its coming to power and the rise in unemployment. Perhaps the party's policies did indeed contribute to unemployment, but that is not demonstrated. And in the last example, time is once again the only link given for the relationship between juvenile crime and working mothers working outside the home.

Our susceptibility to commit the error of false cause is useful in one regard. At times, doctors prescribe sugar pills for patients who chronically complain of ailments. The patient takes the medication (actually, sugar pills) the doctor has prescribed and, feeling better, attributes the cure to the pills, when in fact it is the patient's own psychological powers—faith in the "medicine"—that prompted the cure.

Considering the Alternatives

Allow for alternatives. To forget or ignore choices in stating a solution to a problem or in assigning a cause to a problem may result in the audience being misled or rejecting your argument out of hand. The statement "The players' union should either accept the owners' terms or go on strike," for example, ignores the alternative of continuing to play while seeking negotiated concessions. Similarly, the argument that "Either real estate taxes should be raised or the schools should be closed" ignores the alternative of cutting school costs or the possibility of raising revenue through some means other than property taxes. Such arguments often have an implied "either," as in "(Either) love it or leave it," which ignores the option of not loving whatever "it" is but staying and working to improve "it." Examples of this "either-or fallacy" include "Put up or shut up"; "Sink or swim"; and "Like it or lump it."

Stating All Assumptions

Clearly stating all assumptions will prevent you from inadvertently burying the real issue of your argument. For example, arguing that "Judge Smith should be recalled because he is lenient with drunk drivers" requires establishing that the judge is indeed lenient with drunk drivers and then supporting the idea that recalling the judge is the best way to bring about firmer treatment for drunk drivers. If, however, the arguer sets out to address the question, "Is Judge Smith still being too lenient on drunk drivers?" then he or she commits the logical error of *complex question* by assuming that the judge has been too lenient. Sometimes the problem of unstated assumptions involves the definition of a term. For example, "democracy" is used by communists to include the communist form of government.

Being Fair to the Opposition

An objective, successful argument will deal with issues rather than with personalities. An argument should avoid *abusing the opposition,* or name-calling, as well as *circumstantial attack,* or using the circumstances of the opponent to discredit his or her argument.

For example, there may be many reasons for a person's not being reelected to office. If an incumbent student senator has failed to attend the last six sessions of the student council, you could argue that someone who will represent the student community should be elected, and the incumbent's past performance leads you to conclude that she is not meeting that need. However, if you simply argue that someone should not be reelected because she wears flashy clothing, or because he once flunked out of school, or because she is divorced, the argument is illogical. Abusing the opposition may take subtle forms. Diction with negative connotations needs careful handling. Think, for example, of the connotations suggested by the terms "*crafty* man," "*greedy* administrator," and "*filthy rich* governor."

Using an opponent's circumstances to discredit him or her is equally unfair. If you were to argue, for instance, that Governor Kelly wants a state prison built in Hoop County because his own residence is on the other side of the state, you are using the circumstantial attack. The location of the governor's residence is irrelevant to the merits of the proposed prison site. There may be other reasons, logically sound, for choosing a site other than Hoop County. They might include a greater need for employment in another county or the high population density of Hoop County.

Similarly, when you argue that a former oil company executive should not be appointed to the state energy commission because she would surely favor the needs of her cronies in the oil industry, you are using the circumstantial attack. Former conditions of employment are irrelevant to a person's present honesty or dishonesty. If, on the other hand, you have a letter written by the executive that clearly shows she intends to see that her position will increase corporate profits, you have a valid reason for opposing the appointment.

Arguing Objectively

A danger in treating a controversial issue is that you may have strong feelings about it. Points that are not buttressed by supporting evidence, regardless of how strong your feelings are about those points, may alienate a reader who did not agree with you to start with. Avoid emotion. Objectivity is all important unless your role is no more than that of a cheerleader.

Many attempts to persuade rely on the *appeal to fear.* Insurance companies' advertisements that show a house in flames rely on fear to persuade, as do those of companies that seek to sell automatic garage doors by showing a burglar lurking in the bushes. This is not to say that the products or services advertised lack value; rather, that the objective description of the costs weighed against the advantages would comprise the logical approach. A less subtle use of the appeal to fear pervades the issue of nuclear war and disarmament. A fair approach to the nuclear disarmament issue would require assessing the risks involved in taking either a pro or a con view: are the armaments themselves a deterrent to war, or would a unilateral freeze or unilateral disarmament lessen the risks of destruction even more? But to show a child picking flowers with a mushroom cloud in the background, followed by a voice calling for a unilateral freeze or disarmament, is a patent appeal to fear. The appeal can be used to push either view.

Similar to the appeal to fear is the *appeal to force.* Use of this appeal is often more sophisticated than "Hand over your wallet or I'll put a slug in you!" Though it may be a compelling argument, an appeal to force is not a reasonable one. The person who demands that a foreign government change its human rights policy while threatening to lead a rock-and-bottle-throwing crowd against that country's embassy is invoking the appeal to force.

Although the *appeal to pity* is often as persuasive as the appeal to force, it also violates reason. It is argument by the tear duct rather than by the brain. Charities commonly use the appeal to pity as a means of persuasion;

often this appeal is directed at the audience's sense of guilt as well. As part of a drive to raise money for a starving nation, you are urged to forego a meal a week and send the money saved to an organization that shows you pictures of festering sores and bloated, malnourished toddlers. The same message could more logically appeal to humanitarian principles, the natural reaction most people have to assist someone who has a clear need. It is fully reasonable to make the need known and seek aid to meet it, but sensationally depicting suffering while not objectively picturing the nature and extent of need is, unfortunately, bypassing the reasoned argument, and it may well be less effective. Emotional intensity is difficult to sustain, and some leaders of charitable organizations have noted the public's tendency to get "pity fatigue" and cease support.

Although the appeal to pity is often persuasive and often invoked, it is probably less common than the use of *popular appeal*—an attempt to persuade an audience that because "everybody" is doing something, buying something, or believing something, the audience should also. The argument can take such forms as the following:

> Because most other large cities have imposed an income tax, Gotham should too.

> Sonex sells more televisions than any other brand. Shouldn't you own one?

The appeal is also known as the "bandwagon approach." Sometimes you can literally see this metaphor in operation: witness the soft drink commercial showing a beach buggy loaded with happy people drinking the same brand of cola, or the political campaign parade with the candidate actually riding a bandwagon crowded with his supporters. The bandwagon approach appeals to a person's urge to be part of the group, but it offers no legitimate reasons for doing so. In student writing, the popular appeal may take the form of such arguments as the following:

> Neighboring state universities have schools of veterinary medicine, so ours should too.

> I know that *Night of the Horrible Parakeet* is a good movie because so many people have seen it.

> Professor Plonk is a great teacher because so many students want to sign up for his course.

EXERCISES

1. Identify the errors of logic in the following statements. Then correct the errors according to the principles discussed in this chapter.
   a. A person should not drive while intoxicated because of the possibility of getting a very high fine.

b. The vice president hopes to get the government contract because it will put him in line for a promotion.

c. I would not buy the truck because the owner has shifty eyes.

d. You will get the best deal on a new car from us. We are the largest volume dealer in four states.

e. Professor Smith should give me a passing grade so that I can graduate and get that teaching job offered by my old high school.

f. If you had seen the fire that destroyed the Smiths' house, you would not hesitate to buy our homeowner's insurance policy.

g. Every visitor to Washington should dine at the Sans Amour. The food must be great because many congressmen eat there.

h. Jonathan is nice to his aunt only because he expects to inherit a pile of money from her.

i. Our candidate for president of the student council is best because she advocates the best programs.

j. The supervisor must really like Joe's work. I have never heard him criticize Joe at all.

k. Are you still drinking too much?

l. She is a Scorpio, so it's no wonder she blew the deal today.

m. Never trust anyone over thirty.

n. Every country boy desires to live in New York.

o. The Engineering College is noted for its teaching excellence; therefore, Professor Huckaby over there must be a fine teacher.

p. All right-thinking people will reject the evil that is socialism.

q. You can't believe anything she says. Ten years ago she was convicted of drunken driving.

r. Michael Jackson uses Brand X. Shouldn't you?

s. Professors are expected to spend much of their time publishing. Therefore, you shouldn't go to college because your teachers will be more interested in their publications than they will be in you.

t. All the other kids are doing it—it's okay for me to.

2. Examine the following set of arguments, one of which answers another. Identify any fallacious reasoning in each argument. (The arguments are in the form of letters to the editor of a humanities journal, *The Cresset.* The first is by Mark O. Gilbertson, Department of Theology and Philosophy, Texas Lutheran College. It responds to an article by James Nuechterlein previously published in the journal. The second is by Mr. Nuechterlein, editor of *The Cresset,* in response to Professor Gilbertson.)

Professor Gilbertson's letter:

To the Editor of *The Cresset:*
When moral issues become political footballs, opposing sides tend to resort to simplistic positions and muddled rhetoric. So one looks to responsible journals for recognition of the complexity of the issues and a clarity which will begin to do some unmuddling! It was with that hope that I began reading "The Abortion Muddle." . . . What I encountered, however, was more confusion

than clarity in a not unbiased editorial. Granted, the abortion issue does seem peculiarly able to render one baffled and/or bullheaded, but this is all the more reason to work hard at achieving clarity and sympathetic understanding.

First of all, Geraldine Ferraro's position, which you attack, is an attempt to delimit matters of private and personal choice from those of the public domain and legislation. Whether justifiable or not, this should not suggest, as you indicate, that her position involves "personal opposition to," but "public support of" abortion. Rather, it suggests support for a public policy which allows for some private moral choice in this matter. That her faith commitment would dictate *her* personal choice, and that this particular viewpoint is shared especially by other Catholics, is in no way affected by the Catholic Church's view that this conclusion should be reached by any and all rational persons. The assertion that there are natural (moral) laws is itself a statement of faith of this particular religious community. And of course the question of when a human life, in the sense of a subject of moral rights, etc., begins *is* a matter of theological and philosophical dispute!

Nevertheless, you are right to question the abortion decision as simply a matter of private choice. It is an issue of public concern and, perhaps, even legislative involvement. But the problem is with the *extent* to which it should be considered a matter of private morals or public legislation. This may vary with the circumstances and stage of development of the fetus. Your siding with the "pro-life" argument that it cannot be considered a private issue "because it involves the taking of other innocent life" simply begs the question of the fetus' personhood. You offer no argument. Now, clearly the fetus is a human being in the sense of its being offspring of members of the species *homo sapiens*. But is the fetus at all stages of its development a human being in what might be called the moral sense? Is this being a possessor of rights, or of claims to life, sufficient to outweigh other claims or rights of the mother? These difficult questions are not resolved by talking about fetuses as the "others" that make abortion a public issue.

Second, your dismissal of arguments for the moral justifiability of abortion is unfair. What defense are we given for your claim that "the *only* coherent moral argument in favor of free choice on abortion involves the assumption that fetal life is not human life"? What about the argument that the fetus, though human, is not fully a person with rights? Or the view that its claims to life, as a potential person, are weaker than those of actual persons? Or, the arguments concerning the broader consequences of unwanted children on the world's diminishing resources? These arguments may not establish free choice in every case of an abortion decision, and they may not be conclusive, but are they incoherent?

What does border on incoherence is your drawing a parallel between the choice involved in abortion cases and that denied in such matters as slavery and racial discrimination. In the latter cases clearly we are dealing with full-fledged persons with moral rights; in the abortion issue that is in dispute. If the issue were not so clear-cut as this, you surely would not have what you call the "ambivalence" of the American public. (And on that, why should it be considered ambivalent to oppose a ban on all abortions and yet also oppose abortion-on-demand? That seems to be a perfectly consistent position to me.)

The upshot of all of this would seem to me to be reservation about supporting an amendment which would cater to the kind of muddle-headed campaigning on this issue that we've already experienced. I agree that if we seek an informed consensus of the American people on abortion (a highly unlikely prospect), the only hope is if "the arguments . . . on either side are presented to them with intellectual and moral clarity." But your editorial is a clear indication to me that even the hope of such intellectual and moral clarity is slim indeed!

Mr. Nuechterlein's response:

At the risk of adding to the muddle on this issue, let me respond as briefly as possible to Mark Gilbertson's points.

1. I find it hard to follow Mr. Gilbertson's defense of Geraldine Ferraro. Ms. Ferraro concedes that abortion-on-demand is morally wrong according to her own beliefs because it involves the taking of innocent life, but she supports it as public policy. She defends this apparently contradictory position by attributing her personal views to a "gift of faith" that is hers as a Roman Catholic; not all have that gift, she says, and she does not want to impose her moral/religious beliefs on others. But, as I pointed out, the Catholic position on abortion does not rest on faith. Catholics believe that abortion can be shown to be wrong by the light of reason, unaided by faith. Would it not then follow that Ms. Ferraro has a moral duty to try to show others that abortion-on-demand is objectively wrong, that it is not a purely personal matter, and that it should not be sanctioned in law? Yet she does none of these things. Her position does seem to me to be incoherent.

2. I was wrong, however, to say that the only coherent moral argument in favor of free choice on abortion involves the assumption that fetal life is not human life. Coherence—in the sense of logical consistency—is not the central issue. Many morally frivolous arguments are consistent within their own terms and assumptions. My language in that instance was imprecise, though it did not affect my central argument.

3. Mr. Gilbertson's quarrel with me focuses on the question of whether the fetus—which he concedes is a human being—is a person with moral rights. All his objections save one come down to that issue. (The exception refers to "the broader consequences of unwanted children on the world's diminishing resources." Does Mr. Gilbertson really want to suggest that "unwanted children" can be got rid of because they make a claim on resources that others also make?)

The fetus, Mr. Gilbertson suggests, may lack compelling claims to life because it is not yet a moral personality. (That is not Mr. Gilbertson's term, but it does seem implicit in what he says.) That argument may be intuitively persuasive to many, but consider its implications. If the claims to life of the fetus may be ignored or restricted because of its lack of full moral (or other) development, what of the claims of the newborn infant? Abortion-on-demand allows the killing of human creatures who are developmentally distinct from infants only in the sense that they exist inside the womb rather than outside it. Many pro-choice arguments would in fact justify infanticide as well as abortion.

This suggests that Mr. Gilbertson has his burden-of-the-argument perspective backwards. If we do concede (as he does) that the fetus is a human being, should not the presumption be that it has moral claims to life that cannot rightly be overridden by, say, claims to convenience or privacy or the right of personal choice on behalf of the mother? If we are indeed uncertain as to when life that has legitimate moral claims begins, should we not put the burden of proof on those who would interpret those claims restrictively rather than broadly? That would seem to follow from the common moral perception that protection of innocent life is at the very center of our moral obligations.

Mr. Gilbertson concludes that uncertainty on abortion leads to reservation about supporting the Hatch amendment (which, to repeat, would not ban abortions but would simply leave the matter open for democratic resolution at both the state and federal levels). I find his position logically and morally unpersuasive. Today abortion-on-demand leads to the death of some 1.6 million fetuses per year. Mr. Gilbertson is apparently able to live with that reality with equanimity. I consider it a moral horror.

REVISION EXERCISE

Examine the following argument for logic problems, and revise it so that the argument is stronger.

The state's sales tax on college textbooks should be eliminated. The tax was first levied to raise funds to improve state colleges. If the intent of the legislature was to improve higher education, it certainly makes no sense to have a tax that increases costs for college students. Only an idiot would consider the tax on textbooks reasonable. Students have enough of a burden as it is. The first reason that college textbooks should not be taxed is that the sales tax was intended to help college students. Taking more money away from college students is not the way to help them. It would be easy to exempt textbooks, if not the other things required by college students. Textbooks could be sold only by licensed booksellers who had certified letters from a designated college official specifying the titles of the books that are required for college courses. Those titles then would be exempt. Many college bookstores, I realize, sell many things besides books—sweatshirts, mugs, pencils, even deter- gent. But if separate cash registers were kept for book purchases—or even if a special key were set up—the cash registers could easily be isolated or pro- grammed to ease the job of the sales staff in assessing the amount of sales tax. You might think it would not save each student enough to make the extra bookkeeping worthwhile. But it looks like my expenses for books will be close to $500 this year alone, and the costs will probably go up each of the next three years. The five percent sales tax on that comes to a significant sum for me. Another reason not to impose the sales tax on college textbooks is that there are plenty of other sources of revenue for the state.

CONSTRUCTING AN ARGUMENT

When you write an argument, you usually are defending a conclusion you already hold. That is, before you even begin to plan your writing strategy, you already know about where you want to wind up. You have, in other words, a good idea of the point you want to make. But the success of your argument is not only a matter of explaining your point to your audience. You need also to convince your audience that it is right. Therefore, the writing process for argumentation is one in which you work backward as you inventory and examine the ideas and experiences that have caused you to arrive at your position. At the same time, however, the assertion of that position—your conclusion—must be clear if you are to uncover the reasons on which it is based, for these will ultimately form the evidence on which your case rests.

Argumentation thus involves building a two-part structure: (1) the conclusion (This is *what* I believe) and (2) its basis (This is *why* I believe it). The following diagram illustrates the relationship between the two parts:

CONCLUSION	BASIS
People should be required to retake their driver's test when they are sixty-five.	Statistics indicate that drivers age sixty-five and above have a 20 percent greater chance of being involved in an accident than drivers aged below sixty.

Such an argument is unlikely to convince most readers, and if you were writing this argument, some deliberation would probably cause you to modify the conclusion. Modifying your reasoning is characteristic of evolving an effective argument: you constantly question yourself to test the ability of your conclusion to stand up and to sound fair. In the above example, do you really mean *all* people throughout the United States? What of a person of sixty-five whose driving record is unblemished? Wouldn't such a law be discriminatory? Isn't there a much greater chance of accidents occurring in certain states of high population density? Similarly, examining your basis would also generate questions. For instance, whose statistics are these? What are they based on? Were they nationwide? Is the accident rate for men and women roughly equal?

As you go about constructing and testing an argument, you are really playing devil's advocate with yourself. You are asking the questions that would be posed by someone who holds views opposite from yours. Such self-scrutiny helps you to discover and assert exactly what you believe, to test evidence that will make your conclusion likely, and to ensure that your argument is fair. It also enables you to anticipate objections to your position by opponents, a tactical necessity when you are addressing an especially controversial issue.

Revising as you test and frame your argument frequently will require a modification of your conclusion. You may, for example, make an initial assertion that "Essay exams better reflect a student's knowledge and should therefore replace true-false and multiple-choice tests." But is this true for all courses? For all students? Upon reflection, you may change your assertion to "Essay exams are generally better suited to evaluate performance in senior-level humanities courses at Bollingbroke College than are most objective tests." In other instances, you will find yourself examining your reasons to make sure that they are logical—discard those that do not stand scrutiny. The close relationship between both parts of the argument structure is such that modification of one frequently requires modification of the other.

Constructing an argument involves the following steps:

- Present a conclusion.
- Note your reasons for arriving at the conclusion.
- Test your conclusion by asking questions of it.
- Test your reasons for logic; make sure that they support the conclusion.
- Revise both your reasons and your conclusion, as necessary.

Many of the issues that you will examine in argumentation essays will be more complex than the line of reasoning contained in the previous example. Nevertheless, the process of testing both your conclusion and its basis remains the same. Here, for example, is an example of the beginning stages of a more elaborate argument:

CONCLUSION	BASES
Private education for the elementary pupil is superior to public education.	1. Private education offers greater discipline.
	2. Private education limits the pupil's exposure to undesirable elements.
	3. Private education affords parents the opportunity to select a school on the basis of educational philosophy rather than on proximity to the home.

This argument does not work. First, the conclusion is made ambiguous by the writer's failure to explain "superior." Assuming that what was intended was "academically superior," another problem arises: none of the reasons cited is directly related to academic superiority, and therefore the bases do not support the conclusion. However, the bases do have something in common; that is, each deals with aspects of an educational environment. After spotting this, the writer could revise the conclusion along the following lines:

> Private education provides a superior learning environment for the elementary pupil.

Another option would be to remove the ambiguity in the original conclusion and establish a new set of reasons to support the assertion of "academic superiority," as in the following example:

CONCLUSION

Private education for the elementary pupil is academically superior to public education.

BASES

1. Smaller class sizes in private schools mean greater individual attention.

2. Elementary pupils in private schools consistently earn higher scores on standardized tests than do those in public schools.

3. Greater discipline in the private school results in an environment more conducive to learning.

After you have tested your argument, it is time to consider whether you can support it adequately within whatever limitations you are working with. Constructing an informal diagram may assist you in this. Assume, for instance, that you are writing an argumentation essay of 500 words on the subject of prostitution and that you have framed your argument as follows:

CONCLUSION

Prostitution should be legalized.

BASES

1. Morality cannot be legislated.

2. An individual has the right to control her or his own body.

3. Legalization would reduce the crime related to prostitution.

4. Legalization would reduce the spread of social disease.

You would quickly see that the argument will require discussion of the issue along moral, legal, and social grounds. Furthermore, each of your four bases is itself a conclusion regarding a single aspect of the total issue; accordingly, you would have to supply additional support (what we might call "sub-bases") for each of these conclusions. A final schematic might then look something like this:

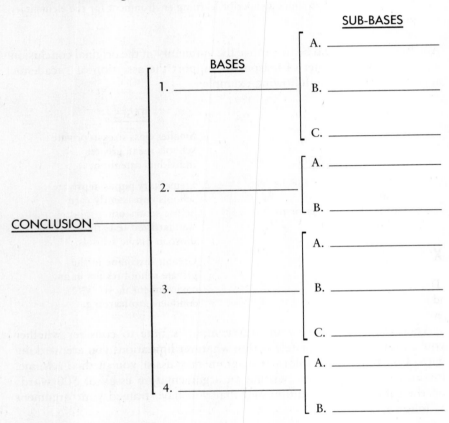

To translate all of this into a convincing argument would be well outside your limitation of length. Were you to attempt to treat the whole argument in 500 words, your essay would be so general as to be unconvincing, especially to readers who opposed your overall conclusion or one or more of the individual conclusions.

You would not scrap your work and begin all over again, however. Instead, as you would when facing a similar problem with any of the other essay types, your recourse would be to employ the principle of ever-narrowing focus. In the case of argumentation, you can further limit your argument by focusing on one of its bases. Here, you might decide to argue that legalizing prostitution would reduce related crime. This, then, would become your major conclusion, and you could rework your argument as follows:

BASES

CONCLUSION

Legalizing prostitution would reduce related crime.

1. Local regulations would protect prostitutes and customers from intimidation, blackmail, and the like.

2. Legalization would eliminate the role of pimps.

3. Prostitutes and their customers could report criminal acts to local authorities without fear of arrest.

4. Legalization would enable police to spend more time on non-vice-related crimes.

EXERCISES

Develop one of the following statements into an argument or counterargument, and illustrate it with a diagram. The statement may be revised to fit your own views.

1. Only a sadist likes to think of a rabbit being blinded by a chemical spray or of a healthy cat or dog being cut up with a scalpel. Antivivisectionists in several states have succeeded in halting the use of animals from local pounds in laboratory experiments. Scientists have no grounds for using live animals in their experiments.

2. Society has a concern about narcotics users only because the users usually have to steal in order to support their habits. If all narcotics became legal and therefore inexpensive, the users could go ahead and kill themselves and the rest of us would not have to worry so much about theft.

3. Group homes for the mentally retarded should not be subject to zoning laws. The county should be able to place such a home in any neighborhood it chooses. There is ample evidence that the presence of such homes does not decrease property values.

4. Developers should not be allowed to build shopping malls unless they contribute to improving nearby road networks to accommodate the increase in traffic the malls bring.

5. The school administration should be responsible for defraying losses that arise from theft in the dormitories.

THE ARGUMENTATION ESSAY ILLUSTRATED

The process of writing an argumentation essay parallels much of the process of formulating an argument. You begin by setting forth your main point—the conclusion of your argument—in the thesis statement and introductory paragraph. The body paragraphs reflect the bases of your argument; they define your stand and provide support to show why your conclusion is sound. As with other essay types, the final paragraph of your argumentation essay may be used to restate, offer recommendations, pose a question, or otherwise provide emphasis for the main point of your argument.

The intricacies of argumentation require ongoing revision in the planning stage (as we have seen) and also in the writing process itself. The following discussion shows how one student went through the entire process of constructing an argument and writing an argumentation essay. The student's starting point was his concern over stories of child abuse, so he thought it would be worthwhile to argue for his view on how to address the problem. Here is his initial argument:

BASES

1. There have been recent news reports of light sentences for child abusers.

CONCLUSION

2. Judges are naive.

We should change the judicial system because it is guilty of failing to punish child abusers adequately.

3. Judges do not want to take responsibility for dealing out appropriate sentences.

4. Society is not being protected.

5. Sterner sentences are necessary.

Upon reexamining the reasons he had noted, the student saw problems with his argument. Reason five, for instance, is a circular argument (restatement in different words) for the conclusion: *Judges are guilty of failure to punish adequately* because *sterner sentences are necessary*. Other reasons overlap or wander into irrelevant issues; for example, reasons two and three explore *why* judges give lenient sentences. Moreover, some generalizations are too broad: the student does not have enough information—just a few recent news stories—to make determinations about all judges or all sentences.

Further thought led the student to reshape the argument according to the following plan:

BASES

1. An adequate sentence for a child abuser is one that affords reasonable protection to society.

2. Current sentences are sometimes inadequate.

3. We should, therefore, promote guidelines for sentences that afford reasonable protection to society.

CONCLUSION

Some judges are failing to punish child abusers adequately; new sentencing guidelines are necessary to afford reasonable protection to society.

The student noted that reason one was an assertion requiring both definition of an "adequate sentence" and discussion of what would constitute "reasonable protection"; reason two would require facts to support it; and reason three would emerge as a conclusion based on the discussion of reasons one and two. Here is an early draft of his essay:

NO QUARTER FOR CHILD ABUSERS

Newspapers recently have carried several stories of child abusers receiving light sentences. I become upset when I read those stories. Child abusers, in my view, should be removed from society until they are clearly no longer threats to innocent children. This whole situation is outrageous! Judges who let these animals out to prey on little kids need to understand that the only reasonable sentence is one that provides long-term protection to potential small victims. In fact, judges who go easy on such scum should be locked up themselves.

Three newspaper reports in the past two weeks alone prove that there is a rampant problem with child abusers. In Los Angeles, a man and wife convicted of killing their fifteen-month-old daughter by soaking the nipple of her bottle in a heroin substitute in order to pacify her were sentenced to three years' probation. In Chicago, a woman whose infant son was kidnapped and murdered after she left him alone while she went out to a bar with friends had child neglect charges dropped because the judge said she had suffered enough. In New York, a father irritated by the crying of his eleven-month-old child scalded her and then shut her in a bureau drawer to suffocate. He received a jail term of only three years because the judge did not want to deprive the man's family of his wages for any longer.

These sentences, or lack thereof, are ridiculous. According to the press accounts, the judge in Los Angeles noted that both parents were heroin addicts and were under the influence of drugs when they administered the heroin substitute to their child. The judge considered this a key point in their defense of "diminished responsibility." In the case of the Chicago mother, I can sympathize with the mother's suffering, but I fail to see why the judge did nothing to punish her for child neglect. In the last case, a brutal murderer will be back on the street in three years, free to harm others and to father more of his own potential victims.

Judges should see that persons who have physically abused children do not get a second chance, whatever the contributing circumstances. Those criminals should be removed from society until they are no longer capable of fathering or conceiving children or until they voluntarily undergo sterilization. Even then, those whose crimes include torture and homicide should be locked away for many, many years to protect innocent children in our society.

The basic plan for the argument is sound, but the first draft has some problems. Note that the title may put readers off because it suggests that the essay may be no more than an emotional diatribe. The introductory paragraph also is colored by name-calling ("animals out to prey," "scum") but really presents no argument or information. The last sentence brings up an irrelevant point: what should be done to lenient judges. The first paragraph in the body begins with an illogically broad generalization: three accounts concerning three cities do not cover enough ground to permit the problem to be termed "rampant." Much more evidence, such as assertions by government experts, would have to be presented before such a generalization would be acceptable. The next paragraph could use a better topic sentence, such as "The sentences were too lenient because the judges ignored the possible consequences for society." The last paragraph of the body would be better if it began with a clear statement of logical relationship, such as "Because of such judicial failures to protect society, we should promote guidelines for sentencing child abusers." Finally, a conclusion needs to be added, recapitulating the argument or otherwise stressing the main point.

Here is a later draft of the essay. Note that it contains changes in addition to the ones noted above:

MORE PROTECTION FROM CHILD ABUSERS

Newspapers recently have carried stories of child abusers receiving light sentences. Sympathy, understanding, and mercy should certainly be elements of consideration for any judge. But the overriding consideration should be the safety of society, especially infants and toddlers, who are poorly equipped to defend themselves. Responsible citizens should begin pressing judges and legislators to maintain sentencing guidelines that take into account the next potential victim of the child abuser.

Many child abusers may be getting off too lightly in our courts. Three recent press accounts suggest that that is the case. In Los Angeles, a man and wife were sentenced to three years' probation after they were convicted of killing their fifteen-month-old daughter by soaking the nipple of her bottle in a heroin substitute in order to pacify her. In Chicago, a judge dropped child neglect charges against a woman whose infant son was kidnapped and murdered after she left him alone while she went out to a bar with friends. The judge said she had suffered enough. In New York, a father irritated by the crying of his eleven-month-old child scalded her and then shut her in a bureau drawer to suffocate. He received a jail term of only three years.

These sentences strike me as too lenient because the judges ignored the possible consequences for society. According to the press accounts, the judge in Los Angeles noted that both parents were heroin addicts and were under the influence of drugs when they administered the heroin substitute to their child. The judge considered this a key point in their defense of "diminished responsibility." In the case of the Chicago mother, I can sympathize with the mother's suffering, but I fail to see why the judge did nothing to prevent her from further child neglect. In the last case, a murderer will be back on the street in three years—free to harm other children and to father more of his own potential victims—because the judge did not want to deprive the man's family of his wages for any longer.

Because of such judicial failures to protect society, we should promote guidelines for sentencing child abusers. Judges should do their best to ensure that those who have physically abused—not just neglected—children do not get a second chance, at least not with their own children. The guidelines should include such options as incarceration for life for the murderers and long sentences for other violent abusers. Sterilization would be another option, particularly for cases of gross neglect.

I am not so much concerned with the specific form of punishment, such as sterilization, which some will applaud and others will judge demonic. I only urge that some forms of sentencing be worked out that ensure far better security for children than was provided in the three instances discussed above.

Writing an argumentation essay involves the following steps:

- Develop a conclusion and its bases.

- Assert the conclusion of your argument in the thesis statement and introductory paragraph.

- Support the bases of your conclusion in body paragraphs that use facts, statistics, and discussion based on observation and experience.

- Emphasize the main point of your argument in a concluding paragraph.

EXERCISES

1. Make a list of all the changes in the above essay not previously discussed. From the standpoints of logic and presentation, explain why each of these was made.
2. "More Protection from Child Abusers" would still profit from one more draft. Decide what additional changes, modifications, and other information would strengthen the argument. Incorporate these into a new draft.
3. Develop an argument in which you either (1) advocate specific sentences for child abuse (or another crime) or (2) take a stand against specific guidelines in favor of making the punishment reflect the particular circumstances of the case. Once you are satisfied with your argument, incorporate it into an essay of about 500 words.
4. Choose a local or other issue, develop and diagram an argument, and evolve the diagram into an argumentation essay of 300 to 500 words.

PART THREE

REVISION

As you have seen, revision is part of every stage in the writing process. It is essential for clarity. It helps you to convey what you intend and to do so with economy, precision, and emphasis. Above all, it helps you to avoid being misunderstood or even embarrassing yourself. By revising as you work—and certainly after completing the first draft of an essay—you will avoid illogic that defeats your argument, paragraphs whose points are not worth making, vague theses causing ambiguity and organizational problems, and stylistic and mechanical difficulties that obscure your message and frustrate your reader.

Few professional writers would submit anything for publication without thorough revision; many, in fact, have noted that revision is the essence of their craft. Nevertheless, inexperienced writers frequently are reluctant to revise. Some lack discipline. Others assume that revision is a last-minute task involving only quick editing and proofreading. And some have every intention of revising, only to be undercut by time or other constraints. Whatever the reason, failing to revise will result in writing that at best *may* get your point across. It probably will not get it across well, and it may ultimately prove to be a waste of your time and that of your audience. The consequences of such writing in both the academic and professional worlds are obvious and equally grim.

Part three provides guidance on how to revise an essay effectively. Note that we begin by examining the whole essay for content and organization before addressing matters of style. Chapters in part three include discussions of the following:

Reviewing content and organization

Achieving sentence variety and emphasis

Strengthening sentence construction

Using effective diction

Using mechanics effectively

11

Revising
the Larger Elements

If you are like most inexperienced writers, you think of revision largely as a matter of style and correctness. Thus, you concentrate on words and sentences. You hunt for a better word, you delete where possible, and you conclude by proofreading for errors of grammar and mechanics. But if you confine your efforts to these smaller elements, you run a grave risk. There is no sense in reworking sentences in an essay when your point is so obvious that the essay has little value, or in seeking a better word when your thesis statement remains unsupported throughout. Revision, therefore, must begin by your examining such large elements as content, purpose, organization, and development.

REVIEWING THE WHOLE ESSAY

Objectivity is essential. Although you have been revising as you went along, getting some distance between yourself and the essay will enable you to approach it as critic rather than as author. Thus, after you have finished your first draft, put it aside for two or three days. When you return to it, imagine that you are reading someone else's work. If time does not permit this much distance, at least take a quick walk or sit back in your chair for a few minutes before donning your critic's hat.

Your first task is to read with fresh, critical senses. Do not get derailed by focusing on the smaller elements or by analyzing your writing; at this stage, you are only trying to get a sense of the essay as a *whole*. How does it read? How does it sound? How does it feel? Is there anything that seems jarringly wrong? Like many experienced writers, you may find benefit in reading the essay out loud. This technique will reduce your reliance on sight—which can play tricks—while permitting you to hear how well the parts of the essay work together.

177

Only after the initial reading should you review your essay with specific aspects of writing in mind. Uppermost should always be the question, "What is my point?" Your overriding concern is how to make that point increasingly effective. Considering the following questions will enable you to spot problems with content and organization so that you may revise accordingly:

1. Does the essay display an introduction, a body, and a conclusion?
    Does the introduction fit the essay?
    Do the paragraphs in the body support the thesis statement and are they well developed?
    Is the conclusion appropriate? Does it emphasize your main point without bringing in new, unsupported generalizations?
2. Has the purpose of communication been met?
    Does the essay appropriately address the audience it is intended for?
    Does it address the subject specified by the assignment?
3. Has the subject been shaped into an appropriate topic?
    Has the subject been sufficiently narrowed? (Or is it still so broad that the reader will be left wondering why some aspects were not covered?)
    Has the topic been narrowed appropriately, given the original assignment?
4. Is the thesis statement clear?
    Does it indicate the topic, its limits, and an organizational plan?
    Do all the topic sentences support the thesis?
    Are other topic sentences (and accompanying development) needed to cover the thesis?
    In other words, does the essay show *unity?*
5. Is the support provided by the paragraphs in the body adequate and sufficiently concrete?
    In other words, does the essay show *precision?*
6. Has the organizational plan indicated by the thesis been carried out?
7. Is the development logical, with each idea leading to the next?
    In other words, does the essay show *coherence?*
8. Have you made a point worth making?
9. Does each paragraph have a topic sentence?
    Does the paragraph deliver what the topic sentence promised?
    Are all points relevant to the topic sentence?
    Are all examples concrete?
    Is the development of each paragraph logical?
10. Have you used a method or methods of development appropriate to your topic?
11. Have you followed logical guidelines that go with a particular method of development? (That is, if you are using classification, have you stated a basis for the classification? If you are using process, have you been consistent in addressing either a participating or an observing audience?)

The following first draft of an essay written by a student illustrates the cardinal role played by the content and organization. As you read, note that there are problems with spelling and punctuation. But first, concentrate on determining the changes that will be necessary to improve the larger elements:

BODY LANGUAGE

In my experience, good teachers tend to show that they are secure. Their self-confidence comes across not only in their display of thorough knowledge of their subjects. But I have also noticed that thier body language—with few exceptions—has something in common, when we are talking about the good teachers, at least. These things are aside from what you'd expect, such as a firm voice and decent dress. There are three areas or kinds of body language that secure teachers have in common, at least of those teachers I've had, because maybe it isn't true in all cases. These three areas I call turf control, stepping up, and hand emphasis.

Secure teachers show a higher range of turf control than insecure teachers do. By "turf control," I don't mean school subject control, but physical area of the classroom control. They mark it out by pacing. There must be something to the idea of territorial control and marking that lots of animals, like lions and leopards and even dogs, do, because I am sure that people do it to. Mr. Brown, for example, who was my physics teacher in high school, use to pace around the whole room. He started out just walking to and fro across the front of the classroom, in the area between the blackboard and the teacher's desk. At first he would go just a few feet in either direction, but as he warmed to his subject, he extended his pacing untill he was going from the windows on one side of the room to the door on the other. By the end of class, he was also walking up and down between the rows of desks in the classroom, and hitting all four corners. In other words, the more at ease he felt, the more area he covered in his pacing. At the opposite extreme was Mr. Smyth, my English teacher, who never stepped from behind his desk. That was just one of the ways he seemed uncomfortable and insecure. He even looked like he was afraid to stand up in front of the class, his voice quavered, and he would always stumble and ramble if anyone asked a question.

Then there is stepping up, as I call it. A good example of this again is Mr. Brown. Sometimes when he wanted to get a rest from pacing around the room during his lecture, Mr. Brown would put his foot up on the trash can; other times he would put his foot on the window ledge, and other times he rested briefly by leaning against the blackboard and putting one foot against the top edge of the teacher's desk.

Ms. Lee, my math teacher, would do the same thing, though only on days when she wore slacks. On the other hand, Mr. Smyth's feet never left the floor. While most of the other good teachers I had didn't go the the foot-lifting extremes of Mr. Brown, it wasn't unusual to see them sit on their desks and put one or both feet on the top of the trash can.

And last there is hand emphasis. Mr. Brown usually walked around with his fingertips touching, almost like in prayer, but he would wave his two hands when he talked about an open question, or poke them forward in jerky motions when he wanted to emphasis some point. Ms. Lee used to point and poke alot, though usually just with her right hand.

Mr. Smyth, however, never took his hands out of his pockets unless he needed to remove one so that he could write on the blackboard.

These are just a few of the ways that confident teachers differ from the ones who don't seem to have much confidence in themselves, though I don't know if it is because they don't know there material very well or because they have stage fright.

A first reading suggested to the student that although her essay was rough, it had structure and a central idea. There was, in short, reason to invest time in careful revision. Then, considering the questions on the revision process listed earlier, she began to analyze and evaluate her essay in terms of content and organization. She determined that her draft did have an introduction (paragraph one), a body (paragraphs two through six), and a conclusion (paragraph seven). She also noted that the essay was appropriate for its context of communication. (The assignment specified an examination of an aspect of education addressed to a general audience of students and teachers.)

Review questions three and four then helped her identify a major problem: the relationship between the topic introduced in the first paragraph and the material developed in the body of the essay needs to be clearer. The student noticed that she had started the essay by addressing the statement "good teachers tend to show that they are secure." She then developed the essay by identifying and explaining three types of body language that suggest self-confidence; for clarity and emphasis, she introduced contrasting behavior by teachers lacking confidence. Nevertheless, the link between security and body language is weak and indirect in the thesis, and she realized that this caused subsequent problems with development. For example, paragraphs four and six lack topic sentences (question nine); paragraph six also lacks development and concrete support (question five).

Based on this analysis, the student determined that she needed to clarify the thesis and adapt the development accordingly. As with all stages of revision, she also found herself paying some attention to problems of wordiness, misspellings, and other elements even as she recast the larger elements; her attention to the stylistic elements may even have helped her clarify her point in her own mind so that she could sharpen the thesis statement. Note how the following introduction shows improvement in several respects other than the clearer thesis:

Among the various teachers I have had, the best ones have shown self-confidence. That sureness has come across not only in their knowledge of their subjects but also in their body language. Unlike those teachers who lack such a characteristic, the teachers who are confident of their subject knowledge and teaching ability have shown that trait in three kinds of body language that I term "turf control," "stepping up," and "hand emphasis."

The new introduction clearly indicates that the thesis, "teachers who are confident of their subject knowledge and teaching ability have shown that trait in three kinds of body language," will be addressed in three body paragraphs of the essay, one for each type of body language.

With this structure in mind (questions six and nine), the student moved on to the group of revision questions concerned with organization and content. She reshaped topic sentences (as suggested by question four) and combined some of the paragraphs in the body to support the topic sentences (questions four, five, seven, and nine). Here is the second draft of the body of her paper:

> Confident teachers show they are in control by establishing their authority over the physical space in the classroom, fixing a wide area of "turf control" by pacing. Mr. Brown, for example, my high school physics teacher, would begin class by pacing across the front of the room, in the area between the blackboard and his desk. At first he would go just a few feet in either direction, but he gradually extended his pacing until he was going from the windows on one side of the room to the door on the other. By the end of class, he was also walking up and down between the rows of desks in the classroom and hitting all four corners. The more at ease he felt, the more area he covered in his pacing. At the opposite extreme was Mr. Smyth, my English teacher, who never stepped from behind his desk, and who showed insecurity in several other ways, such as a trembling voice and stumbling, rambling answers to questions.
>
> "Stepping up" is another kind of body language used by teachers who are self-confident. Mr. Brown was also a good example of this. Sometimes when he wanted a rest from pacing around the room during his lecture, Mr. Brown would put his foot up on the trash can. Other times he would put his foot on the window ledge, and sometimes he would rest briefly by leaning against the blackboard and putting one foot against the top edge of the teacher's desk. Ms. Lee, my math teacher, would do the same thing (only on the days she wore slacks). I also remember that other self-confident teachers used to sit on their desks (in between pacings) and prop their feet against the top of their trash cans. In contrast, insecure Mr. Smyth never took his feet off the floor, except to walk out of the room at the end of class.
>
> Another form of body language used by confident teachers is "hand emphasis." Mr. Brown usually walked around with his fingertips touching, almost like in prayer, but he would wave his two hands when he talked about an open question, or poke them forward in jerky motions when he wanted to emphasize some point. Ms. Lee used to point and poke a lot, usually with her right hand. Mr. Smyth, however, never took his hands out of his pockets unless he needed to remove one so that he could write on the blackboard.

Pleased with the improvement in both the introduction and body paragraphs of her essay, the student then examined the conclusion. She realized that other than enabling her to end the essay, it accomplished little. The greater clarity in the thesis statement and the increased precision caused by well-developed supporting paragraphs, however, helped her broaden the implications of her observations as she revised the conclusion. To gain greater emphasis, she also added a quotation:

> "Attitude," according to *Webster's Dictionary,* refers to "the posture of a figure" as well as to "a feeling or mood." Maybe the definition should be broadened to include the motions of the hands and feet, since they may show a person's feelings or mood as well as the person's words do. Though I have not observed other authority figures as closely as I have teachers, I suspect that they, and most of us, may show much about their self-confidence just by their body language.

The process of revising for larger elements involves the following steps:

- After completing the first draft, put it aside until you have gained some distance and objectivity.

- Then read the draft as critic, concentrating on the essay as a whole.

- Review the essay in light of the content and organization questions listed earlier.

- Consider breaking the questions into groups, beginning with the broadest issues of structure, purpose of communication, appropriate topic, and thesis statement (questions one through four).

- Revise the essay according to your responses to these questions.

- Repeat the process as you move down the list of other questions.

EXERCISES

These exercises trace the revision of a student's essay through three drafts.

1. Read the following first draft and then review it with specific reference to the content and organization questions listed earlier. Respond also to the questions that follow the draft.

First Draft

LAMBS TO THE SLAUGHTER

Today's college students are exploited by large class sizes, and being forced to buy books and materials that they do not need.

From the Ivy League to the Pacific Eight, many college students attend classes that have too many people in them. This causes problems in the education they receive, problems that stem from the impossibility of class discussions in these large classes. The teacher, because of class size, can only lecture. He doesn't have time to answer students questions, even if they were encouraged to ask them, which they aren't.

The result of all this is lectures that often just skim the surface of the material, bored students, and finally objective tests that only require you to fill in the blanks or match answers to questions. Alot of these students work many hours each week so that they can afford to attend college. Many of their parents scrimp and save to help put their offspring through college. And all they get are huge classes and tests that demand nothing more than memorization.

The other thing that causes college studnets to get ripped off is professors who make their classes buy books and materials that they do not need. In alot of cases, a professor will demand that his class buy a book and then only use the book once or twice during the semester. In other cases, a professor will have his students buy a book and then simply tell them to read around in it. The students don't know what they're supposed to read. They don't know why they should read it. But they do it because the professor says they should. The worst example of this is the professor who makes his students buy a book that he has written only so that he can make money from the sales. He has no intention of using the book in class but he has every intention of using the money he gets from it's sale!

Most college students are interested in learning. They deserve better than they often get. What needs to be done is to make class sizes smaller and to force professors to order only books and materials that the content of the course requires.

QUESTIONS

a. With specific reference to the revision questions, list the strengths of this draft.
b. List the weaknesses.
c. Aside from problems of style, which of the large element weaknesses is the most damaging? Why?
d. In previous chapters, it has been noted that an audience forms an opinion of a writer based on what the writer has said and how the material has

been presented. After evaluating this draft, what is your picture of the writer? Explain.

2. Here is the second draft. Again, review it in light of the content and organization questions. Additional questions follow the draft.

Second Draft

LAMBS TO THE SLAUGHTER

The ever-increasing cost of a college education has resulted in many students questioning whether or not they are getting what they pay for. Some students believe that they are being exploited by colleges that make large classes standard and by professors who force them to buy books and materials that they do not need.

College classes of 100 to 600 have become the standard in many of the nation's schools, with the result that students are being deprived of the educational opportunities that should be part of learning. Because they cannot possibly answer all the students' questions in such classes, professors often do away with discussion, and the class becomes nothing more than a thrice-weekly lecture directed at a sea of faces. The result is often boredom, students sit passively as words echo all about them, the professor has no opportunity to engage in debate with active and interested students, and the intellectural stimulus and depth that is part of discussion is lost. The ultimate exploitation occurs during examinations. The class size often forces the professor to give objective tests consisting of true-false or multiple-choice questions. Thus, examinations become nothing more than regurgitation sessions, and those students who sincerely want to investigate an area of knowledge are left with nowhere to go. "The answer to number ten is a"; "number two in column b matches number seven in column a." Sadly enough, it is the student most in need of small classes—the freshman and sophomore—who is shunted into Introduction to Psychology with an enrollement of 300, and into Introduction to Biology with 250 students.

Equally upsetting to many of today's students are thoughtless professors who demand they buy unnecessary textbooks and materials. With the average hardback text costing at least $20 (paperbacks are a few dollars less), students are reluctant to buy books that will be of little use to them. Yet in one of my recent classes, I was told to buy a text costing $22.95, that the class would use it from time to time. I bought the book. The professor referred to it twice during the rest of the semester. In other instances, a text appears on a course syllabus, the professor tells the class to "read around in it," and the students buy it. But they are never told what to read or why. When one of my friends complained to a professor who was guilty of this practice, the professor simply brushed the complaint aside with the remark that "it's a good book to have around." Serious as such instances are, they pale next to the practice which some professors use: forcing the class to buy a book written by the same professor. Naturally, there is nothing wrong with this practice providing that the book will be used in the class. However, a number of professors demand that students buy their texts simply to make money from the sales.

The $6,000 to $10,000 per year that students pay for a college education is high enough. Like everyone else, students are exploited by inflation and the cost of living. But for their money, they deserve an educational experience not found in large classes, and they do not deserve to be exploited by thoughtless and, at times, unscrupulous professors.

QUESTIONS

a. Have the weaknesses you identified in the first draft been overcome?
b. Is this draft structurally better than the first draft (revision questions one, four, six, and nine)?
c. Is the thesis statement adequately supported in the body (question five)? Are the examples sufficiently concrete?
d. As this is an argumentation essay, is the method of development appropriate (question eleven)?
e. Are you convinced by the argument? Why or why not?
f. After evaluating this draft, has your picture of the writer changed? Explain.

3. Here is the student's third draft. Review it to determine if all the weaknesses identified by the content and organization questions have been remedied. Again, respond to the questions that follow the draft.

Third Draft

LAMBS TO THE SLAUGHTER

The rising costs of a college education have prompted many students to ask if they are getting what they pay for. At State University, tuition has gone up over sixty percent in the last three years; the cost of certain basic texts, according to the manager of the bookstore, has increased about 30 percent in that same period. But as the prices rise, value for money declines for the students, who increasingly are exploited by large classes and by being forced to purchase texts that they do not need.

The large sizes of several of my classes deprive students of participation, dialogue, and other important learning opportunities. In my biology lecture section, for example, there are at least 250 students. Last Tuesday the professor lectured on bivalves; twice I had difficulty understanding her because she spoke so rapidly, but she never noticed my raised hand, and I was unable to get my questions addressed. After class a line of students approached her with questions. I didn't have time to wait since I had only ten minutes to get to my Introduction to Psychology class. I never did get my questions answered, and I must admit that I no longer can recall exactly what they were.

If the biology class reveals the problem, the psychology class underlines the result. When I arrived, I took my seat among 300 other students. The lecture was boring—in part because the professor was so far away that many students couldn't even see his facial expressions. Students near me were snoring, writing letters, and reading the student newspaper. And why not? In my psychology course (like my biology course), I am given only multiple-choice tests for ease of grading. On these, I regurgitate memorized facts; I am never asked to synthesize information in a discussion, and therefore I get no instructor reaction to my general ideas. I think much of my tuition is wasted.

The forced purchase of unnecessary books complements the exploitation. My psychology text cost me $22.95 (plus tax). I have never had a specific assignment from it, and the objective tests in the course are only over the material the professor has lectured on. I must admit, though, that the professor told the class to "read around in it." I'm not sure what this means, what to read, or why. When my friend Jim asked the professor why the class had to buy the book, the response was that "It's a good book to have around." While this may be an extreme case of thoughtlessness, it is quite common for students to be required to buy an expensive text and then be assigned only one-tenth of it for class. My friend Ann bought a $20 book for her Music Appreciation course last year and was assigned only two of the twenty-one chapters.

The $6,000 to $10,000 per year that students pay for a college education is high enough. There should be value for money. But value is certainly not found in classes whose size precludes participation and fosters testing that measures only an ability to memorize and guess, or in the forced purchase of texts whose major accomplishment is to add to the student's frustration.

QUESTIONS

   a. Review this draft with specific reference to each of the revision questions. Do you find any major problems remaining?

   b. The examples and details in this draft are more concrete than in the previous ones. What effect does this have on the credibility of the argument?

   c. Are you convinced by the argument? Explain.

   d. Finally, what picture of the writer is likely to emerge after an audience has read this essay? How does it compare/contrast with the pictures you had after reading each of the two previous drafts? What are the reasons for the change?

SHARPENING IDEAS

Revising the larger elements will also help you write more thoughtful essays. If you examine the first drafts of both the previous essays ("Body

Language" and "Lambs to the Slaughter"), you will conclude that their content probably would not have held an audience's interest. The subsequent drafts, however, evolved into well-supported observations likely to engage most people involved in education. The evolution occurred as the revision questions caused the writers to test what were initially only partly defined ideas. Only after these ideas were refined were the writers able to articulate them with clarity and insight.

Whatever you write about is likely to become more sophisticated as you revise. Reviewing an essay for content and organization requires that you analyze the relationships between topic sentences, as well as the material that makes up the topics themselves and their supporting detail. If you notice that connections are unclear and assertions weak, the problem may be that your points remain fuzzy in your own mind. Subjecting your first and subsequent drafts to the content and organization questions will help you clarify an idea in your mind, thus enabling you to express it with emphasis and precision.

The following is a first draft of an essay by a student writer. If you examine it with reference to the revision questions, you will see that it requires quite a bit of reworking. Nevertheless, you may detect an idea in this draft that, if explored, would make for a perceptive essay.

HAIR TODAY

The Edenton Kwik-Kut is tacky, and it has undergone a real transformation since I first remember going into it fifteen years ago. It used to be known then as the Edenton Barber Shop, simpley enough. I guess the changes reflect how the community has changed, and its just like a rolling stone gathers no moss. It is a bit more sophisticated now, at least pretty much. There are still some rough edges that show its past.

I must have been about 4 or five years old the first time I remember going to get a haircut at the Edenton Barbershop. My father took me. There was one barber, old Ed. He had a burr haircut around the sides of his head and was bald on top. The shop had old magazines around and I would look at the pictures while I waited, and a deer head was on the wall too. The shop smelled nice, and the floor was always littered, Ed and the customers usually chatted. Mostly about local things.

The barbershop was remodeled not long ago and alot of changes can be seen, now the Edenton Kwik-Kut. Now alot has changed of the basics. There is an attempt to make the place look like it has a modern, big city kind of atmosphere. There are two new men running the place. The hair cuts are now called styling and now the charge is $10 not $1.50. Instead of the shop being an all-male stronghold, there are now female customers and the reading matter is different. The place also smells like hairspray, the floor is alot cleaner, and there is a picture on the wall not a deer head.

Things have changed. I don't know if I'd call it progress, however. There is no more hair tonic, just scented shampoos. Now big wash basins and chairs that tilt back, so you can hang your head over the basin while its being wetted down before cutting.

The essay has an introduction, a body, and a conclusion of sorts (revision question one). The introduction gets off to a bad start, however, as the writer confesses uncertainty over the relationships between ideas ("I guess the changes reflect how the community has changed"), and this uncertainty is reflected in the rest of the ambiguous introduction. The lack of clarity becomes pronounced when we consider question four. The writer's thesis is vague, its significance undisclosed, and other than suggesting that the essay will contrast the past with the present, no organizational plan is presented. Similar problems occur in the body, paragraphs two and three. Both have topic sentences (question nine), but they are vague and neither provides sufficient development or concrete support (question five). (In paragraph two, for example, which "old magazines" are we supposed to envision? What was the substance of conversations about "local things" that we are supposed to overhear?) Finally, there is a degree of coherence as the essay moves from the past to the present (question seven) and attempts to contrast the old with the new (question eleven). However, the writer's point remains vague throughout, and therefore the reader ultimately is unsure if it is a point worth making (question eight).

The second draft that follows reveals that the writer has begun to address some of the larger elements that hampered his first draft. As you read, note also the recurrent nature of the revision, reflected in the writer's efforts to improve diction and other stylistic aspects of his essay. Again, however, concentrate on the larger elements of content and organization.

HAIR TODAY

The Edenton Barber Shop has undergone many changes in the past fifteen years, and the business has grown more sophisticated.

Fifteen years ago the Edenton Barber Shop was a dusty and leisurely hangout for the men of the town. My earliest memories are of a forty-five minute haircut I received while listening to old Ed, the barber, chat with waiting male customers about the high school football team and an accident outside the town that killed a drunk teenage driver. The patrons would chat while paging through old, ragged issues of *Field and Stream* and *Outdoor Life,* and gaze at the deer head on the wall. The wooden floor was strewn with dust balls and hair clippings—wet and slick with oil. The shop smelled of the cracked leather furniture and dust, but mostly of talcum powder and rose-scented hair tonic applied so liberally to each customer's head. At the end of my biweekly grooming, I paid $1.50.

Today, the Edenton Barbershop is called the Kwik-Kut and the name isn't the only thing that has changed. The wooden floor is now covered by shiny blue vinyl tiles, and the stuffed leather chairs have been replaced by shiny chrome and canvass ones. Old Ed has been replaced by Jules and Maurice, and both men and women come to the place. *Field and Stream* and *Outdoor Life* are also gone, replaced by recent issues of *People* and *Good Housekeeping.* In place of the stag's head is a plastic-framed print, and the aroma of hair spray and shampoo hangs in place of the familiar smell of hair tonic. Some of the conversation still concerns local sports and auto accidents, but the women have added hair styles, clothing sales, and juggling home and career to the topics of discussion. The shop is cleaner and the service is faster. But now each patron pays $10 or more.

The changes show the changes that the town of Edenton has itself undergone in the last fifteen years. More women have moved into occupations once held only by men—bankers, doctors, lawyers—just as they have moved into the barbershop. Many of the wooden buildings in the business district have been replaced by new buildings. The changes have replaced personableness with speed and artificial efficiency.

The second draft is much improved. The improvement is largely the result of a more specific and direct thesis statement and topic sentences that better reflect the purpose of each paragraph. This specificity has, in turn, enabled the writer to develop the body more fully with concrete details that enable the audience to visualize the past and the present.

Despite these improvements (and others that you probably have noticed), the essay remains unsatisfying. The problem is still the writer's uncertainty about the significance of his topic (question eight). In its present form, the fact that the Edenton Barbershop has changed and become more sophisticated is likely to be of interest only to those who know Edenton. For the rest of us, the response is likely to be "so what?" Yet, if we examine the writer's conclusion, we see that there is something else here—despite the brightness and efficiency of the new, the old had certain qualities that we will miss. With this thought, writer and reader can meet, for all of us have at one time or another experienced a sense of loss as things have changed.

Recognizing the importance of the conclusion, the writer did a final revision. As you review it, note that the introduction now reflects the realization of his previous conclusion and that it has been broadened to capture reader interest. Furthermore, just as the revision questions enabled the writer to discover more clearly what he wanted to convey, so have they enabled him to write a conclusion that is significantly more reflective because it offers a social comment that takes the reader well beyond the confines of the writer's own experience.

HAIR TODAY

Even as the simplicity of the burr haircut belongs to another era, the relaxed informality of yesterday's barbershop has been replaced by the efficiency of professional hair stylists. The changes of a generation are reflected in the chrome and glass of the Kwik-Kut, once known as the Edenton Barbershop. The dazzle of the new has come with a price, however, for with the passing of the simpler ways we also may have lost that which was most genuine and human in our experience.

The Edenton Barbershop had a leisurely pace and a comfortably seedy decor. The one barber, old Ed, always took at least forty-five minutes with scissors and comb to trim the head of any man or boy. He used to chat in a monotone with long pauses about high school sports and wrecks on the highway. Waiting patrons would exchange comments with him while they paged through old, ragged issues of *Field and Stream* and *Outdoor Life,* occasionally pausing to gaze at the stag's head on the wall above the mirror behind Ed's chair. The wooden floor was strewn with dust balls and hair clippings—wet and slick with oil. The shop smelled of cracked leather and dust, but mostly of talcum powder and rose-scented hair tonic splashed liberally on each customer's head. For the grooming ritual Ed charged $1.50.

When the Edenton Barbershop became the Kwik-Kut after Ed died, the huge, new, shiny mirrors installed along all the walls soon reflected more than changed hair styles. About twenty minutes is required for a haircut and styling, accomplished by a variety of razors and a blow dryer. Jules and Maurice, the new owners, clip men and women. They make little effort to chat with the customers, apparently preferring to let the waves of piped-in easy rock communicate for them. In place of *Field and Stream* are recent issues of *People, Computer World, Psychology Today,* and *Modern Woman,* and instead of leather chairs there are seats of shiny chrome and canvas. Where the stag's head used to gaze back at the customers now hangs a plastic-framed print of a Toulouse Lautrec poster, and the scent of hair spray and natural herbal shampoo has replaced the rose-oil hair tonic and talcum powder. The men still talk of local sports and auto accidents when they meet someone they know, but this conversation mingles with women patrons discussing hair styles, how to juggle home and career, and the advantages of private schools over public ones. Meanwhile, the dust balls are gone, and Jules routinely sweeps up the hair clippings once an hour. The grooming ritual now costs $10.

I don't mind all the changes that have occurred in Edenton in the past fifteen years. Women have moved into the barbershop just as they have moved into new professions. And I don't mind that some of the dilapidated wooden businesses have been renovated with concrete and glass. However, the faster pace, the higher prices, and the plastic and chrome of the Kwik-Kut are indicative of an artificiality and efficiency that I could live without.

Your treatment of any topic may become more thoughtful if you carry out the following procedures as part of the process of revising the larger elements:

- Answer simply and directly the question, "What is my point?"
- Check that the thesis statement clearly asserts that point.
- Ask, and answer, why your point should be important to the audience.
- Consider giving some emphasis to the general and universal in your introduction and conclusion to enhance audience involvement.
- Check that the relationship between the main idea and all supporting ideas is clear—that each topic sentence is directly linked to the thesis statement.
- To help the audience identify with your topic and ideas, check that all supporting details are concrete and specific.

REVISION EXERCISE

The following draft of a student essay shows promise in organization and content. Give it a careful initial reading and then review it according to the revision questions for the larger elements. Then go over it again, this time with specific reference to the suggestions made in this section and the procedures outlined in the box above. Revise the draft accordingly.

CALL OF THE WILD

Thoreau praised nature because he found it a sort of sacred refuge from society, and I am finding myself in agreement with his feelings. I agree with Thoreau not because I see nature as some sort of holy temple but because it offers some quiet where I can at least hear myself think.

I cannot seem to get away from racket. I live in Atlanta, where it is warm enough most of the year that many people drive around with their windows down. It is almost impossible to walk down the street without someone driving by with the car stereo cranked up and the music assaulting my ears. "UH HHH NEEEEED YAAAHHH T'NIIIIGHT. . . ." My apartment offers no refuge either. Next door is a jazz freak who considers it his life's mission to turn up the bass until our common wall is reverberating. On the other side is a family with a four-year-old and a six-year-old, who hate each other. They spend their lives screaming or being screamed at by their parents. "HEATHUH, Y'ALL

QUIT BEIN' UGLY WITH KRISTY OR I'LL . . ." The rest of the time they devote to crying—not polite sobs but caterwauling.

There is no relief in the suburbs. I recently visited a friend who lives in a development in the suburbs, feeling that this would be a break from the honking horns and other assorted noise of the city. Wrong. People do not really live in the suburbs, they exist only to take part in a concert of bellowing lawn mowers, screaming children, and neighborly shouting. "Hey, Charlie, what's happening?" "Yuh missed a weed, Pete!" "Howzaboutabeer?" I have nothing against neat lawns and the American dream from about midmorning to six at night. I hate them after those hours, especially when one of the good neighbors decides to provide a lawn mower serenade at ten at night.

So I retreat. I get in my car, turn the radio on softly, and drive northeast until I see the pine trees and the hills. I look for a quiet road, park the car, and walk. I'm with a sun that soothes, wind that caresses, and the sounds of birds and insects. Sometimes I pack a lunch and some books, and the day finds me happily leaning against a tree a mile or two from a road, book before me and sandwich in hand.

Although I am willing to keep retreating to escape the noise, I more and more resent having to do it. I guess people were a lot more considerate when the world was not so crowded, but even in Thoreau's time it must have been crowded enough.

12
Achieving Sentence Variety and Emphasis

Inexperienced writers sometimes think that a "good" sentence style is one that is marked by variety, one that does not follow the monotonous Dick-and-Jane pattern of an elementary school reader. And, indeed, a good sentence style does show variety, but it also shows proper emphasis: the parts are arranged so that the most important element stands out. In revising the sentences in your essay for variety and emphasis, make sure that (1) each sentence is structured so that its meaning is clear and its most important element is appropriately positioned, and (2) each sentence appears within the context of a variety of sentence lengths and structures.

Examine the following paragraphs, both on the same topic. Each presents the same information, though the sentence styles are radically different.

> Some people think that reading the newspaper obituary page is simply morbid. I don't read it because I enjoy finding out who died. I read it because I can learn bits of history from it. I often discover persons who were famous for their accomplishments in another generation. Reading about them helps me fill in the gaps in my knowledge. The gaps are in the time between history books I have studied and the period when I first began paying attention to current events and newsmakers. Last week I read about a once famous medical researcher. I also read about a military hero in World War II. I read about an advisor to President Roosevelt, too.

> Although some people think that reading the newspaper obituary page is simply morbid, I don't read it because I enjoy finding out about who died; rather, I read it because I can learn bits of history from it: I often discover persons unknown to me but famous for their accomplishments in another

generation, and reading about them helps me fill in the gaps in my knowledge (gaps between the history books I have studied and the period when I first began paying attention to current events and newsmakers). Last week I read about a once famous medical researcher, a military hero in World War II, and an advisor to President Roosevelt.

The first paragraph is too simple. Short sentences, all in the pattern of subject-verb-object, give a monotony to it. A revision of the first, and an improvement, the second paragraph suffers from a different problem. Although it consists of only two sentences, the first one is so long and involved that the reader may get lost in the jungle of clauses and phrases and have to read the paragraph at least twice to follow the thought, even though each of the sentences is grammatically correct. The following revision is an improvement over both of the paragraphs above, for it has variety without extreme complexity or tiresome simplicity.

Some people think that reading the newspaper obituary page is simply morbid, but I read it because I can learn bits of history by doing so. I often discover persons unknown to me but famous for their accomplishments in another generation. By reading about them, I am able to fill the gaps in my knowledge— gaps between the history books I have studied and the time I first began paying attention to current events and newsmakers. Last week, for example, I read about a once famous medical researcher, a military hero of World War II, and an advisor to President Roosevelt.

The discussion in this chapter presents different means of obtaining variety and emphasis, something you will want to check as you compose and revise. Of course, any of the types of sentences discussed will be ineffective if all the other sentences around it are of the same structure and length.

VARYING SENTENCE TYPES

Simple, Compound, Complex, Compound-Complex Sentences

You can achieve emphasis by varying the types of sentences within a paragraph. A sentence consists of at least a single independent clause. According to the number and kind of clauses they contain, sentences may be classified as *simple, compound, complex,* or *compound-complex.* Mixing the four types of sentences appropriately, as you write and revise a paragraph, can provide variety in sentence length as well as in complexity. Variety in the type of sentence you use will change the rhythm within a paragraph and keep the reader from becoming numbed by prose that would otherwise have the quality of a metronome beat.

A simple sentence contains a single independent clause:

He never cheats on tests.

A compound sentence contains at least two independent clauses:

He never cheats on tests, and he always writes well-organized essays.

A complex sentence contains an independent clause and one or more dependent clauses:

When Harvey finished with the hair dryer, I got to use it.

A compound-complex sentence consists of one or more dependent clauses and two or more independent clauses:

When Agnes handed in her test, she looked apprehensive, but she strode out of the room confidently.

Questions and Exclamations

Another means of providing suitable variety to your sentences is to make occasional use of questions and exclamations. A rhetorical question (one that the writer answers or that already has an implied answer) can be useful particularly to lead into or to conclude a discussion. An exclamation may also be appropriate for achieving sentence variety. However, because exclamations draw such strong attention to themselves, they can easily become distracting unless used very sparingly.

Observe how the following passage from a student essay makes use of a variety of sentence types. The second passage shows the labels for each type.

The overthrow of the Duvalier regime in Haiti focused considerable international attention on the plight of that country in both economic and human terms. News footage of jubilant citizens in Port-au-Prince was accompanied by a stream of statistics in the press, which noted, for example, that the country's per capita income level is only about $300 per year. Haiti's trade deficit, moreover, has gone from $27 million in 1975 to $146 million, and the average life expectancy is about fifty-two years. Almost 90 percent of its children are undernourished. The reports imply that the country's economic plight has been caused by its mismanaged government, and some observers now believe that a national recovery is suddenly possible if there is an infusion of Western aid. Hasn't that often been the response of the West? What has often happened in the past, however, is that most economic aid has not reached the masses of people, who will probably continue to live in isolation and distrust of the government. Although outside aid will probably increase, most citizens may have little cause to be jubilant, and the traditions that have caused persistent poverty are likely to continue. The answer is that economic aid alone is not enough!

The overthrow of the Duvalier regime in Haiti focused considerable international attention on the plight of that country in both economic and human terms. [*Simple Sentence*] News footage of jubilant citizens in Port-au-Prince was accompanied by a stream of statistics in the press, which noted, for example, that the country's per capita income level is only about $300 per year. [*Complex Sentence*] Haiti's trade deficit, moreover, has gone from $27 million in 1975 to $146 million, and the average life expectancy is about fifty-two years. [*Compound Sentence*] Almost 90 percent of its children are undernourished. [*Simple Sentence*] The reports imply that the country's economic plight has been caused by its mismanaged government, and some observers now believe that a national recovery is suddenly possible if there is an infusion of Western aid. [*Compound-Complex Sentence*] Hasn't that often been the response of the West? [*Rhetorical Question*] What has often happened in the past, however, is that most economic aid has not reached the masses of people, who will probably continue to live in isolation and distrust of the government. [*Complex Sentence*] Although outside aid will probably increase, most citizens may have little cause to be jubilant, and the traditions that have caused persistent poverty are likely to continue. [*Compound-Complex Sentence*] The answer is that economic aid alone is not enough! [*Exclamation*]

TRANSITIONAL WORDS AND PHRASES

Transitional words and phrases are devices that give coherence between sentence parts, between sentences, and between paragraphs.

Within a sentence, coordinating conjunctions (*and, or, but, nor, for, so, yet*) and correlative conjunctions (*either . . . or, neither . . . nor, not only . . . but also, both . . . and*) can be used to show addition, contrast, or alternatives of thought embodied in words, phrases, and clauses. (Appropriate use of these conjunctions is discussed later in this chapter.)

To link a thought from one sentence to the next, there are a variety of transitional words and phrases. Depending on the relationship of the thoughts, the transition will usually serve one of several purposes: addition, contrast, alternative, sequence, cause-effect, restatement. The following is a list of transitional words for each of these purposes:

Addition: *and, moreover, also, in addition, as well as, equally, furthermore, too, again, at the same time, while, similarly, likewise, anyway, in any case*
Contrast: *but, nor, however, yet, nevertheless, on the contrary, otherwise, in contrast, on the one hand . . . on the other hand, still, conversely, although, in spite of, even though, though, regardless, notwithstanding*
Alternative: *or, alternately*

Sequence: *first, second, third (etc.), finally, last, next, then, afterwards, formerly, soon, meanwhile, now, in the past, once*
Cause-effect: *thus, accordingly, as a result, hence, therefore*
Restatement: *on the whole, in general, generally, in short, in sum, that is, in other words, for example, indeed, in other words, pronouns such as he, she, it, that, those.*

Here is the same passage you examined earlier. As you read it this time, however, note the transitional words and phrases that are highlighted.

The overthrow of the Duvalier regime in Haiti focused considerable international attention on the plight of that country in *both* economic *and* human terms. News footage of jubilant citizens in Port-au-Prince was accompanied by a stream of statistics in the press, which noted, *for example,* that the country's per capita income level is only about $300 per year. Haiti's trade deficit, *moreover,* has gone from $27 million in 1975 to $146 million, and the average life expectancy is about fifty-two years. Almost 90 percent of its children are undernourished. The reports imply that the country's economic plight has been caused by its mismanaged government, and some observers now believe that a national recovery is suddenly possible if there is an infusion of Western aid. Hasn't that often been the response of the West? What has often happened in the past, *however,* is that most economic aid has not reached the masses of people, who will probably continue to live in isolation and distrust of the government. *Although* outside aid will probably increase, most citizens may have little cause to be jubilant, and the traditions that have caused persistent poverty are likely to continue. The answer is that economic aid alone is not enough!

VARYING SENTENCE BEGINNINGS

You can also achieve sentence variety by varying sentence beginnings, starting your sentence with an adverb, a subordinate clause, a conjunction, a modifying phrase (one that serves the functions of an adjective or adverb), or an absolute. (An absolute is a construction that is independent from the rest of the sentence, such as "*The crop having failed,* the farmer declared bankruptcy.") Here are some examples:
Opening with an adverb:

Occasionally I had to borrow money.

Suddenly the door banged open.

Opening with a subordinate clause:

When the letter arrived, I was too nervous to open it.

Because we had a flat tire, we got home late.

If she teaches the course, I shall sign up for it.

While the organ played, the monkey did tricks.

Opening with a conjunction or conjunctive adverb:

But he never appeared.

And he kept his promise.

However, the cost was too high.

Nevertheless, you failed to keep the bargain.

Opening with a modifying phrase or absolute:

In an hour, we located the park.

The game having ended, we left for the restaurant.

To prepare the fish, you should use olive oil.

Having chased me out of the yard, the dog returned to the porch.

Watching the cat's shadow, the bird looked tense.

COORDINATION

Coordination is the linking of similar elements within a sentence, such as words, clauses, and phrases. Coordination can thus provide variety in sentence construction, reduce repetition, and place sentence elements in a logical relationship that will improve audience comprehension. For coordination to be correct, (1) the proper coordinator must be used, and (2) the coordinated sentence elements must be of equal importance.

As mentioned earlier, there are several coordinating conjunctions, and each of them indicates a special relationship between the elements of a sentence.

"And" indicates that the two related elements are of equal value and complementary in meaning:

I'm going to buy him a sweater, *and* he can wear it on Sunday.

"But" indicates that two related clauses are of equal importance but contrasting in intention:

I'm going to buy him a sweater, *but* he can't wear it on Sunday.

"Or" indicates an alternative or choice between elements of equal value:

I'm going to buy him a sweater, *or* he will buy one himself.

"Nor" is the negative counterpart of "and." Like "and," "nor" joins an element of equal value with the first element, but "nor" indicates negation. When the second element contains "nor," "not" or "neither" must appear in the first element:

I cannot buy him a sweater, *nor* can I pay for his dinner.

When the elements linked by coordinating conjunctions are independent clauses, a comma precedes (*not* follows) the coordinating conjunction, as in the example sentences above. When the coordinating conjunction joins words or phrases, rather than independent clauses, no comma is needed: (See also the discussion on the use of the comma in a series, in Chapter 15.)

She turned on the radio *and* the television.

He looked at the child *and* walked away.

Notice how coordination can reduce repetition. Compare the following with the two sentences above:

He turned on the radio. He turned on the television.

He looked at the child. He walked away.

SUBORDINATION

The purpose of subordination is to show, within the same sentence, the importance of one element in relation to another. (You may also wish to consult the discussion of transitions earlier in this chapter.) Subordination may be carried out by the following methods:

1. Begin the less important clause with a subordination-marker word, such as the following:

although	unless	as
though	whether	when
since	so that	where
because	before	while
if	after	until

Note how subordination is used to combine two sentences:

Original:

I wanted to meet him. I did not have a chance.

Combined:

Although I wanted to meet him, I did not have a chance.

2. Use *who, which,* and *that* to introduce the subordinate clauses:

I bought the book at the university bookstore. It is having a sale.

I bought the book at the university bookstore, *which* is having a sale.

3. Use phrases that contain a nonfinite verb form, participles (-ing or -ed form), or the infinitive ("to" followed by the verb, "to go"). Notice how subordination is used to combine the following sentences:

Original:

The sparrows' nest was in the shutters. Their loud songs woke me early every morning.

Combined:

Singing loudly from their nest in the shutters, the sparrows woke me early every morning.

Original:

There is a simple way to improve home security. Buy a dog that has a loud bark.

Combined:

To improve home security, buy a dog that has a loud bark.

If a subordinate clause uses a subordination-marker word and precedes the main clause, it is normally followed by a comma:

Although I like hamburgers, I can't afford to eat them.

Since he is not here yet, why don't we leave?

If you don't like the candidate, you shouldn't vote for her.

Wherever they found termites, they sprayed insecticide.

EXERCISES

1. Determine whether or not the following sentences are properly coordinated. (Is the most appropriate conjunction used? Are the coordinated statements closely related and of equal importance?) Correct any errors that you find.
    a. I voted for the man, and I still don't like him.
    b. He took the course four times, and he may have to take it a fifth.
    c. I didn't vote for her, but I've only lived in her district for a year.
    d. A good means of learning to succeed is to study three hours a night, and I haven't been able to do that.
    e. In order to save gasoline, don't drive when you can walk, but always consider the extra time that walking requires.
    f. Visit us again, and we always love to see you.
    g. I am not going to quit, nor shall I ask for a promotion.
    h. She will drive the blue sports car, or she will use her limousine.
    i. I did eat their porridge, but I did not kill them.
    j. Jason married Katharine, whom he had known for only three days, and they learned to love one another.

2. Explain whether the subordination properly emphasizes the more important element in each of the following sentences and revise those that use subordination improperly:
    a. She had just arrived in class when word reached her that she had won the lottery.
    b. In addition to losing his arm in the accident, he had to have four stitches in a cut on his leg.
    c. After graduating from college, she became an assistant to the senator.
    d. Until he learns to get to places on time, he will remain unemployed.
    e. According to the surgeon general, cigarette smoking is dangerous to your health.
    f. I was only mildly surprised when the doctor said my wife had delivered triplets.
    g. When gun powder exploded without causing the musket to fire, the expression "a flash in the pan" came into being.
    h. The couple always sits in row E when they attend the basketball game.
    i. You shouldn't have agreed to come if you dislike Afghan cooking.
    j. The exterminator set roach traps throughout Quentin's house whenever he found roach tracks.

PARALLELISM

You can often make a sentence flow smoothly and provide extra emphasis by placing certain clauses, phrases, or words conveying concepts of equal value in parallel grammatical form. Parallelism is the repetition of similar (or "parallel") constructions in different sentence parts. For example, in the sentence "I bought *a coat, a purse,* and *a ring*" the italicized elements are parallel, each italicized element consisting of an indefinite article ("a") and a noun. Parallelism also appears in longer elements, such as clauses and sentences, as in the following example:

> When I started shift work, I began losing sleep. When I started losing sleep, I began losing my cheerfulness.

Note that the two sentences have parallel clauses ("When I . . . ," "When I . . .") and are also parallel in that each begins with a subordinate clause and each is a complex sentence (a dependent clause and an independent clause). Parallelism of sentence pairs is not a grammatical necessity but sometimes helps to provide emphasis—the effect is noticeable to a reader whether he or she recognizes that "parallelism" is at work. Sometimes, as the following discussion indicates, parallelism is necessary to keep sentence parts logically related.

Grammatical Class

The process of making individual words parallel involves placing them in the same grammatical class. For example, to convey information about your favorite pastimes, you might state:

> My favorite pastimes include *photographing* wildflowers, *playing* the bassoon, and *jogging* in the park.

Here the verbals (gerunds, which are verbals used as nouns) are parallel in the -ing form. Another means of stating the information (though less specifically) is to use parallelism of nouns:

> My favorite pastimes include *photography, music,* and *exercise.*

Repetition

Sometimes parallelism consisting of repetition can lend emphasis to a statement or to a series of statements. For example, you might give the following explanation for your opinion of a movie:

> The plot, the characters, and the photography were all poor.

Using parallelism with repetition adds emphasis:

> The plot was poor, the characters were poor, and the photography was poor.

Using parallel sentences and increasing repetition makes the statement stronger:

> The plot was poor. The characters were poor. The photography was poor.

Parallelism can also be effective with subordinate clauses:

> I thought *that* she had caught the ball, *that* we had won the game, and *that* we were the new champions.

Remember, however, that if it is not to lose its emphasis, repetition should be used sparingly.

CORRELATIVES

Understanding parallelism when using correlative conjunctions ("either . . . or," "neither . . . nor," and "not only . . . but also") can help you maintain smooth and logical sentence elements. The following statement lacks parallelism:

> She *not only* lost her money *but also* her keys.

For the clauses to be parallel, "lost" should come before "not only" in the first clause so that the same parts of speech follow each correlative:

> She lost *not only* her money *but also* her keys.

The sentence above can also be made parallel in other ways:

> She not only lost her money but also lost her keys.

> Not only did she lose her money, but also she lost her keys.

The same logic of parallelism applies to "either . . . or" and "both . . . and":

> Either she lost her money, or she lost her keys.

> She lost either her money or her keys.

> She both lost her money and lost her keys.

> She lost both her money and her keys.

LOGICAL CATEGORIES

Logical categories are a necessity in parallelism. Consider this sentence:

Germans, bankers, and Canadians gathered for the meeting in Geneva.

The categories in the series—Germans, bankers, and Canadians—are not parallel: some Germans and Canadians are also bankers. For the categories to be logical and parallel, the sentence should be revised as follows:

Germans, Canadians, and bankers *of other nationalities* gathered for the meeting in Geneva.

COMPARISONS

Comparisons employing "more . . . than" require parallel constructions. It is wrong, for example, to say:

I find *more* enjoyment in listening to the music of Beethoven.

This is an incomplete statement; necessary for logical completion is a parallel "than" complement:

I find *more* enjoyment in listening to the music of Beethoven than in listening to that of Gilbert and Sullivan.

All comparisons, not just those employing "more . . . than," must be stated fully. For example, it is illogical to state the following:

Her views on foreign policy oppose the *president*.

It is the president's views that are being opposed, not the president himself. Logically, the statement should read:

Her views on foreign policy oppose the *president's*.

GRADATION

Arranging elements of a series in the order of their importance can give special emphasis to the final element:

His lack of a sense of responsibility left his wife puzzled, his friends frustrated, and his supervisor angry.

In the above sentence, the series is arranged according to intensity. In the sentence below, the elements in the series go from smaller to larger:

> The tax reform issue grew in popularity throughout the city, the county, the state, and the country.

INVERTED WORD ORDER

Inverting normal word order, like other devices for emphasis, should be used sparingly, since more than infrequent use of this device will simply produce an overall effect of awkwardness. When used appropriately, however, inverted word order can provide strong emphasis.

Normal pattern:

> She stepped in front of the irate customer.

Inverted:

> In front of the irate customer she stepped.

Normal:

> No other teacher ever won such admiration.

Inverted:

> Such admiration no other teacher ever won.

Normal:

> The dog stood by the table, eating the last of my sandwich.

Inverted:

> By the table stood the dog, eating the last of my sandwich.

In revising for variety and emphasis, see that sentences are structured so that:

- They are clear.
- The most important elements are appropriately positioned.
- There is variety in length and structure.

EXERCISES

Correct the faulty parallelism in each of the following sentences:

1. Corn products, wheat products, oat products, and Cheerios are my favorite breakfast foods.
2. John likes to cook, reading historical novels, and classical music.
3. His eyes grew brighter and brighter, his cheeks redder and redder, and his knees weaker.
4. I remember my college years as being happy and carefree, and the sadness that came when I graduated.
5. The children were running, laughing, and the parents were screaming.
6. We picked tomatoes from the garden, apples from the orchard, and went home.
7. I will either call you tonight or first thing tomorrow morning.
8. The trees are lofty and beautiful, the sky is blue and clear, and the grass is green but feels prickly.
9. This issue is of paramount concern to the legislators, the taxpayers, and to welfare recipients.
10. They are enjoying football more.

REVISION EXERCISES

Revise each of the following paragraphs to improve sentence variety:

1. In crossing the railroad, I found many tracks. I tried to avoid one engine. I was knocked down by another. I was dragged a distance of a block or more. I got cuts on my face and hands, and I got coal ashes in the cuts. I didn't get any broken bones, and that was eight years ago. It took me two years to recover though.

2. The personal computer industry has brought manufacturers sudden fortunes as well as sudden bankruptcy: technological developments have come with such rapidity that some manufacturers who had made important breakthroughs and watched huge upsurges in sales develop were surprised only a few months later when a rival company achieved a technological breakthrough that made the first company's advance obsolete; each of the manufacturers, in other words, has remained vulnerable to rapid advances by a rival. Prospects, moreover, are that such marketing instability will continue for the industry.

3. He was a good boy until he got to card-playing and drinking. He didn't like to work after that, and he often stayed out till morning. He'd sleep late, and I couldn't wake him. The farm got run down, and the family got further in debt. We sold the farm, and we bought a house in town. He got worse than ever. He couldn't do any work. He wouldn't do anything but gamble and drink. Sleeping off his hangovers in the street finally solved the problem. A garbage truck ran over him one Monday morning.

13
Strengthening Sentence Construction

Once you are satisfied with the larger elements of content and organization, and after you have improved sentence variety and emphasis, your revising should involve reading your essay over to uncover any awkwardness in sentence construction that is obscuring your meaning. Root out the faulty grammar that lets a sentence say something you do not intend. Make your sentences work for you to keep the logical relationships among your concepts clear and to avoid distracting your reader with usages that are unconventional.

The discussion that follows treats some of the main ways that sentences can be strengthened. Not all the ways will be of equal importance to all writers. The discussion reflects a conservative view of what is acceptable written English in forums where people write for an educated, nontechnical audience.

POINT OF VIEW

A writer has the option of presenting material from various points of view: the first person ("I" or "we"), the second person ("you"), or the third person ("he," "she," "it," or "they"). Here *point of view* is used only in the sense of *person;* do not confuse *point of view* with *viewpoint,* which suggests "attitude" or "feeling."

Perspective

In order to maintain continuity, many writers use a single point of view throughout an entire piece of writing. Though point of view, or perspective, can shift within an essay—or even a paragraph—a single perspective should always be maintained within a single sentence. Writing informally from personal experience, you may use the first person, "I" and "me." (If you employ the highly general third-person point of view, "one," you may unintentionally sound pompous in an otherwise informal discourse.) If you shift from "I" to the audience's point of view, "you," you may not only distract readers but also place them in a perspective that they find difficult to accept.

The following sentence, for example, shifts point of view from the first person to the second person:

> What *I* learned from my last party is that *you* should never hide out in someone else's closet.

Here is the same sentence revised:

> At my last party, I learned that I should never hide in someone else's closet.

Many writers restrict use of the "you" point of view to a process paper, in which they wish to give the audience a sense of participation in working through a process together. They also restrict the "one" point of view to formal reviews and reports, in which a feeling of formality is appropriate.

Direct and Indirect Discourse

Another aspect of point of view requiring continuity is the use of either direct or indirect discourse. Direct discourse is a direct quotation—as in "He asked, 'Why not?' " By contrast, indirect discourse is a restatement from the perspective of the listener—"He asked if I was going." Notice the awkward shift in the following sentence:

> My friend *asked me to go* on vacation with him and *would I share* expenses.

This sentence would be clearer if amended to either of the following:

> My friend asked me to go on vacation with him and to share expenses.

(Both parts of the request are in indirect discourse.)

> My friend asked, "Will you go on vacation with me and share expenses?"

(Both parts of the request are in direct discourse.)

REVISION EXERCISES

Revise the following sentences to correct any problems with point of view:
1. I enjoy visiting Niagara Falls because one feels the power of nature there.
2. By attending the revival, I learned that you should obey the Ten Commandments.
3. She asked would I like to follow her.
4. When a person graduates from college, you find that jobs are still scarce.
5. We had trouble locating a police officer; one is usually not there when you need him or her.
6. She asked me would I buy a subscription.
7. One often requires assistance when he or she is visiting a foreign city for the first time.
8. She indicated her strong dislike for the other lawyers in our office, but you never know when your opinion is likely to change.
9. I have a terrible time understanding assembly kits, and it seems to me that manufacturers intentionally aim to confuse you.
10. Your insurance policy should provide full coverage if a vandal shatters your windshield or even steals your fog lights.

PLACEMENT OF MODIFIERS

Modifying (describing or limiting) words, phrases, and clauses should be placed as closely as possible to the word, phrase, or clause being modified. Normally, the modifier immediately follows the term modified, but sometimes it is necessary for the modifier to precede the term modified.

Misplaced Modifiers

A misplaced modifier is one that modifies the wrong element in the sentence, usually because the modifier is placed far from the element it was intended to modify. The following sentences contain misplaced modifiers:

A dog ambled past the schoolyard fence *that had foam on its mouth*. (Misplaced clause)

Nancy is the most interesting person in the office *as an editor*. (Misplaced phrase)

The woman called a physician *with the flu*. (Misplaced phrase)

Bruce *only* loved his wife. (Misplaced word)

Sometimes misplaced modifiers do no more than make a sentence read awkwardly; at other times, they cause confusion, sometimes amusing confusion. In either case, the process of correcting misplaced modifiers involves placing the modifying phrase as closely as possible to the term modified. Here are the sentences corrected:

A dog *that had foam on its mouth* ambled past the schoolyard fence.

(The original sentence reads as if the fence had foam on its mouth.)

As an editor, Nancy is the most interesting person in the office.

(The original sentence reads as if the office is an editor.)

The woman *with the flu* called a physician.

(The original sentence reads as if the physician had the flu.)

Bruce loved only his wife.

(The original sentence reads as if the only thing Bruce did was love his wife; the revised sentence limits the category of those he loved to his wife alone.)

The last example points up the care that is necessary with such modifiers as "only," "just," and "merely." Consider the different meanings conveyed by repositioning "only" in the following sentences:

Agriculture will worsen only gradually.

Agriculture will only worsen gradually.

Only agriculture will worsen gradually.

The first sentence conveys the idea that agriculture will not worsen rapidly, but slowly. The second sentence indicates that agriculture has no prospects other than to worsen gradually. The third sentence indicates that agriculture alone—not similar facets of the economy—will worsen gradually.

Dangling Modifiers

A dangling modifier is a modifier that does not clearly and logically refer to some word in the sentence. The following sentences have dangling modifiers:

After two martinis, the waiter brought us menus.

Watching for cars, the road looked safe to cross.

Having arrived at the shore, the motel was a welcome sight.

While watching television, the news of the general's death startled us.

Being new to the job, the boss assigned Carla to break me in.

To cook in the Chinese manner, a bottle of peanut oil must be kept handy.

Here are the sentences corrected:

After we had had two martinis, the waiter brought us menus.

(The original sentence reads as if the waiter had had the martinis.)

Watching for cars, the children thought the road looked safe to cross.

(The original sentence indicates that the road is watching for cars.)

Having arrived at the shore, we thought the motel was a welcome sight.

(The original sentence indicates that the motel arrived at the shore.)

While watching television, we were startled by the news of the general's death.

(The original sentence indicates that the news was watching television.)

Because I was new to the job, the boss assigned Carla to break me in.

(The original sentence reads as if the boss was new to the job.)

To cook in the Chinese manner, you should keep a bottle of peanut oil handy.

(The original sentence requires the bottle of peanut oil to do the cooking.)

As the above sentences indicate, you correct a dangling modifier by supplying a subject for it to modify logically.

Squinting Modifiers

A modifier that can logically attach to the words or phrases on either side of it is a squinting modifier. For example, the following sentence poses a problem:

They decided on Tuesday to visit the castle.

Is Tuesday the day that they made the decision, or is Tuesday the day on which they planned to visit the castle? To clear up the ambiguity, the writer could have amended the sentence in one of two ways:

On Tuesday, they decided to visit the castle.

They decided to visit the castle on Tuesday.

REVISION EXERCISES

Revise the following sentences to correct any errors in placement of modifiers:
1. Shuddering convulsively, the pill was popped into the patient's mouth.
2. When a poor immigrant boy of ten, my father took me to my first baseball game.
3. While reaching for the telephone, the keys fell from her hand.
4. They ate the hot dogs with relish.
5. Joe bought a Ford from the used car salesman with bucket seats.
6. Cruising at 3,000 feet, the people looked like ants.
7. To play the scene correctly, words must be enunciated with precision.
8. The couple went to the party on the bus.
9. The university counselor is very understanding when crying and upset.
10. Standing before her threateningly, the guitar was gripped as if she would use it as a weapon.
11. The dog, chewing the cookie, showed no interest in whether the postman intended to pass through the gate holding the can of pepper spray.
12. In March the tour group, left stranded because of the airline strike, was unable to leave until April.
13. Schneider only was excited by the thought of getting his income tax refund.
14. To go to the mall on Tuesday, we decided to take a subway and then a bus.
15. He just identified Joe as being at the scene of the crime.

SENTENCE FRAGMENTS

During revision, check your essay for undesirable fragments—incomplete sentences written and punctuated as if they were complete—and then reread what you have written in reverse, from the last sentence to the first. This practice helps you to see statements that are out of context and to identify more easily those sentences that are incomplete. Examine the common types of fragments discussed below. Although they may seem relatively easy to recognize, they can be quite troublesome to identify when in context, for they often read as extensions of the sentences that follow or precede them.

Verbal Phrases

Sentence fragments often arise from use of a verbal rather than a finite verb. A *verbal* is a form that is derived from a verb but operates as another part of speech. It has uses that are appropriate, but serving as the main verb is not one of them. Examine the following fragments involving verbals that wrongly serve as main verbs:

She headed for the door. *The argument being over.*

How to select a motorcycle. That is the purpose of the magazine article.

Voting. That is our duty.

The fragments above may be corrected by connecting the verbal phrase to the sentence it relates to, by changing the verbal to a finite verb, or by supplying additional elements to make the verbal phrase into an independent clause. Here are the sentence fragments corrected:

She headed for the door, the argument being over.

(The verbal phrase is joined to the existing sentence.)

She headed for the door. The argument was over.

(The verbal is replaced by the finite verb *was.*)

The purpose of the magazine article is to discuss how to select a motorcycle.

(The verbal phrase is combined with the existing sentence.)

Voting is our duty.

(The verbal phrase is combined with the existing main clause.)

Prepositional Phrases

A prepositional phrase that stands alone is a sentence fragment. Such a fragment can be corrected by joining the phrase to the clause containing the element that the phrase modifies. The following are fragments in which prepositional phrases stand alone:

He loved his job. *From the start.*

She placed the money where she thought it would be safe. *Under the pillow.*

The car was parked illegally. *In a loading zone.*

Here are the fragments corrected:

He loved his job from the start.

She placed the money under the pillow, where she thought it would be safe.

Or:

She placed the money where she thought it would be safe—under the pillow.

The car was parked illegally in a loading zone.

Subordinate Clauses

A subordinate clause, like a prepositional phrase, belongs with a main clause because the subordinate clause serves as a part of speech in relation to a main clause. Standing alone, a subordinate clause is a fragment. The following are examples:

I had no money left for books. Since I had spent my last cent on tuition.
                               (adverbial)

The rain lasted for three days. While I sat around indoors.
                                (adverbial)

The most expensive piece was the necklace. Which I bought.
                                           (adjectival)

The car stalled on the beach. Where I left it.
                              (adverbial)

When the promotion was delayed. That is when I decided to look
          (adverbial)
for a new job.

The fragments above can be corrected by joining the subordinate clauses to the appropriate main clause:

I had no money left for books, since I had spent my last cent on tuition.

The rain lasted for three days, while I sat around indoors.

The most expensive piece was the necklace, which I bought.

The car stalled on the beach, where I left it.

When the promotion was delayed, I decided to look for a new job.

Compound Predicates

Sometimes a sentence has two main verbs, as in the following:

He *ran* and *screamed* at the top of his voice.

If the second verb is detached in a separate sentence and the subject is not repeated, a fragment results.

Incorrect: He ran. And screamed at the top of his voice.

Correct: He ran. And *he* screamed at the top of his voice.

Here are examples of compound predicates in sentence fragments:

She did not meet him. And did not want to.

The refrigerator broke down. But was easy to repair.

The book was popular. And made the best-seller list.

Here are the fragments corrected by being joined to the main clauses:

She did not meet him and did not want to.

The refrigerator broke down but was easy to repair.

The book was popular and made the best-seller list.

Compound Objects

Sometimes, like compound predicates, compound objects are separated from their clauses and become fragments. Here are examples:

Everything he earned went for their vacation. *And their extra taxes.*

(Compound object of the preposition *for.*)

The professor assigned three research papers. *And two lab reports.*

(Compound object of the verb *assigned.*)

The office meeting provided a chance to discuss personnel problems. *But not salary inequities.*

(Compound object of the verbal *to discuss.*)

Here are the fragments corrected by being joined to the main clauses:

Everything he earned went for their vacation and their extra taxes.

The professor assigned three research papers and two lab reports.

The office meeting provided a chance to discuss personnel problems but not salary inequities.

REVISION EXERCISES

1.   Rewrite the following fragments to make them complete sentences:
     a.   Especially after John's friends showed up at her house.
     b.   A notice having been slapped on the window.
     c.   In the beginning of the month of April, in 1984.
     d.   Where the row of ash trees meets the white fence.
     e.   Because my brother is not my keeper.
     f.   The problem being that he is incompetent.
     g.   A travel guide to the great Italian city of Rome, the scene of so many intensely romantic adventures.
     h.   Which I have never been guilty of before.
     i.   Standing apart from the crowd and content in my decision.
     j.   Without the report having been completed.
     k.   After buying a new house, two BMW 528 sedans, a new lawn mower, and an Apple computer.
     l.   This being that consumers are pressed for time and are therefore unable to compare prices.
     m.   Needing a job for which she was desperate and was willing to go any place to relocate.
     n.   The trash can lid, blowing down the street, amid the wild wind of March in the upper reaches of the Ohio valley.
     o.   Following their loss to Tech.
     p.   Considering that no one showed up for the meeting.
     q.   Heritage Mall. A great place to shop.
     r.   The fuzzy rat, a delightful—though misunderstood—pet.
     s.   Since I had last dined on Korean food.
     t.   Because the job required too much.
2.   Revise the following paragraph to correct any sentence fragments. Join the fragments to the existing sentences or rewrite them as complete sentences:

The shortage of student housing. This has been a problem on this campus for years. The cause of this shortage being the fact that the state won't build dormitories. This is because the president and some deans own local rooming houses. And apartment complexes. They want to be able to continue charging really high rents. And have full occupancy. Thus, no cheap dormitory rooms.

FUSED SENTENCES

During revision, check to see that your sentences are not fused. Each independent clause should have punctuation that separates it from other independent clauses or sentences. Examine the following:

The man knocked on the door he was selling gopher tonic.

Though two independent clauses appear in the statement, there is no indication of the point at which the first unit of thought ends and the next begins. To clarify the relationship between the two thoughts, the statement can be rewritten in a number of ways:

The man knocked on the door. He was selling gopher tonic.

The man knocked on the door; he was selling gopher tonic.

The man knocked on the door, and he was selling gopher tonic.

The man who knocked on the door was selling gopher tonic.

The man who was selling gopher tonic knocked on the door.

The first two choices are satisfactory because the period and semicolon provide adequately strong pauses; the audience is signaled that a separate and significant unit of thought is to follow. The third choice is grammatically correct, though the resulting sentence seems wordy. The fourth and fifth choices economically embed one clause—now a dependent clause—in the other; they are also grammatically correct. In revising fused sentences, determine how best to emphasize the more important clause. (Note the different emphases in four and five.) But keep in mind that sometimes the two clauses may be equally important. In such cases, employ a coordinating conjunction.

COMMA SPLICES

Another problem to check for in revision is the comma splice. Comma splice refers only to a specific type of comma error: the use of a comma alone to separate two independent clauses not joined by a coordinating conjunction. For example:

The man knocked on the door, he was selling gopher tonic.

The simplest means of correcting the comma splice is to use a semicolon or a period in place of the comma:

The man knocked on the door; he was selling gopher tonic.

The man knocked on the door. He was selling gopher tonic.

Comma splice errors occur frequently with *conjunctive adverbs* ("however," "therefore," "besides," "indeed," "in fact," "also," "moreover," "furthermore," "nevertheless," "still," "thus," "hence," "consequently," and "accordingly"). A conjunctive adverb is not the same as a coordinating conjunction, which always is positioned between the two independent clauses it links. Rather, a conjunctive adverb can take different positions within the second clause. When a conjunctive adverb appears at the beginning of an independent clause, the word must be preceded by a semicolon and followed by a comma. When a conjunctive adverb appears within the clause, it is both preceded and followed by commas. Comma splice constructions occur when a conjunctive adverb begins an independent clause but is preceded by a comma instead of a semicolon. Compare the following:

COMMA SPLICE	COMMA SPLICE ELIMINATED
I am a writer, however, none of my stories has been published.	I am a writer; however, none of my stories has been published.
	or
	I am a writer; none of my stories, however, has been published.

COMMA SPLICE	COMMA SPLICE ELIMINATED
There was no snow last weekend, therefore, we could not go skiing.	There was no snow last weekend; therefore, we could not go skiing.
	or
	There was no snow last weekend; we could not, therefore, go skiing.

REVISION EXERCISES

1. Revise the following to correct for fused sentences and comma splices:
    a. The game was important for our school's reputation, it was being broadcast over national television.
    b. I was lying on the floor then I decided to get a snack.
    c. Ben awakened from a deep sleep, and then he made breakfast.
    d. William descended on his in-laws as Melissa arrived at her cousin's in Mississippi Karen went back to college.
    e. You left the room you weren't properly dressed.
    f. He had just bought a new car and a secondhand boat then his boss fired him.
    g. I was standing in the elevator with nothing on but my thermal underwear I really felt embarrassed.
    h. We must unite against the tobacco industry's immensely powerful lobby, it's continuing to promote a substance research has shown is a killer.
    i. Joan clumped up the stairs, she was eager to get home and begin her new computer program.
    j. The man screamed long and loud, however, no one came to his aid.
    k. Elizabeth giggled she was beginning to let the wine show through her normally sophisticated demeanor.
    l. This typewriter lacks a number of the features I've come to expect in an expensive machine, furthermore, the keyboard somehow feels wrong.
    m. The bird flew in the window it was looking for any kind of food it seemed to be starving, it looked pathetic.
    n. Bruce distrusted the sales pitch, nevertheless, he desperately needed a new vacuum cleaner.
    o. Sarah applied only to four universities, in fact, she initially considered applying only to one then she changed her mind.
    p. The metropolitan transit authority is overcharging non-rush-hour customers why shouldn't they get a break if they're willing to use the subway during quiet times after the commuters have gotten to work?
    q. The man cursed in anger he had been passed over for promotion again.
    r. We do not look at television, thus we are not interested in subscribing to cable TV.
    s. The senator showed great courage in participating in the country's space program he deserves a medal.
    t. "I demand that I be given a new hearing, I'm innocent," the defendant asserted.
2. Revise the following paragraphs to correct any errors of fused sentence or comma splice:
    a. The parking lot behind the shopping center is rarely used by shoppers, instead, it has become something of a race track and autocross rally site. Since last spring, when a woman was struck by a speeding motorcycle, shoppers have refused to park in the back lot. Occasionally, however, a

stranger intent on finding a parking space on a Saturday afternoon will venture into the rear lot he or she will be unaware that it has become a playground for the motorized reckless society.

b. I remember when no businesses stood on the corner except a gas station and a feed store that was just five years ago. Now it is difficult to recognize despite the street signs. What was once peaceful and rural has become the site of a major hospital the medical center is known all over the state. And the facility has provided jobs for many people in the area, however, the increase in traffic congestion has been a drawback in the eyes of many.

REFERENCE AND AGREEMENT

Because errors in reference and agreement can cause not only distraction but misunderstanding, check your essay carefully for these errors when revising. Be aware that certain words *refer* to other words in the surrounding context. When the word to which reference is made occurs first in the sentence, it is called an *antecedent*. Problems of reference and agreement occur largely with pronouns and their antecedents, and between subjects and verbs of sentences.

Pronoun and Antecedent

A pronoun must *agree* with its antecedent in number (singular or plural) and in gender (masculine, feminine, or neuter). Pronouns must also *refer* clearly to their antecedents. Consider this sentence.

Mary told Joan that she lacked a sense of humor.

Because "she" has no antecedent to which it clearly refers, the reader may be confused as to who needs the sense of humor. Rewording with a single pronoun clears up the faulty reference:

Mary chided Joan on her lack of a sense of humor.

Or, perhaps:

Mary said, "Joan, you lack a sense of humor."

Agreement errors signify a lack of clarity in language use, as in the following:

The present school system exceeds *their* normal operating capacity.

"System," the antecedent of "their," is singular, but "their" is plural. The reader may be led to conclude that a plural referent for "their" exists in an earlier statement. Upon discovering no plural antecedent, the reader has no choice but to impose his or her own logic on the statement and conclude that the pronoun "their" should be "its." The agreement error causes distraction if not irritation.

Problems with *remote antecedents* can arise with the pronouns "it," "that," "this," "these," and "those." Consider the following:

> The current war in Albania has caused severe problems for the American government as well as for the Canadian government. We Americans cannot tolerate this.

The referent for "this" is so remote that you cannot identify any precise antecedent. Amended, the last sentence should read "We Americans cannot tolerate this war."

Give special attention to the antecedents "everyone," "no one," "one," "a person," and "each." These referents are singular, but the common tendency is to regard them as plural.

INACCURATE	REVISED
The income level of a person has nothing to do with *their* room assignments.	The income level of a person has nothing to do with *his or her* room assignment.

In the inaccurate sentence, the plural pronoun "their" is used as the referent for the singular antecedent "a person."

Gender-Neutral Pronouns

Gender-neutral language has become preferred usage. Traditional usage, which employs "he" and "him" to refer to any person regardless of sex in a generic context, is seen as conveying sex bias. (For example, "The passenger must place *his* luggage under the seat.") To avoid offense and sex stereotyping in pronoun usage, choose "he or she" or "his or her" or "him and her" and make use of plural terms.

> The passenger must place *his or her* luggage under the seat.

> Passengers must place *their* luggage under the seat.

Another way to convey objectivity is to alternate male and female referents. For example, in an essay discussing the rising costs of automobile insurance, you might use the masculine pronoun in a paragraph describing the rises a consumer has seen in his premium changes over a three-year period and the feminine pronoun in a subsequent paragraph on what measures a consumer can take to lower her costs.

Subject and Verb

A sentence's subject and verb, like pronouns and their antecedents, must be in agreement. If the subject is singular, the verb must be singular; if the subject is plural, the verb must be plural.

Here is a list of certain subject-verb combinations that often cause problems.

If "and" combines two or more elements in a subject, the verb should be plural:

The Smiths and their pet dachshund *are* going to Europe.

If "or," "nor," "either . . . or," or "neither . . . nor" combines two or more singular subjects, the verb will be singular:

March or April *is* a good month for scheduling a long weekend.

Neither rain nor snow *keeps* the campus police from taking their walks.

However, if one subject is singular and the other plural, the verb agrees with the closer of the two subjects:

Either the teacher or the students *are* going to be dissatisfied.

"Each," "every," "nothing," "no one," "everyone," and "someone" require singular verbs:

Everyone *needs* clean air to breathe.

Nothing *is* going to prevent her from graduating.

Someone *has* played a trick on us.

Collective nouns (such as "herd," "majority," "family," "couple") and nouns of quantity that are followed by prepositional phrases take singular verbs when they refer to a single unit:

The audience *was* thrilled with the performance.

The committee *plans* an elaborate investigation.

Ten gallons of gasoline *is* all the tank holds.

Three minutes of the second period *remains*.

But when a collective noun or noun of quantity refers to individuals within a group rather than the group as a unit, a plural verb is required:

A majority *were* unable to leave their houses because of the snow.

Four quarts of milk *are* in the refrigerator.

When "there" begins a sentence, it is followed by a singular or a plural verb, depending on whether the subject of the sentence is singular or plural:

There *is* a hole in the wall.

There *are* holes in the wall.

A relative pronoun ("that," "which," "who") takes a singular or plural verb, depending on whether the antecedent is singular or plural:

He will sell the prize chicken that *was* raised on his farm.

He will sell the prize chickens that *were* raised on his farm.

The law, which *is* unfair, needs to be repealed.

The laws, which *are* unfair, need to be repealed.

I gave food to the beggar who *was* poorly dressed.

I gave food to the beggars who *were* poorly dressed.

"Any," "some," "none," "all," "more," and "most" take either singular or plural verbs, depending on their context:

Any of these answers *is* correct.

Were any of you able to attend the lecture?

Of the 300 students, some *are* not going to graduate.

Some of the food *has* spoiled.

All of our hopes *were* fulfilled.

All of my money *was* lost.

Do not mistake the object of a preposition for the subject of the sentence:

One of the hamsters *was* sick.

REVISION EXERCISES

1. Revise the following sentences to overcome problems with reference and subject-verb agreement:
   a. The times she attended was the most enjoyable.
   b. Each person should understand that their problems do have solutions.
   c. No one ever likes to turn their back on a person in need.
   d. The Bacons and their son agrees to vote for the Republican.
   e. The problems with the men the two sisters married are quite complex; I don't even like to discuss them.
   f. Neither Ed nor Willard were in class today.
   g. Joe, along with his family, are attending the state fair.
   h. Every one of the Smiths go to church on Sunday.
   i. The army is building their own defenses.
   j. A writer like Chaucer or Shakespeare were well known by their contemporaries.
2. Revise the following paragraphs to correct any errors of pronoun reference and agreement:
   a. Finding that the hubcaps had been stolen left Mitchell angry. He had an idea who had done it but knew someone would have to step forward and offer their help in identifying the thief. He wished he knew if the hubcaps could be sold easily.
   b. Wandering through the mall, Melissa saw her father looking in the pet shop window at a long-haired white kitten. He appeared to be transfixed, and Melissa knew then that when she arrived home, another pet would have joined the family.
   c. The grocery store clerk seemed tired. All evening he had been lifting gallon jugs of milk, which left his arms feeling rubbery. Then he had an hour of helping the cashiers, loading groceries into bags for shoppers. They often were rude and expected him to drop all his other responsibilities whenever a customer checked out. Sometimes they expected him to carry the groceries to the walk and load them into the cars. This was the reason he decided this was his last night on the job.
   d. I hate to fly. Once when I, together with my sister and cousin, were waiting in the airport lounge, a stranger bored us with a story about how he overcame his fear of flying. He noted that he never flies without wearing his favorite pair of argyle socks, which don't go with very many of his conservative business suits.

VERB TENSE AND MOOD

Because verbs carry the action of your sentences, they need to function well together. In addition to indicating action or state of being, verbs also reveal tense—the time the action took place (*past* tense), takes place (*present* tense), or will take place (*future* tense). Verbs, with their auxiliaries, may also indicate whether the action has been completed (*perfect* tense) or is in progress (*progressive* tense).

PRESENT: I accomplish
PRESENT PROGRESSIVE: I am accomplishing
PRESENT PERFECT: I have accomplished
PAST: I accomplished
PAST PROGRESSIVE: I was accomplishing
PAST PERFECT: I had accomplished
FUTURE: I will accomplish
FUTURE PROGRESSIVE: I will be accomplishing
FUTURE PERFECT: I will have accomplished

To avoid distracting the reader, maintain a logical, consistent sequence of tenses from clause to clause and from sentence to sentence. In revising, check particularly for shifts from past to present and from present to past. Note, for example, the tense shifts in the following paragraph:

> As the month of November *progressed,* the anticipation I *feel begins* to grow. I *am* aware that at the end of this month would come the day I *had* been waiting for since last March. It *was* growing more difficult to pay attention to my school assignments as I *thought* of the mountains and cooler temperatures. Soon the ski slopes *would* again *be* open.

In the first sentence, the tense shift from the past to the present is illogical and distracting. Moreover, the tense shift in the first sentence, coupled with the present tense in the second sentence, causes confusion about "this month": does the writer mean the past November, or is she referring to the present time at which she is writing the account?

Here is the paragraph revised. Note that there are several changes to help keep the time sequence clear.

> As the month of November *progressed,* the anticipation I *felt began* to grow. I *was* aware that at the end of that month would come the day I *had* been waiting for since last March. It *was* growing more difficult to pay attention to my school assignments as I *thought* of the mountains and cooler temperatures. At the end of November, the ski slopes would again be open.

The Historical Present

Writers sometimes use the *historical present* in a narrative to create a sense of closeness between the reader and events that took place in the past. This use of the present tense usually occurs in works of literature and in literary criticism. The first of the two paragraphs that follow is a historical account of a village gravedigger; the second is a brief literary analysis. Both use the historical present:

He *works* incredibly hard and with great independence, travelling from village to village on a moped to the carrier of which *is* tied a gleaming spade and fork. He *drives* well out towards the centre of the road and the Anglo-American traffic *has* to swerve and swear to avoid him. Quite a lot of people *recognize* him, however, for he *is* a famous person, and *give* him a wide berth. They *know* they *are* seeing Time's winged chariot with a two-stroke.

Ronald Blythe, *Akenfield, Portrait of an English Village*

Chaucer's Wife of Bath *shows* how a person can have many faults, yet remain cheerful and likable. The Wife *tells* how she mistreated her five husbands, and, in essence, *seems* to be asking if among the pilgrims there *is* a volunteer for the role of sixth husband. The implied request *is* mirrored by the actions of the loathsome hag in the Tale the Wife *tells*.

The Subjunctive Mood

Formal usage, and sometimes informal usage as well, requires the use of the subjunctive mood when *a wish* or *conditions contrary to the facts* are referred to. The following sentences properly employ the subjunctive mood:

I wish I *were* rich.

If he *were* (not *was*) coming, he would be here by now.

Were (not *was*) the point untenable, John would not stand by it.

Becky would attend the convention if more money *were* (not *was*) in the travel fund.

ADJECTIVES AND ADVERBS

Adjective Degrees

Adjectives have two degrees, comparative and superlative. Use the *comparative degree* (signaled by *-er* or *more*) only when making a comparative statement about *two* objects, persons, or concepts:

Of the two texts, Rita's is the *better* one.

Milton's poetry evokes *more* interest than Dryden's.

John is *happier* than anyone else I know.

Use the superlative degree (signaled by *-est* or *most*) to make a comparative statement about *more than two* objects, persons, or concepts:

Of the five texts, Rita's is the *best*.

Of Dryden's play, Wordsworth's sonnet, and Milton's epic, the *most* interesting work is Milton's.

John is the *happiest* of the three.

Adverb Degrees

Like adjectives, adverbs have two degrees. The comparative degree is marked by *more* and the superlative by *most:*

You drive *more* recklessly than he.

Of all my friends, you drive the *most* recklessly.

Adjective-Adverb Confusion

Use adjectives to modify nouns and pronouns. Use adverbs to modify verbs, adjectives, and other adverbs. Do not confuse the adjective and adverb forms.

INCORRECT	CORRECT
Wayne did his job *good*. (Adjective modifying verb)	Wayne did his job *well*. (Adverb modifying verb)
Wayne did a *real* good job. (Adjective modifying another adjective)	Wayne did a *really* good job. (Adverb modifying adjective)

REVISION EXERCISES

1. Revise the following to correct for problems in the use of adjectives and adverbs in the following sentences:
    a. John sure knows how to drive a truck!
    b. The man sat continuous atop the flagpole for three days.
    c. Drowning the cat was a real bad thing to do.
    d. The Smiths determined to fix up the house as good as their finances permitted.
    e. Kate's head felt poor when she awoke.

    f. Tennis and basketball are enjoyable sports to watch, but I like to watch basketball the most.

    g. Of the three brothers, John is the more likely to do good in school.

    h. Fred complained of feeling nauseous.

    i. I sometimes forget to do my math assignments very careful.

    j. Mr. Scott is the less helpful of the three teachers.

2. Revise the following paragraph to correct any problems with misuse of adjectives and adverbs:

The worse job I ever had was in a hardware store. People would come to me to complain about shoddy construction in their houses and expect me to feel badly about their problems. If I recommended a real good plumbing compound and the customer didn't follow directions and applied it to a wet joint, then I got the blame. If I sold someone floor tiles and he or she dropped the box and cracked the tiles, the easier thing to do was to come back and complain that I sold him or her broken tiles. And if the person acted real angry and spoke cruel, the manager said I was supposed to answer polite. I didn't do well at that part of the job.

14

Using
Effective Diction

When you are writing, you cannot communicate with your audience except through an effective choice and arrangement of words, and you should remember that your audience cannot see your facial expressions or hear your tone of voice. Thus, to enable your audience to envision what you are seeing, you need to provide guidance through a careful selection of words that are appropriate within your writing context, even though you may not be conscious of choosing the "best" words as you compose a first draft. Revising for appropriate diction is probably the revision step that you will repeat most often.

Revising for good diction means finding not *a* word or phrase but *the best* word or phrase to communicate your message to a specific audience. In some instances, good diction may mean selecting a simple, everyday word rather than an unfamiliar or pretentious one, such as the word "stole" instead of "arrogated" or "appropriated." In others, it means avoiding vague expressions like "a meaningful dialogue" or rejecting jargon such as "interfacing to maximize feedback." But perhaps most importantly, good diction reflects your respect for your audience's intelligence, your intent to clarify rather than obscure your message, and your desire to present information or ideas honestly and in a manner that will not be misleading.

There is no one method for achieving good diction, as the choices open to you will depend in every instance on your writing context. Notice, for example, the difference in diction in the following presentation of similar information in different contexts. The first example is the opening of Abraham Lincoln's address at Gettysburg:

Fourscore and seven years ago our fathers brought forth on this continent, a new nation, conceived in Liberty, and dedicated to the proposition that all men are created equal.

229

Appropriately formal for the occasion of dedicating the Civil War battlefield, such diction would sound pretentious in more casual circumstances. Writing on the same day, a journalist or historian might have worded the statement more simply:

> Eighty-seven years ago our nation was founded on the basis of liberty and equality.

Whatever your writing context, your message will be communicated in a style that is emphatic and persuasive if you present that message with special attention to language that is simple, fresh, specific, and honest.

SIMPLICITY

Avoid cluttering your writing with words that lack precision. Not only does every word you use count, but every ineffective word hurts. Have no fear of saying things simply, in language suitable for your audience. From your experience as a reader, you know that it is difficult to understand writers who are vague or wordy or otherwise clumsy with language. As you learn to handle language with control, you will appreciate how the "right word" is worth looking for, while three or four poor substitutes cannot really do the job.

When seeking to determine whether your language is suitable for your audience, ask yourself two questions: "Have I used words that express my idea clearly and that my audience will be likely to understand?" and "Have I chosen words because they communicate my idea, not because they show my audience how much learning I have?"

Using the Common Word

If you write about "equitation" instead of "horseback riding," you may be unintentionally saying to your audience, "You can see how smart I am by the big word I know, and some of you are going to have to guess what my topic is or else wait until you have read a third of my essay to find out." You may also be forgetting about the importance of appropriateness for a given audience. For instance, the term "heart attack" would be readily understood by most readers. For an audience of physicians, however, "coronary thrombosis" or "coronary infarction" would be more precise and more appropriate.

Specialized language addressed to nonspecialists can sound pretentious as well as unclear. Here is a sentence, written by a psychologist, that is unlikely to be understood except by other psychologists—and even they may have trouble:

The technique of paired comparisons of plastic forms in testing oral stereognosis . . . has apparently eliminated problems of intersensory contamination inherent in earlier methods.

The psychologist could have revised the sentence without *jargon* (specialized, technical language) so that it would have been understood by the members of almost any audience:

By placing two plastic objects of different shapes in a person's mouth, I can objectively test the person's ability to recognize objects by sense of touch.

As you can see, a first step in revising for simplicity is to select the common word that most accurately conveys the idea or concept you are discussing. Use technical terminology only if there is no precise, common-word substitute, and define the term the first time you use it unless you are writing for an audience of experts.

Writing with Economy

A second step in revising for simplicity is to substitute, whenever possible, a single word for a phrase—so long as the substitution does not make it more difficult for the audience to understand what you are saying. Deleting unnecessary words is important for three reasons: (1) it saves the audience time; (2) it aids clarity; (3) it helps you suggest that you are direct and efficient and that you are *not* pompous or pretentious.

Let's take a practical example. Assume that you are a business executive who has just received a job application that begins as follows:

It has come to my attention that you seek to ascertain the potentiality of someone becoming an employee of your corporation.

Your reaction would be negative. The applicant has taken twenty-one words to say what could be said in about twelve. She has wasted your time, and she obviously is writing from a dictionary rather than from her mind. Had the applicant written, "I wish to apply for the position of accountant," you probably would have continued reading her application.

Substituting Active for Passive

A third step in revising for simplicity is to consider substituting the active voice for the passive. *Voice* is not the same as *tense*, which indicates whether something happened in the past, present, or future. Rather, voice indicates whether the *subject* (usually the first noun element in the sentence) *acts* or is *acted upon*—whether the subject *performs* the action or *receives* the action. For example, "Senator Kathleen Garvey delivered the keynote address" is in the active voice; Senator Kathleen Garvey, the subject, performs the action. However, the passive statement, "The keynote address was delivered by Senator Kathleen Garvey," has the subject "address" being acted upon. Note that the active statement has the greater simplicity: not only is the same amount of information presented in fewer words, but the writer is forced to present *all* the information. That is, had she used the passive, she might simply have stopped after writing "The keynote address was delivered," and the audience would gain no knowledge of the *agent* (who did the delivering?).

Sometimes, however, you may find the passive useful for achieving variety or for giving special emphasis to the person or thing that receives the action. For instance, "Duane was hit in the face by the bat" properly emphasizes the victim rather than the agent. As a general rule, however, substituting the active voice for the passive will give your writing a greater degree of simplicity, action, and directness.

FRESHNESS

Effective writing sounds fresh rather than trite. Fresh diction involves setting aside tired, shopworn expressions. For example, "He was as angry as a wet hen" could be freshly stated, "He was like an erupting Mount Saint Helens." "Noisy people were packed in the auditorium like sardines in a can" could be restated, "The noisy, crowded auditorium was like a seal rookery." Using fresh expressions will keep your audience interested and increase its respect for you.

Rejecting Clichés and Fixed Phrases

To achieve freshness will require some mental energy. Your first step is to check your essay for clichés and fixed phrases. Because many such expressions are familiar elements in everyone's vocabulary, you may have to exert some effort to notice them. Clichés are common expressions, platitudes (flatly uninteresting observations), adages, and bits of folk wisdom used so often that they have become tiresome. You have heard many of these over the years:

I'm so hungry I could eat a horse.

. . . as big as a house

. . . as flat as a pancake

. . . a sight for sore eyes

. . . nip in the bud

The grass is always greener on the other side.

There's no sense in reinventing the wheel.

It is important to use fresh expressions not just because worn-out ones may bore your audience but also because overused expressions are often imprecise. For example, the politician who says that union members will have to "bite the bullet" to help get inflation under control is not identifying exactly the sacrifices he expects the union members to make. Suppose, however, that the same politician were to say, "XYZ Union members will have to hold their wage demands below 7 percent if they want to help get inflation under control." In the second case, precise and useful information firmly holds the audience's attention, while also suggesting that the speaker has given the topic serious thought.

Examples of fixed phrases are "due to the fact that," "in the event that," "at this point in time," "in terms of," "in all likelihood." In revising, you will find that you can simply drop such phrases or else find shorter substitutes. For example, "because" is a ready substitute for "due to the fact that"; "if" can be used instead of "in the event that"; "now" or "then" can replace "at this point in time"; "regarding" or "as to" substitute for "in terms of"; "probably" is a less wordy way of saying "in all likelihood."

Using Figurative Language

Your writing can be more vivid if you use appropriate figurative language—language that provides a comparison, describes something as if it were some *other* thing. Using figurative language, however, usually involves careful deliberation in order to find comparisons, and thus incorporating figurative language into your essay is frequently a part of revision rather than of the first draft stage. Nevertheless, wisely chosen figurative language can give your writing uniqueness, and it is therefore in your interest to set aside time for thinking about it during revision.

Your ability to see a likeness in unlike things also can give your audience a new perspective. Through reliance on sensory experience, you can add interest, freshness, and perhaps even humor to your essays. In addition, because figurative language relies on association, it is economical.

A word of caution, however: be careful not to overuse figurative language. Unless it is used sparingly, figurative language may become distracting. And in some situations—such as those in which the audience wants only simple, straightforward facts—figurative language may be inappropriate.

Among the kinds of figurative language available to you are: *metaphor, simile, personification,* and *allusion.*

Metaphor

A metaphor is a comparison of things that are apparently dissimilar. A metaphor provides comparison without using "like," "as," or other words that announce a comparison is being used.

His ears are flags.

The university is an octopus wrapping its tentacles around my checkbook.

Simile

A simile compares two apparently dissimilar things, softening the comparison by using the qualifiers "like" or "as." Instead of saying "A *is* B" (metaphor), the simile says "A *is like* B" (or "A is *as* B").

He returned her dropped handkerchief as if it were a wet diaper.

The pet shop owner wheezed and whined like an asthmatic guinea pig.

Personification

Personification is a figure of speech that is particularly useful for emphasis. To personify is to speak of an abstraction or nonhuman thing as if it were a person, as in the clichés "Father Time" and "Mother Nature." Personification can effectively endow nonhuman things or abstractions with human characteristics, as in the following:

The automatic dishwasher gargled, then spit the sudsy water into the sink.

Bright pink walls shouted at us as we entered the lounge.

The wind reached its chill fingers between the buttons of my coat.

Allusion

An allusion acts as a kind of metaphor. It is an implied comparison of something with an historical or literary subject or event. For example, you might say that someone's powers of oratory are "Churchillian," suggesting that the person has the exceptional speaking ability of a Winston Churchill. If you call Lebanon a "new Vietnam," you are helping bring to mind the possibility of another seemingly unresolvable and costly conflict. Your allusions, however, should remain in the realm of knowledge that your audience is likely to possess; if you use allusions that are too specialized or obscure, you run the risk of the audience failing to grasp your point. Here are examples of appropriate allusions, since they involve comparisons with entities likely to be recognized by nearly any reader:

> Mr. Higgins, like Ebenezer Scrooge, demands long hours for low pay.

> Although not a Beethoven, Vaughan Williams has composed music of enduring popularity.

> The Zerlon Company's machine, the Edsel of typewriters, is experiencing poor sales.

> A chamber of gothic horrors, my grandmother's attic resembles a creation from the mind of Edgar Allan Poe.

The Mixed Figure of Speech

In revising your essay for effective diction, check for mixed figurative language, that is, language that gives the audience two or more dissimilar images in rapid succession. Suppose, for example, you wrote the following:

> The professor, a mean old bear of a man, roared directions at the students in a voice as clear as a bell.

This sentence suggests to your audience an absurd image of a bell-shaped bear roaring like a lion; the mixed figure causes distraction from the point you are trying to make. While figures of speech can make writing more vivid, remember that it is far better to make a literal statement than to use figurative language that does not present a distinct image consistent with your intention.

SPECIFICITY

By employing specific, precise diction, you can achieve both freshness and clarity. One noted scholar of the English language, S. I. Hayakawa, stated that language offers various means of conveying substantially the same information. You may see these means as a ladder of abstractions. Note that the following sentences range from *abstract* to *concrete*:

1. I like beauty.

2. I like beautiful things.

3. I like beautiful flowers.

4. I like beautiful roses.

5. I like long-stemmed American Beauty roses.

6. I like the long-stemmed American Beauty roses arranged in a vase in the window of Mrs. Murphy's living room.

At different times, each level may be appropriate. Levels five and six are most effective as supporting development, yet level six is the more specific because it refers to certain flowers and to no other ones. By presenting supporting information on the sixth level, you will be using concrete detail, which will make your writing precise, emphatic, and interesting.

But the six-step ladder has, so far, taken care of only the noun in step one, "beauty." There are also different degrees of *intensity* for the verb "like." And when you are striving for true precision, you can analyze "like" in a similar manner, questioning yourself as follows: "Precisely how did I feel when I saw those roses last Saturday? Did I want to bring my friend to see them also? Did I want to stand looking at the flowers for ten or fifteen minutes? Or did I simply admire them in passing and hurry on home for lunch?" You might then turn to a college dictionary and examine the list of synonyms under the "like" entry: "love, enjoy, adore, savor, relish, fancy, dote." (Most dictionaries provide synonym lists.) Having determined the various shades of meaning—and, in particular, the different levels of intensity—of each of the verbs, you may decide to assert, "I *enjoy* the three long-stemmed American Beauty roses in the window of Mrs. Murphy's living room." By selecting "enjoy" you will convey the notion of simple appreciation. "Adore" would suggest extreme fondness. The other synonyms may also seem not quite accurate or appropriate.

Remember that verbs often have synonyms that suggest varying degrees of intensity; adjectives and nouns usually have synonyms with varying degrees of abstraction. If you are to select the words that most accurately and appropriately reflect your meaning, you need to grapple with the question, "Precisely what do I mean?"—and answer the question through your attention to diction.

HONESTY

Your audience has the right to demand that you, as the writer, be honest. As you revise, try to catch expressions or usages that are common in speech but sound exaggerated in writing. For example, were you really "shocked" to learn that your favorite bakery had closed? Is the death of a parakeet a "tragedy"? Compose and revise to show your audience the same respect that you would expect were you one of its members.

A writer's tendency toward exaggeration may stem partly from constant exposure to various forms of advertising. But consider your own response to being told that a certain detergent will get your clothes "whiter than white." What is your attitude toward a bank that claims to offer "free" checking and then triples its charges for printing your checks? And what is your reaction to seeing a new car advertised for $7,995, only to find that the price does not include transportation charges, dealer preparation, or options already installed—all of which bring the real price to about $12,000?

You are unlikely to mislead your audience intentionally, but if you fail to choose your words carefully, that could be the result. If, for example, you make a statement such as "I enjoy living in the dormitory because everyone there is so friendly," you are probably being misleading because at least a few dorm residents could be characterized as "unfriendly" or at least "shy." What about statements such as "Bill despises Professor Cummings" or "I think Erin is the most wonderful person in the world"? As you can see, being honest in choosing your words—as well as your concepts—means being honest with yourself. And if you appear less than candid to your audience, you run the risk of alienating it.

Checking for honesty involves identifying *overstatement,* points that you have exaggerated or idealized. Take particular care to be honest in developing such topics as a religious experience, a kindly grandparent, university food, a death or funeral (mourners tend to idealize the character of the deceased), a favorite book, a sports event in which you starred—any topic about which you have strong likes or dislikes, any topic about which society has formed strong attitudes (patriotism, motherhood, communism).

Denotation, Connotation, and Slanted Diction

Words have both denotative and connotative meanings. Denotative meanings are the dictionary definitions of a word. Connotative meanings are the associations that cultures or individuals attach to a given word. For example, "mother" may connote warmth and security for you; but for some person whose mother tied him to a playpen for his first five years of life, "mother" may well carry associations of frustration and fear. Generally, though, choose words according to the public, or cultural, connotations that they will be likely to carry for an audience.

Examine the way that connotation operates in the following statements, which convey essentially the same denotative information:

1. John is scatterbrained.

2. John is muddleheaded.

3. John is disorganized.

4. John is unsystematic.

Slanted diction is word choice that suggests a strong bias in the writer's attitude toward his subject. Diction slanted positively often appears in advertisements. One stereo manufacturer, for example, claims that its receivers "have brought an exceptional level of high fidelity to car stereo. Not just with advanced features, but with truly fine specs and, of course, terrific sound." Words such as "exceptional," "advanced," "truly fine," and "terrific" have little or no meaning in the advertisement context, but they do show strongly favorable attitudes that are intended to sway the audience.

Notice how American humorist H. L. Mencken uses diction slanted negatively in the following passage:

> Virginia is the best of the South today, and Georgia is perhaps the worst. The one is simply senile; the other is crass, gross, vulgar and obnoxious. Between lies a vast plain of mediocrity, stupidity, lethargy, almost of dead silence. In the North, of course, there is also grossness, crassness, vulgarity. The North, in its way, is also stupid and obnoxious. But nowhere in the North is there such complete sterility, so depressing a lack of all civilized gesture and aspiration.
>
> "The Sahara of the Bozart"

Sometimes, however, slanted diction is less obvious than in the Mencken passage. Note the differences in attitude conveyed by "spy" as opposed to "traitor"; "upset" as opposed to "falling apart"; "mentally ill" as opposed to "insane"; "special education" as opposed to "education for the retarded."

Diction that carries highly emotional connotations has a place in persuasive writing, but it must be combined with believable supporting detail. Believable supporting detail can make an emotional topic move an audience; exaggerated supporting detail may cause the topic to slip into the pit of *sentimentality* (indulging in an emotion for its own sake). There is genuine feeling—not sentimentality—in the way John Malcolm Brinnin concludes his description of the death of his friend Dylan Thomas, the noted Welsh poet:

> In Dylan's room nurses were dismantling the oxygen tent and clearing away other instruments. He had stopped breathing, one of them told us, while she was bathing him. As she was about to turn him over on his right side she had heard him utter a slight gasp, and then he had become silent. When the nurses left us alone, Liz sat down in the chair in which she had watched all the nights of his dying. Dylan was pale and blue, his eyes no longer blindly searching but calm, shut, and ineffably at peace. When I took his feet in my hands all the warmth was gone; it was as if I could feel the little distance between his life and death. Liz whispered to him and kissed him on the forehead. We stood then at the foot of his bed for a few very long minutes, and did not weep or speak. Now, as always, where Dylan was, there were no tears at all.
>
> *Dylan Thomas in America*

Whisper, kiss, gasp—these and other words carry connotations of strong emotion. But the emotional diction in the passage combines with believable detail—the nurses dismantling the oxygen tent and clearing away the instruments, Liz sitting down in the chair, the narrator holding the poet's feet, the two people standing silently at the foot of the bed. The combination of specific detail and emotional diction makes the passage convincing and moving. Compare the Brinnin passage with the account below, which, because of exaggerated detail seems sentimental and unconvincing:

> To punish her daughter, a mother refused to kiss the girl at bedtime. The weeping child finally fell asleep that gray morning, and she never woke again, never! Grief is unavailing now! She lies in her little tomb. There is a marble urn at the head, and a rose bush at her feet; there grow sweet summer flowers; there waves the grass; there birds sing their matins and their vespers; there the blue sky smiles down today, and there lies buried the freshness of my heart.

> Adapted from *Ladies Home Journal,* as recounted in S.B. Shaw,
> *Touching Incidents and Remarkable Answers to Prayer*

Effective diction results from:

- *Simplicity*
  Use the common word.
  Express yourself in the fewest words necessary.
  Rely on the active voice.

- *Freshness*
  Reject clichés and fixed phrases.
  Use appropriate figurative language.

- *Specificity*
  Use concrete nouns.
  Use verbs with the right degree of intensity.
  Consult dictionary synonym lists to find the precise word.

- *Honesty*
  Consider precision as well as denotation and connotation of words.

EXERCISES

1. Examine each of the following sentences for wordiness, floweriness, and pomposity. Restate each briefly and simply:
   a. In terms of grading, he is an easy teacher.

b.   She was ill-disposed to reject the potential career proffered by the organization.

c.   I watched the sun set on the Lincoln Memorial, fading pink with the last illumined billows of clouds in the sky, as Old Glory flapped gently in the breeze.

d.   After perusing the library's various and multifaceted tomes, I have, I believe, arrived at the inescapable conclusion that it is indeed worthy of my donation of $50,000.

e.   On the basis of having examined your missive, I feel compelled to do everything in my power to ease your financial encumbrance.

f.   In terms of the school budget, and with regard to the fact that those of us assembled at this time and place are passionately interested in and committed to our children's educational well-being, we find it incumbent upon ourselves to pledge that we will judiciously, meticulously, and honestly administer the duties and responsibilities which we have with all due regard taken.

g.   The inebriated clerk misappropriated the company's funds.

h.   The pet shop was seen to contain a rather large variety of different sorts of puppies, all of which were registered.

i.   The art exhibit in Johnston Hall is that which one may refer to as magnificent.

j.   Having practiced till noon, by then she had the ability to be able to serve the ball with a lot of accuracy.

2.   Identify which of the following sentences are in the active voice and which are in the passive. Rewrite the passive sentences in the active voice and the active sentences in the passive voice; determine which voice is more effective in each case.

a.   The audience liked the play.

b.   The speech was delivered to Congress by the President.

c.   A teller embezzled money from the bank.

d.   The valuable diamond ring was discovered by a man cleaning the rug.

e.   Mermaids are believed in by few people.

3.   A *mixed* figure of speech combines two or more images in a way that appears incongruous or awkward. Describe the problem that occurs in each of the following:

a.   His jowls, which gave him the appearance of a bloodhound, swung like hammocks when he walked.

b.   She was on the road to recovery even though the doctor's diagnosis wasn't even in the ballpark.

c.   The police officer treed the criminals, who were like sitting ducks on a pond.

d.   The old battle-ax gave sugarcoated advice.

e.   His voice, soft as silk, cut through the air like a knife.

4.   Below is a list of clichés and fixed phrases. Write a substitute for each cliché or phrase that clarifies it or makes it fresher or more precise.

a.   quiet as a mouse

b.   solid as a rock

c.   fell like a ton of bricks

d.   equally as good as

e.   in the same boat

   f.   center around
   g.   in connection with
   h.   in back of
   i.   kind of different
   j.   pretty as a picture
5. For each of the following abstractions, construct a list of words ranging from the less abstract to the concrete:
   a.   vehicles
   b.   sports
   c.   plants
   d.   music
   e.   beverages
6. Find synonyms for the following verbs and arrange each list of synonyms according to intensity:
   a.   hate
   b.   run
   c.   injure
   d.   play
   e.   see
7. Describe how each of the following statements is an exaggeration that needs qualifying:
   a.   Sunsets are beautiful.
   b.   Politicians are crooks.
   c.   The sea is our ally.
   d.   Man is loneliest in a crowd.
   e.   Universities are cultural centers.
8. Write out the denotative meaning of each of the following words and then list several connotations of each:
   a.   politician
   b.   beach
   c.   freedom
   d.   intellectual
   e.   scientist
9. Explain how connotation is or is not appropriate in the following figures of speech:
   a.   The bridge builder's career spanned decades.
   b.   The exquisite dinner had more aromas than a locker room.
   c.   The punch tasted like the water from a defrosted refrigerator.
   d.   The fisherman was happy as a clam.
   e.   The mayor has been doing a fine job. If she can get the new sewage plant financed, that will be the icing on the cake.
10. Construct a statement personifying each of the following:
   a.   winter
   b.   thirst
   c.   a telephone
   d.   a computer
   e.   the sun
11. Construct both a simile and a statement of allusion to describe each of the following:
   a.   a friend's face

b.   a wartime disaster
c.   a favorite aged relative
d.   your hometown
e.   a political campaign

REVISION EXERCISES

Revise each of the following passages to correct inappropriate figurative language and to improve freshness, economy, simplicity, and honesty.

1.   The gift shop had no other customers on that winter day in January. The Christmas shopping season, like all good things, had come to an end, and hardly anyone came to the shop after Christmas. At that point in time, Mr. Garr felt sorry for Mr. Wiggins, the shop owner. Mr. Garr went into the shop and selected for purchase a small, scented candle that was not very large but cost over five dollars. He made the purchase out of charity, though he thought he was being charged too much. Later he learned that Mr. Wiggins netted $100,000 a year, mostly from sales in the Christmas season of November and December. That knowledge presented a terminus to Mr. Garr's charitable impulses, so to speak.

2.   Understanding why people vote the way they do is like trying to find a needle in a haystack. Some people will vote for a candidate just because she's a woman—regardless of what she stands for—and others will vote for her opponent just because he's not a woman—regardless of what he stands for. I guess it could probably be said in such a case that the bottom line is a kind of sex discrimination—for both sets of voters, it would seem.

3.   A big lesson in life is if you are just able to learn that from defeat it is possible to learn character and that how you play the game is more important than winning. Every lost game has a silver lining if you can pull a victory of character building out of the jaws of defeat.

15

Checking Mechanics

It is inefficient to spend time and energy planning and writing an essay, only to type it hurriedly and rush to submit it. Time spent revising and polishing can make the difference between a successful written communication and a piece of writing that does not quite jell. It can also reveal errors or sources of possible confusion or distraction that you will want to fix before giving your work to someone else to read. As perhaps your last task in the revision process, you need to become your own proofreader. In this role, you read through the essay checking the nuts and bolts of punctuation that hold the language together.

It is best to stick to conventional usage in capitalizing, punctuating, and the like, for two reasons. First, you run the risk of making a poor impression on your audience members who know the usual practices and may become alienated if you do not observe them. You are writing not to alienate your audience but to draw it toward your line of thinking. Second, following standard usage leaves you free to devote your energy to questions of thought and of language. At the same time, use of conventional mechanics offers you considerable control over your writing, as is shown in this discussion.

THE COMMA

A comma indicates a pause between sentence parts. It is possible to "listen" for places where a comma is required, but in general you can gain greater control of your writing through conforming to the accepted uses of the comma.

With Coordinating Conjunctions

▶ Place a comma before coordinating conjunctions ("and," "but," "or," "nor") to separate independent clauses in compound sentences:

I thoroughly enjoyed our recent meeting, and I want to thank you for the useful information you gave me.

Charles eagerly sought membership in the country club, but he was dismayed to discover its social bias.

The Irish cannot unite behind a common view of the English, nor can the Scots agree on one view of the Irish.

The comma is optional when the independent clauses are short:

The sky is blue and the sun is shining.

Elvis stayed but Carol went home.

▶ Place a comma before coordinating conjunctions to separate independent clauses in a compound-complex sentence:

The photography book had a high price, but it was expensive to produce.

The children who were in the play stayed indoors to rehearse, and the rest of the class went outside to the playground.

With Adverb Clauses

▶ Place a comma after introductory adverb clauses:

As soon as we heard the cannon, we realized that all was lost.

If we attempt to debate the speaker, we will have to be sure of our facts.

When the General Assembly returns to the Hall of Nations, the press gallery will be full.

Omit the comma when the adverb clause that follows the independent clause is essential to sentence meaning:

Wilson stole third while Barringer waited for the ball.

The crowd roared as the umpire signaled "Safe!"

▶ Place a comma before an adverb clause that follows an independent clause when necessary for clarity or smoothness:

> I understand that many people find the president unappealing, although I think him a man of great charm.

> The Republican Party must unite behind its candidate, because this election is the most significant in years.

With Transitions

▶ Place a comma after transitional words or phrases:

> In the first place, Roberts fails to understand the concept he is dealing with.

> In fact, doesn't she deserve a scholarship?

With Introductory Phrases

▶ Place a comma after long introductory or modifying phrases:

> Yearning for its master, the dog stopped eating and drinking.

> To enlist the cooperation of oil-rich nations, we will reevaluate our tariff program.

With Interjections

▶ Place a comma after a mild interjection that opens a statement:

> Oh, did you see that car?

> Yes, we do have what you require.

With Series

▶ Place a comma between items in a series:

> Pick up the bottle, raise it to your lips, and swish the liquid over your tongue.

> We devoured candy, plums, and yams.

(Some popular publications consider the comma preceding the conjunction optional; however, the preferred form is to retain the comma.)

Generally, omit commas when items in a series are joined by conjunctions:

> Violence or drought or poverty or inflation or drugs—which will be the focal point of the next decade?

Sometimes it is necessary to place a comma between items in a series that is joined by conjunctions to avoid ambiguity or confusion:

> She attended William and Mary and Emory and Henry and the University of Oregon.

In this sentence, commas are needed to distinguish the "and" in the names of the institutions from the conjunction "and":

> She attended William and Mary, and Emory and Henry, and the University of Oregon.

▶ Place commas between two or more adjectives that equally and independently modify the same noun:

> The heavy, short man was eating cheese.

> Goldie, my beautiful, friendly retriever, died this morning.

In the sentences above, a comma is indicated only when both adjectives refer directly to the noun. When the first adjective modifies the whole idea that follows, it is not separated from the second adjective by a comma:

> The sad short story made me cry.

> Look at these beautiful blue jeans!

There are two tests that can help you decide whether a comma is needed between two adjectives. If the adjectives can be reversed and still make sense, or if "and" can be inserted between them, then the adjectives can be separated by a comma.

In the following sentences, note that the tests are applied (reverse the adjectives, insert "and") and the adjectives are shown as coordinate:

> She ate the *cold, sweet* plums.

> She ate the *cold* and *sweet* plums.

She ate the *sweet, cold* plums.

Examine the following sentences, and note that inserting "and" and reversing the adjectives shows the adjectives are not coordinate.

He holds radical political views.

He holds radical and political views.

He holds radical, political views.

With Nonrestrictive Elements

▶ Place commas around nonrestrictive phrases and clauses:

Byron Maguire, a noted actor, is my uncle.

Mrs. Brown offered the Waldorf salad, made with fresh apples, to the entire team.

Do not place commas around restrictive clauses and phrases:

He tripped over the box that was full of turtles.

The carpenter on the ladder dropped his hammer.

With Contrasting Elements

▶ Place commas around contrasting elements:

She comes from Minneapolis, not Chicago.

Churchill, not Eisenhower, saved Europe.

With Localities

▶ Place commas around the parts of an address or geographical location:

I grew up in Stone Harbor, Cape May County, New Jersey.

The Millers' address is 143 Beach Street, Houston, Texas.

Most government buildings in Washington, D.C., are open to tourists.

With Titles

▶ Place commas around a title or a degree that follows a proper name:

Jennifer Townsend, M.A., was the keynote speaker.

The chairman of the board, J. Randolph Jones, Sr., called the meeting to order.

Greg Dunning, M.D., and Mary Williams, Ph.D., are the authors of this article.

With Dates

▶ Place commas around the parts of a date:

The building was dedicated on July 13, 1944.

January 21, 1986, is the date on his letter.

If the day is given before the month, omit the comma:

The last entry in the journal is dated 3 October 1859.

If the day is not given, the comma following the month is optional:

I haven't seen her since June 1986.

In December, 1980, my family moved to California.

With Salutations

▶ Place a comma after the salutation in an informal letter:

Dear Hepsibah,

My dear Aunt Mildred,

THE COLON

With Independent Clauses

▶ Place a colon after an independent clause to announce that clarifying material follows:

What separates Chaucer from his contemporaries is his deep appreciation of the wide variety of English life: he welcomes the genteel with the bawdy, the spiritual with the worldly.

The following delegates from the Tenth Congressional District voted "aye" to the controversial resolution: Barry Adams, Heather Fulton, D. Jason Landis.

With Quotations

▶ Place a colon before a formal quotation when the quotation is a complete sentence. The quoted statement following the colon begins with a capital letter:

Perhaps John F. Kennedy said it best: "Ask not what your country can do for you; ask what you can do for your country."

Mary Wollstonecraft took a balanced view: "The two sexes mutually corrupt and improve each other."

With Numbers, Biblical References, and Salutations

▶ Place a colon between hour and minute, between Biblical chapter and verse, and after a formal letter greeting:

8:45 A.M.

Luke 2:13

Dear Mr. Turner:

THE SEMICOLON

With Independent Clauses

▶ Place a semicolon between independent clauses not connected by a coordinating conjunction:

The candle was lit; there still was insufficient light for reading.

The cat was a gourmet; he demanded shrimp, scallops, and lobster.

▶ Place a semicolon between two independent clauses linked by a conjunctive adverb. A comma follows the conjunctive adverb:

The ever-expanding Soviet navy may prove troublesome to the West; in fact, it is now the largest military sea force in the world.

Angela called her broker immediately; however, her purchase order was too late.

With Series

▶ Place a semicolon between elements in a series when commas appear within an individual item in that series:

Hamilton bought three new pets: Clarence, a goldfish; Seymour, a scorpion; and Magnolia, a mouse.

Seated on the platform were Senator Joseph Smith, from Cambridge, Massachusetts; Mayor Mary Grove, from Hartford, Connecticut; and Professor Carlos Martinez, from Albany, New York.

THE PERIOD

With Sentence Endings

▶ Place a period at the end of all sentences except questions or exclamations:

There is nothing so appealing as the mating song of the hornbilled egret.

"Virginia Woolf's life is really a study of contrasts," claimed Professor Snort.

With Abbreviations

▶ Place a period after an abbreviation:

Dr.	Sr.
Ms.	R. E. Jones
B.A.	Ave.

Current usage allows omitting the period from certain abbreviations, particularly those of organizations and agencies:

NATO	UNESCO
FBI	NAACP

With Indirect Questions

▶ Place a period (not a question mark) after an indirect question (a declarative statement that concerns a question):

> She wanted to know if Congress would continue the education funds.

> The district attorney asked Randolph the source of his income.

THE QUESTION MARK

With Direct Questions

▶ Place a question mark after a sentence that asks a direct question:

> Are you going to the party?

> "Do you really think," he asked, "that the government will fail?"

With Implied Uncertainty

▶ Use a question mark to imply uncertainty concerning dates or facts:

> Bede, 673(?)–735

> Eric the Red, born 950(?)

THE DASH

With Interruption

▶ Place a dash before and after a parenthetical statement that clarifies a sentence:

> The black mass—a corruption of the Christian service—continues in parts of Eastern Europe.

> The basics of democracy—equality, choice, expression, freedom—are still thriving in our country.

With Qualification

▶ Use dashes to indicate strong hesitation or doubt:

> They will arrive at nine—I hope.

> You are an honest person—aren't you?

THE HYPHEN

With Word Division

▶ Place a hyphen between syllables of a word when your margin does not leave you room to write the entire word on one line:

>   secre-   handker-
>   tary   chief

Do not hyphenate single-syllable words even if they are long ("thought," "could," "straight"), and do not hyphenate words so that a single letter is set off ("a-bove," "weight-y"). If you are not sure how to divide a word, check the dictionary.

With Two-Word Adjectives

▶ Place a hyphen between two-word adjectives that function as a single adjective:

> They sat on the moss-covered stone and ate their lunch.

> The air-conditioned theater is always crowded in the summer.

With Compound Words and Numbers

▶ Place a hyphen between the elements in compound words and numbers:

> My mother-in-law gave me another new tie.

> Sparta was a Greek city-state.

> Thirty-seven students have signed up for the new class in astrology.

With Prefixes

▶ Place a hyphen after prefixes followed by proper nouns, and after "ex" and "self":

"You are un-American," stated Senator Pringle.

As France entered the post-World War I period, her citizens rallied around the new government.

He is an ex-union official.

Snodgrass, forever suffering the pain of self-doubt, became entirely superfluous within the organization.

THE EXCLAMATION POINT

With Exclamatory Sentences

▶ Place an exclamation point after exclamatory sentences:

Touch me and I'll scream!

With Interjections

▶ Place an exclamation point after an emphatic interjection:

Damn! The hot rivet fell inside my shoe.

We're having deep-fried artichokes for brunch? Great!

PARENTHESES

With Enumeration

▶ Place parentheses around numerical or alphabetical points within a sentence:

There are three central questions we must confront if this project is to be successful: (1) the total cost, (2) the required number of manhours, and (3) the long-range effects on the international market.

With Explanatory Elements

▶ Place parentheses around material that explains but is not essential to the meaning of a sentence. Sometimes an entire sentence, with appropriate punctuation, may be placed in parentheses:

> The character of Sherlock Holmes ("Elementary, my dear Watson") was actually drawn from a man known to Sir Arthur Conan Doyle.

> Because of the North Sea oil fields, Aberdeen (population 190,200) became Scotland's first "boom town."

> You may need additional information. (If so, consult the card catalog.)

BRACKETS

With Direct Quotations

▶ Place brackets around material not part of a direct quotation but added for clarification:

> "I believe," said the ambassador, "that he [the foreign minister] is a loyal friend of the United States."

The Latin word *sic* in brackets in a direct quotation indicates that an error appears in the original source:

> Her journal entry for April 24, 1869, reads, "We leave today for Calafornia [*sic*], a long and perilous journey."

QUOTATION MARKS

With Direct Quotations

▶ Enclose direct quotations (the exact words and punctuation of the speaker or writer) in quotation marks. When using a quotation within your own sentence, quote only the words that belong to the secondary source:

> Ibsen maintained that "all men require a pleasing illusion to make the ugliness of reality more palatable."

"There are two major problems plaguing the nation," Mary Coats explained. "The first is inflation; the second is unemployment."

Indirect quotations (that is, restatements of the original words of someone else) do *not* take quotation marks:

Mr. Jackson said, "The divorce rate in America is a symptom of the nation's moral degeneration." (direct quotation)

Mr. Jackson said that he considers the divorce rate in America to be symptomatic of the nation's moral laxity. (indirect quotation)

▶ Quotations within quotations should be indicated by single quotation marks:

At the convention, the speaker told the members of the N.E.A., "I disagree with Professor Jamison's charge that we are 'a bunch of muddleheaded intellectuals' who 'cannot separate theory from reality.'"

With Titles

▶ Place quotation marks around the titles of essays, magazine articles, chapters of books, short stories, and individual poems.

MacQuirk's new essay, "A New Theory of Relativity," is not as thorough as Rankin's "Understanding Relativity."

Hemingway's "Indian Camp" is my favorite short story.

The class read Sylvia Plath's excellent poem "The Stones."

With Other Marks

▶ Place the period and the comma inside quotation marks:

"I believe," said John, "that we are on the brink of disaster."

▶ Place the colon and the semicolon outside quotation marks (unless they are part of the quotation itself):

The novelist accused her audience of "ignorance that is an insult to the arts"; I noted, however, that some of her comments were also ignorant.

He claimed that "we are a lost civilization": morally and spiritually we are bankrupt.

The speaker, attacking the quality of education in the contemporary classroom, stated, "We have only three options: reorganize our schools; hire better teachers; establish appropriate funds for necessary materials."

▶ Place the question mark inside the quotation marks when the quotation itself is a question and outside the quotation marks when the quotation is included within a question:

"Do you love me?" he asked.

Did the courtship proceed "with all deliberate speed"?

THE APOSTROPHE

With Possessives

▶ Use *'s* with singular nouns that do not end with *s* to indicate possession:

John is Bill's brother.

The book's jacket is gorgeous.

▶ To make a singular noun ending with *s* possessive, use the apostrophe alone or *'s:*

I enjoy reading Dickens' (*or* Dickens's) novels.

The duchess' (*or* duchess's) estate is now a public trust.

▶ Place the apostrophe after the *s* to form the possessive of plural nouns:

The Smiths' house is for sale.

The players' shirts were stolen.

▶ Place *'s* after the last letter of plural nouns that do not end with *s* to show possession:

The children's bicycles are in the yard.

The geese's honking kept us awake.

▶ Use *'s* to form the possessive of indefinite pronouns:

Someone's coat is on the floor.

Is everybody's work finished?

Do not use an apostrophe with possessive pronouns:

I'm not sure whose turn it is.

He picked up his book; she picked up hers.

The decision was both theirs and ours.

With Some Plurals

▶ Use the *'s* to form the plural of words being referred to as words:

Jack has five misspelled *separate's* in his paper.

How many *yes's* do I hear?

▶ Use *'s* after letters of the alphabet and numbers to form their plurals:

Richard's three F's made his father angry.

Paula's 7's are poorly formed.

With Contractions

▶ Use the apostrophe to show contractions in words and dates:

I'm meeting Jill at 2 o'clock.

She's a member of the class of '86.

ITALICS AND UNDERLINING

With Titles

▶ Underline (to indicate italic type) the titles of books, magazines, newspapers, pamphlets, videotapes, long poems, films, plays, and works of art:

Although originally produced in 1939, *Gone with the Wind* continues to attract the moviegoing public.

We are going to read Milton's *Paradise Lost* in literature class next term.

I subscribe to *Time* and *Ms.*

With Foreign Words and Phrases

▶ Underline (to indicate italic type) foreign words that have not become part of the English language:

The candidate, summing up his successful campaign, said, "*Veni, vidi, vici.*"

The speech was delivered *tout d'une tirade.*

With Words, Letters, and Figures

▶ Underline (to indicate italic type) words, letters, and figures referred to as such:

You spelled Mississippi with too many *s*'s.

John's *7*'s look like *1*'s.

The word *tranquillity* means different things to different people.

CAPITALIZATION

▶ Capitalize proper nouns:

Margaret Fuller	Los Angeles, California
John the Baptist	University of Michigan
Hudson River	Bell Telephone Company
Fifth Avenue	United Nations

▶ Capitalize adjectives derived from proper nouns:

Shakespearian	Greek
Californian	Platonic

▶ Capitalize specific events or periods in history, months, days of the week, and holidays:

> the Civil War   Monday, April 24
>
> the Stone Age   Christmas

▶ Capitalize titles immediately preceding a name:

> President Lincoln   Reverend Witherspoon
>
> Dean Smithers   Captain Pierce

▶ Capitalize abbreviations immediately following a name:

> John L. Meadows, Jr.   J. P. O'Malley, D.D.S.
>
> Margaret Winkler, Ph.D.   Arthur Roth, M.D.

▶ Capitalize the first word in every sentence.

▶ Capitalize all words in a title, except articles, the "to" of infinitives, conjunctions, and prepositions—unless these appear as the first or last word in a title:

> *An Inquiry into the Assassination of President William McKinley*
>
> "In Darkness and Confusion"

▶ When quoting a complete sentence, capitalize the first word and any other word that the author capitalized:

> Citing the current campus crisis, Dean Blather wrote: "Action must be taken now if the University is to survive."

Capitalization is not necessary when incorporating a quoted phrase into your sentence:

> The creature laughed at "this strange little planet."

▶ Capitalize abstract nouns when they are personifications:

> the stench of Pity
>
> the rape of Romance

EXERCISES

1. Insert commas where they are needed:
    a. Today is January 13 1987.
    b. "Oh I really do like chocolate" squealed the child.
    c. He was the son of a merchant from London and he married the daughter of a merchant from Brussels.
    d. Please bring in the groceries especially the sack with the ice cream in it.
    e. She prided herself on her athletic ability particularly her skill in basketball soccer and polo.
    f. Chris not Susan smoked all Marty's cigarettes.
    g. Budapest Hungary was poorly represented at the conference.
    h. Rasputin who was purported to be the queen's lover exerted great influence in czarist Russia.
    i. The thatched roofs were very very flammable.
    j. And now ladies and gentlemen here is Walter Schmurtz the anchorman for the six o'clock news team.
    k. The third assault was led by Philip Augustus King of France.
    l. Accordingly we should enlist the cooperation of the commissioner of revenue.
    m. To keep his treasure safe the king hired six guards.
    n. I don't in fact plan to attend the class reunion.
    o. The child was an angel but an angel with fangs.

2. Correct the punctuation and capitalization problems in the following:
    a. Bill is this Mikes' pen or is it Gretchens'.
    b. That you lisp, George is nothing to be ashamed of.
    c. Ugh, the cheese in the cellar turned rancid, I knew I shouldn't have left it there.
    d. The train arrived at 4 35, John my boyfriend wasnt on it, he came on the bus the next night.
    e. Is it your turn or our's to bring refreshments?
    f. Shots rang out and general Lee shouted "no surrender".
    g. Do'nt get the idea that you're here for a vacation you are'nt.
    h. He divorced punctuality, and married eccentricity.
    i. James Madison the fourth president of the United States courted and married: the beautiful Dolley Madison.
    j. consider the following proposition; i have two coins totaling fifty five cents one of the coins is not a nickel. What are the two coins.
    k. He caressed her lovingly. all the while munching on a candy bar.
    l. Country music defies classification to analyze it is to spoil it.
    m. While composing his symphonies Beethoven was deaf.
    n. Bankruptcy obliged the family to move from Berlin Germany, on August 17 1808, when Mary celebrated her tenth birthday and look for a new home near Billings Montana.
    o. cheer up cried Heathcliff!
    p. Mr Moore the president of Union bank, Ms Nathanson the stockbroker,

and Ella Snyder PhD the famous botanist combined their efforts in the third annual greater Gibson county talent show.

q. There are four steps to washing your dog—1 immerse the animal 2 scour it thoroughly with soap 3 dry it off 4 comb its fur.

r. His most recent novel, "Beyond the Horizon," was acclaimed by critics. (See the review by Waldo Flink in Time, December 20 1986.)

s. It was not; however, the flood that made me late.

t. At four am Linus tumbled out of bed; went to the kitchen; then realized his clock was on eastern standard time.

REVISION EXERCISES

Revise the following paragraphs so that standard rules of punctuation are followed:

1. When I was graduating from high school like everyone else I had to submit to the embarrassment of the graduation portrait—a special problem was the attitude of my parents who insisted that I get my hair done in what mother called a grown up professional style. Dad meanwhile worried about the length of my dress and he said You cant wear slacks that day. Well I said after these problems are worked out Ill arrive at school with 300 other students and die of embarrassment because I will look like I'm thirty years old or worse.

2. The role of land is extremely important to the Canob indians descendents, according to Harriet Greenfern. In her book, The Canob Psyche she notes that almost 40 percent of all land occupied by these people is too steep to farm but they cling to it despite it's not having economic value. Ms. Greenfern notes that an ancient Canob poem, titled Tree gods has a line in it that tells just how important the land is: 'My soil—I die for it'. Today eking out a subsistence in the poor rocky soil at the base of the mountains is a way of life that gives these descendents of the ancient Canobs an average life-span of forty years. They refuse to leave however for the few factory jobs available on the plain preferring slow starvation to leaving behind ground theyve been taught to consider sacred.

Appendix A

Understanding Grammar

To understand the sentence and its components, a knowledge of the terminology describing the basics can be quite useful, especially when you find it necessary to revise your sentences. Not only can a working knowledge of the sentence parts help you understand how to improve clarity, but it can also aid you in correcting or amending poorly or improperly structured sentences. Some of the terms are necessarily defined by use of other terms; some are explained through examples. If you need explanation of a term used to define another term, you may wish to consult the index.

NOUNS

A *noun* is conventionally defined as the name of a person, place, or thing. However, a working definition is that a noun is any word that can fit into the following blank: the _____.

Types of Nouns

Proper noun: a word that names a specific person, place, or thing.

> *Jean* is from *Quebec.*

Common noun: a word that names a general category or class of persons, places, or things.

> Put your *coat* in the *closet.*

Collective noun: a word that names a group or collection (and usually takes a singular verb or prounoun).

> The *committee* plans to present *its* report at the next meeting.

(In this case, *commitee* is considered a unit.) It would be correct to write "The *committee have* returned to their homes," since the committee is considered to be composed of several persons. Because such usage is unusual, you would be less likely to distract the reader if you wrote instead, "The *committee members have* returned to their homes."

Concrete noun: a word that names something that can be perceived by the senses.

George smelled *smoke,* but he did not see a *fire.*

Abstract noun: a word that names something that is intangible and cannot be perceived by the senses.

Ms. Carr took great *pride* in her daughter's *intelligence.*

Functions of Nouns

Subject: a noun about which a sentence or clause makes a statement. (The subject usually appears near the beginning of a sentence or clause.)

John is hiding in the closet.

Possessive: a noun that serves as a modifier of another noun and indicates ownership.

The guest broke *Greg's* bottle.

Object of a preposition: a noun that is linked to another sentence element by a preposition.

I am going to *California* for the *summer.*

Direct object: a noun that receives the action of the verb.

Abigail wrote the *book.*

Indirect object: a noun that indirectly receives the action of the verb and states to whom or for whom something is done. (When the indirect object follows the direct object, the prepositions *to, for,* or *of* are used. When the indirect object precedes the direct object, the preposition is understood.)

Joan hit the ball to the *fielder.*

Joan hit *him* the ball.

Sam bought a new tie for his *friend*.

Sam bought his *friend* a new tie.

Pat asked a tough question of the *theologian*.

Pat asked the *theologian* a tough question.

Predicate noun (also called *predicate nominative* or *subject complement*): a noun that appears in the *predicate* and is equivalent to the subject. (The main verb in a sentence containing a predicate noun is *be, seem,* or the equivalent.)

Frances is the *captain*.

EXERCISES

1. Identify the nouns in the following:
    a. Gail put the ship back in the bottle.
    b. Anxious that he would miss his appointment, the man pressed the accelerator to the floor and the car leapt forward.
    c. Clarence, anticipating his mother's response, covered his ears as her shriek reverberated around the room.
    d. The council will unveil its recommendation this afternoon.
    e. He lifted the weight as his muscles bunched and strained.
    f. Wayne prepared the sandwiches, Joe tossed the salad, and Jill tapped the keg of beer.
    g. The woman's smile fluttered Tim's heart.
    h. Bill's fear of appearing in public offset his skill as a violinist.
    i. The wildlife agency pressed its case in the courts.
    j. I returned last night from Colorado, and I will leave tomorrow for the Orient.
2. Identify each subject in the following by underlining it once and each object (including objects of a preposition) by underlining it twice:
    a. The pen scratched the top of the desk.
    b. I hate phone calls late at night.
    c. The traffic jam made the sales representative late.
    d. Late hours did not affect her.
    e. His shirts were stained with oil.
    f. Ten persons died in the accident.
    g. There was a large hole in the lawn.
    h. She asked him for a new typewriter.
    i. For the first week, he came to class regularly.
    j. Suddenly the laughter stopped.

PRONOUNS

A *pronoun* is a word that stands in the place of a noun or noun element (a phrase or clause functioning as a noun). Pronouns therefore function in sentences in the same ways that nouns do.

Simple personal pronoun: a direct substitute for a noun.

Subject:	I	we
	you	you
	he, she, it	they

He likes ice cream.

They decided to cancel the meeting.

Object:	me	us
	you	you
	him, her, it	them

Tom called *her* for the assignment. (direct object)

The judges awarded *him* first prize. (indirect object)

Sally can't go to the movies with *us*. (object of preposition)

Possessive:	my, mine	our, ours
	your, yours	your, yours
	his; her, hers; its	their, theirs

Is this book *yours?*

Their new apartment has five rooms.

Reflexive personal pronoun: a pronoun that indicates that the subject of the clause acts upon itself (*myself, yourself, himself, herself, itself, ourselves, yourselves, themselves*).

He blamed *himself* for the accident.

Did you hurt *yourselves?*

Intensive personal pronoun: a pronoun used to intensify or emphasize its antecedent. Intensive personal pronouns have the same forms as reflexive personal pronouns.

I built the table *myself.*

The students *themselves* graded the exam papers.

Impersonal pronoun: the pronoun *it,* with no antecedent (nothing preceding to which *it* refers). An impersonal pronoun may stand in place of a clause or phrase that follows the main verb, operating as the subject of the sentence.

> *It* was wrong for him to laugh.
> (*Compare:* For him to laugh was wrong.)

> It was appropriate that she got a raise.
> (*Compare:* That she got a raise was appropriate.)

An impersonal pronoun may also refer to an understood concept.

> *It* is hot in Mexico.
> (*Compare:* Mexico is hot.)

Demonstrative pronoun: a pronoun that calls attention to or points out the thing being referred to (*this, these, that, those*).

> *This* is the book I told you about.

> *Those* aren't my glasses.

Relative pronoun: a connective that joins a *dependent clause* to an *independent clause,* normally having the immediately preceding noun or noun substitute as its antecedent (*who, whoever, whose, whom, whomever, that, what, whatever, which, whichever*).

> The queen honored the man *who* axed Sir Mortimore.

> John loved the girl *whom* his mother picked.

> They live in a town *that* has no sidewalks.

> The trees, *which* are yellow, are full of spiders.

Who is used for the subject in a clause and *whom* for the object. Note that, in formal English, *who, whose,* and *whom* refer only to persons, and *that* and *which* refer to nonhuman concepts.

Interrogative pronoun: a pronoun that introduces a question; it has the same form as a relative pronoun, except for the *-ever* words.

Who is knocking at my door?

Which is the most difficult test?

Indefinite pronoun: a pronoun that does not refer to a particular person or thing (*none, both, one, each, all, any, few, some, much, more, many, several, something, someone, somebody, anything, anyone, anybody, everything, everyone, everybody*).

Someone left an umbrella in my car.

Helen did *much* of the work herself.

EXERCISES

1. Identify the pronouns in the following:
    a. We left from there yesterday.
    b. Are you going, too?
    c. They accepted responsibility for the accident.
    d. Was it theirs or yours?
    e. It was, she thought, appropriate to reduce senior citizen fares by 20 percent.
    f. These belong to Cathy.
    g. "Whatever can you mean?" he inquired.
    h. Which of the two arguments is the more compelling?
    i. The climate, which was marked by damp days and chilly evenings, ruined her health.
    j. Bob did most of the typing himself.
2. In the following, identify each pronoun used as a subject by underlining it once and each pronoun used as an object by underlining it twice.

    Example: <u>She</u> gave <u>him</u> the book.

    a. You can tell me if it's correct.
    b. Why did he tell her?
    c. That is the purpose of the course.
    d. He gave the answer, which was wrong.
    e. Whom shall I say is calling?
    f. The car belonged to her.
    g. I was unsure who was to blame.
    h. Someone left a purse in the bus.
    i. There were two awards for him.
    j. They bought the tickets yesterday.

ADJECTIVES

An *adjective* is a word that modifies (describes or limits) a noun or pronoun. A working definition is that an adjective is any word which you can fit into this blank: the _____ (noun).

Descriptive adjective: names a quality or condition of the noun or pronoun it modifies.

> The *small* boy wore a *red* jacket.

Limiting adjective: points out or identifies the noun or pronoun it modifies or indicates number or quantity.

> *My* house is the *third* one from the corner.

Indefinite, possessive, relative, demonstrative, and *interrogative pronouns* sometimes serve as limiting adjectives.

> *Few* students attended the lecture.

> *My* house has no electricity.

> I located the man *whose* wallet was found.

> She wore *that* hat to the opera.

> *What* reason did you give?

Adjectives that are also pronouns agree in *number* (singular or plural) with the noun or pronoun they modify.

> *These* hats are made in China.

> *This* dog is Warren's.

Though adjectives usually precede the word modified, they may also appear following, or in the *post position*.

> Patsy likes her meat *rare*.

> The dog, *large*, *black*, and *menacing*, appeared suddenly.

Degrees of Comparison

Positive: a modification that simply suggests how the thing modified is different or distinct from other things like it.

The *black* dog is named Porthos.

Comparative: a modification designated by *-er* or *more* and used to differentiate two items.

Of the two paintings, Rob prefers the *larger*.

Esther is *more* confident than Leona is.

Superlative: a modification designated by *-est* or *most* and used to differentiate one item from among more than two items.

Of the five chairs, Bryan's is the *most* comfortable.

Jimmy is the *strongest* boy in the school.

EXERCISES

1. Identify the adjectives in the following:
    a. The tall, gangling athlete wore a green sweater that was three sizes too small.
    b. She ran quickly and gracefully after the crowded trolley car.
    c. Bill claimed Professor Simonson's test was unfair.
    d. I called after the man whose umbrella hit me in the face.
    e. The small coral snake can deliver a fatal bite.
    f. Becky's, rather than Suzie's, was by far the better effort.
    g. My dog has deep brown eyes, an energetic tail, and complete loyalty.
    h. That man is a fool.
    i. This book is more comprehensive than that one.
    j. The manager displayed little enthusiasm for my proposal.
2. In the following, identify each adjective used in the positive degree by underlining it once, each used in the comparative degree by underlining it twice, and each used in the superlative degree by underlining it three times.

Example: The young woman, who was older than I was, gave the best speech of all.

    a. You will never meet a kinder man.
    b. The fever got worse that night.
    c. Long icicles hung from the roof.
    d. We had a better time last summer.
    e. The highest peak was a real challenge.
    f. The store had never had such slow business.
    g. The high cost of insurance made the car unaffordable.
    h. Fresh water will always be in short supply.
    i. A good swim was the best exercise, he thought.
    j. The chair, old and musty, sat in the darkening room.

VERBS

A *verb* is a word that states an action or asserts a condition. It may or may not have a direct object (that is, may be transitive or intransitive); it may state an equivalence between subject and predicate (linking); and it may indicate whether the subject acts or receives action (that is, it may be active or passive).

Transitive verb: requires a direct object to complete its meaning.

> Travis *threw* a ball into the pond.

Intransitive verb: is complete without a direct object.

> The sun *appeared*.

Some verbs may be transitive or intransitive, depending on the context. For example, in the following sentences, the verb "paint" is transitive in the first sentence and intransitive in the second.

> Calvin *paints* guinea pig hutches.

> Donna *paints* beautifully.

Linking verb: states equivalence between subject and predicate or states a condition of the subject by connecting it to the predicate. A linking verb is always intransitive.

> Carol *became* the chief architect.

> Elmer *is* the winner.

> Karen *seems* pleased with her roommate.

Active voice: subject performs the action indicated by the verb.

> The dog *smelled* a beaver.

Passive voice: subject receives the action indicated by the verb.

> The beaver *was eaten* by a fox.

Auxiliary Verbs

An *auxiliary* or *helping verb* combines with a main verb (1) to indicate tense, (2) to form the passive voice, (3) to help form negative statements, (4) to add emphasis, or (5) to ask questions.

Richard *was* provided help with his homework.
(Auxiliary indicates past tense, passive voice)

A pork chop *is* tied around Simon's neck.
(Auxiliary indicates present tense, passive voice)

Tyler *did* not enjoy visiting his friend.
(Auxiliary used with negative)

You *do* eat bananas often!
(Auxiliary indicates emphasis)

Do you eat bananas often?
(Auxiliary indicates question)

Modal: an auxiliary that indicates condition, such as ability, obligation, permission, possibility, or habit is termed a *modal*. Some auxiliaries that function as modals are *can, must, may, should, would.*

She *can* do the algorithm.
(Modal indicates ability)

He *must* be on schedule.
(Modal indicates obligation)

You *may* park in my driveway.
(Modal indicates permission)

This antique *may* be for sale.
(Modal indicates possibility)

You *should* feel ashamed.
(Modal indicates obligation)

She *would* arrive by noon each Wednesday.
(Modal indicates habit)

Principal Parts

The *principal parts* of a verb—the present infinitive, the past tense, and the past participle—supply the basic forms for the different tenses of the verb.

Regular verbs: form the past tense and the past participle by adding *-d* or *-ed* to the present infinitive. Most verbs in the English language are regular.

PRESENT INFINITIVE	PAST	PAST PARTICIPLE
laugh	laughed	laughed
walk	walked	walked
hope	hoped	hoped

Irregular verbs: form the past tense and the past participles in some way other than adding *-d* or *-ed* to the present infinitive. The following is a brief list of examples of the three principal parts of some verbs that are irregular and often misused.

PRESENT INFINITIVE	PAST	PAST PARTICIPLE
do	did	done
get	got	got (or gotten)
go	went	gone
eat	ate	eaten
lay	laid	laid
lie	lay	lain
set	set	set
sit	sat	sat

For both regular and irregular verbs, the past participle is used with an auxiliary (*have, had*) to form additional past tenses of the verb (*have laughed, had eaten*).

Mood

Mood is a verb property that indicates whether the speaker is expressing a command; a fact or question; or a wish, supposition, or uncertainty.

Imperative: makes a request or gives a command.

> *Attach* the gas line to the fuel pump. (Note that the imperative implies the subject "you.")

Indicative: states a fact or asks a question.

> We *fed* cornflakes to the owl.

> *Was* he ready on time?

Subjunctive: expresses a wish, supposition, or uncertainty.

> I wish that I *were* rich.

> Suppose that you *were* he.

> If it *were* to snow on Saturday, we could go skiing.

Verbals

A *verbal* is a form that is derived from a verb but operates as another part of speech. It may appear as a *participle,* a *gerund,* or an *infinitive.*

PARTICIPLE

A *participle* is a verbal that operates as an adjective. It may appear in present, past, or perfect form.

Present participle: a verbal ending in *-ing.*

> Jennifer's business is a *going* concern.

> Lend a *helping* hand.

> There is a goldfish in your *swimming* pool.

Past Participle: a verbal in the form of the third *principal part* of the verb.

> The *lost* dog was hungry.

> Hector drove a *stolen* car.

> Judy handed in her *written* work.

Perfect participle: a verbal in the form of auxiliary + *-ing* + past participle (active) or in the form of auxiliary + *-ing* + *been* + past participle (passive).

> *Having gone,* Suzie missed the ice-cream truck.

> The blind man crossed the street, his dog *having led* him there before.

> Their liquor *having been drunk,* Paula and Linda left the party.

GERUND

A *gerund* is a verbal that operates as a noun. It may appear in present or perfect form.

Present gerund: a verbal in the form of the first *principal part* + *-ing.*

> *Swimming* is my favorite pastime.
> The coach prefers *losing* to *winning.*

Perfect gerund: a verbal in the form of auxiliary + *-ing* + third *principal part* (active) or in the form of auxiliary + *-ing* + *been* + third *principal part* (passive).

> The couple argued over *being divorced.*
> The senator was glad at *having been saved* from scandal.

INFINITIVE

An *infinitive* is the present-tense form of a verb preceded by *to* (sometimes, however, *to* is understood rather than openly stated). As a verbal, an infinitive may operate as a *noun, adjective,* or *adverb.*

Noun infinitive:

> To *sing* and (*to*) *dance* was all the happy frog desired.

Adjective infinitive:

> Few persons find time *to read.*

Adverb infinitive:

> John went *to complain.*

Verb Phrases

Participial phrase: consists of a participle, its modifiers, and an object. It operates as an *adjective.*

> *Anticipating a barrage of mortar fire,* the troops ducked for cover.

> Mr. Jones saw the thief *hiding from the police.*

A *nominative absolute* is a special kind of participial phrase that grammarians have traditionally claimed is grammatically unrelated to the rest of the sentence; the nominative absolute does in fact operate adverbially, serving the function of answering a *why* or *when* question.

> *His partner having wrenched his knee,* the tennis player called off the match.

Gerund phrase: consists of a gerund and, sometimes, its modifiers and an object. It operates as a *noun.*

Being respectful is important.

Bill enjoys *watching Bowling for Dollars* with the vice president.

Infinitive phrase: consists of an infinitive, and, sometimes, its modifiers and an object. It operates as a *noun,* as an *adjective,* or as an *adverb.*

To *dine with Allison* is a true pleasure.

Few people find the time *to read.*

Archie retired *to wax his moustache.*

EXERCISES

1.   Underline the main verb once and the auxiliary verb twice in the following:

Example: She is authorized to sign the deed.

    a.   Charley was denied promotion.
    b.   Governor Smith admonished her legislative aide.
    c.   A sling was tied around the sick child's neck.
    d.   The train halted.
    e.   The choir sings off-key.
    f.   Do you come here frequently?
    g.   Must we return to Cousin Henry's right away?
    h.   You should stay.
    i.   He laughed at the man but cried at himself.
    j.   Candice was given a million dollars to do with as she pleased.

2.   In the following, underline each main verb once and each verbal twice.

Example: Her picture was the winning entry.

    a.   Having dined, we sat waiting for the speech to begin.
    b.   With a rousing cheer, the crowd welcomed the team.
    c.   After paying the fee, we entered the pool area.
    d.   The decaying remnants of the fruit strewed the ground.
    e.   Before writing the article, the journalist did little research.
    f.   Bedridden, the old man had not eaten for days.
    g.   Lacking change, I was unable to phone.
    h.   The ripening grain swayed in the sun.
    i.   To climb the hill was our task.
    j.   The lost cat reappeared the next morning.

ADVERBS

An *adverb* is a word that modifies (describes or limits) a *verb, adjective,* or another *adverb.* Adverbs have relative freedom of position in the English sentence but usually appear near the word modified. An adverb may be defined as a word that answers one of the following questions: Where? When? How? Why? How long? How often? How much? (Some adjectives, however, also respond to the last three questions.) Many adverbs are marked by *-ly.*

John ran *upstairs.*
(Adverb answers the *where* question)

Judith ate fish *yesterday.*
(Adverb answers the *when* question)

The cannibal ate the missionary *zestfully.*
(Adverb answers the *how* question)

Vengefully, Roland struck the target.
(Adverb answers the *why* or *how* question)

It seems that we must wait *forever.*
(Adverb answers the *how long* question)

We sell books *frequently.*
(Adverb answers the *how often* question)

Amy had *scarcely* slept.
(Adverb answers the *how much* question)

Note the difference between *there* as an adverb of place (in answer to the *where* question) and *there* as an *expletive* (an expletive is a filler in the word order, itself empty of meaning; it stands in the place of another word or phrase as does the impersonal *it*).

Set the book *there.*
(*There* is an adverb)

There is a communication problem.
(*There* is an expletive. *Compare:* A communication problem exists)

Note that *there* as an expletive cannot stand as a sentence subject. The usual subject and verb order are reversed, so you must take care to see that they agree in number.

> There *is* a *book* on the credenza.

> There *are books* on the credenza.

Degrees of Comparison

Positive: a simple modification of the verb.

> We must wait *forever*.

Comparative: a modification designated by *more* and used to distinguish between two items.

> Jeff learns *more quickly* than Mary does.

Superlative: a modification designated by *most* and used to distinguish one item from among more than two items.

> Of the three, Jeff learns the *most quickly*.

Conjunctive Adverbs

> See page 278.

EXERCISE

Identify the adverbs in the following:
1. John dialed the secret combination gleefully.
2. Quickly and accurately, Karen responded to the question.
3. Mr. Cummings bounded along lightly.
4. Confidentially, Claudia asked that she be dropped from the team.
5. The man placed his hat carefully upon his head, adjusted his tie precisely, and walked out of his house purposefully.
6. Place the exam papers here.
7. Of the drama club members, Burton learns his lines the most slowly.
8. Michael had suddenly grown pale.
9. We must return tomorrow.
10. They cried piteously, "We have been robbed!"

INTERJECTIONS

An *interjection,* a word or phrase conveying emotion, is grammatically independent of any sentence that may accompany it.

Hurrah! Our team won!

Oh, I don't care.

Excellent! What a fine movie!

CONJUNCTIONS

A *conjunction* is a word that connects words, phrases, or clauses.

Coordinating conjunction: a connecting word (*and, but, or, nor*) conveying the idea of equal importance for the items connected.

Mr. Halligan vacuumed the floor *and* washed the windows.

The livingroom was clean *but* not the kitchen.

Correlative conjunction: a coordinating conjunction that is used in paired form (*either . . . or, neither . . . nor, not only . . . but also, both . . . and*).

Bob will *either* attend summer school *or* go to the beach.

Sue looked *not only* tired *but also* worried.

Neither job *nor* family could keep her from the golf course.

Subordinating conjunction: see *relative pronoun,* page 266.

Conjunctive adverb: an adverb that acts as a conjunction, joining two independent clauses (*however, therefore, besides, indeed, in fact, also, moreover, furthermore, nevertheless, still, accordingly, consequently*).

The train was late; *consequently,* I missed my appointment.

John is an excellent tennis player; *in fact,* he has won many tournaments.

The doctor is busy today; *however,* he can see you tomorrow.

PREPOSITIONS

A preposition is a word that operates to connect a phrase or embed it within a clause; prepositions signal meanings of time, space, direction, agency, or some other relation that the connected or embedded phrase has to a verb, noun, adjective, or adverb in the clause. A *prepositional phrase* consists of a preposition, its object, and any modifiers of the object; the phrase may operate as an *adjective* or as an *adverb*.

> Milton worked *in the dark*.
> (Prepositional phrase used adverbially)

> His problem is a matter *of chronic self-abuse*.
> (Prepositional phrase used adjectivally)

EXERCISE

In the following, underline each interjection once, each conjunction twice, and each preposition three times.

Example: Oh, I left the money and the checks in my room.

1. "Never!" he shouted. "I'll wait for the next bus home!"
2. After the race, the winner collapsed and died.
3. The rent or the insurance is certain to increase; however, we should be able to afford the cost.
4. Not only the television but also the camera and radio were missing.
5. Okay, it's time for everyone to leave.
6. On top of the dresser rested a photograph of the grandfather.
7. Until the committee meets, the policy will not be changed, but most of us cannot wait for two more weeks.
8. Take however long is necessary, but try not to be late.
9. For three days we rested; in fact, we should have rested longer.
10. Neither the trophy nor the prize money made her willing to compete in the next contest.

CLAUSES

A *clause* consists of a *subject* and a *predicate*. Both the subject and the predicate may be spoken of as *simple, complete,* or *compound.* The *subject* is the noun or noun substitute (pronoun, phrase, or clause that operates as a noun) about which the clause makes a statement. The subject usually appears as the first noun element in the clause. The *predicate* is the verb and any modifiers and objects that apply to the verb or to one of its objects.

Simple subject: the noun or noun substitute about which the clause makes a statement.

>   The *man* in the car drives too fast in school zones.

Complete subject: the simple subject plus the words that modify it.

>   *The man in the car* drives too fast in school zones.

Compound subject: two or more subjects joined by coordinating conjunctions.

>   The *man* and his *wife* drive too fast in school zones.

Simple predicate: the main verb of the clause.

>   The man in the car *drives* too fast in school zones.

Complete predicate: the simple predicate plus its complements, modifiers, and objects.

>   The man in the car *drives too fast in school zones.*

Compound predicate: two or more predicates joined by coordinating conjunctions.

>   The man in the car *drives* too fast in school zones and *stops* without warning on freeways.

Types of Clauses

Dependent (subordinate) clause: serves the function of a *noun, adjective,* or *adverb* in relation to an *independent clause;* it may not stand alone as a sentence.

>   Ben likes *whatever he reads.*
>   (Noun clause)

>   Dot is in love with the man *who delivers pizza.*
>   (Adjective clause)

>   *When Linda is ready,* we can leave.
>   (Adverb clause)

>   I am in agreement with *what Bruce said.*
>   (Noun clause)

Restrictive clause: an adjective clause that limits the noun or noun substitute that it modifies. A restrictive clause is not set off by commas; it is essential to the meaning of the noun or noun substitute and cannot be omitted.

Children *who wear galoshes* catch few colds.

Nonrestrictive clause: an adjective clause that provides additional information about a noun or noun substitute while placing no restrictions or limits on what it modifies; that is, the information provided by the nonrestrictive clause is not crucial to identifying the noun or noun substitute modified.

Lettuce, *which contains vitamin C,* should be fed to your guinea pig regularly.

Independent clause: a clause capable of standing alone as a sentence.

Jenkins hit the ball.

Jenkins hit the ball and ran to first base.

Jenkins hit the ball, and *he ran to first base.*

If you want sentimental poetry, *read Julia Howell.*

Although Gomez is a clever debater, *Schultz can defeat him handily.*

The colonel and the general do each put marshmallows in their cocoa; however, *they try not to let anyone know.*

EXERCISES

1. Identify the clauses in the following:
    a. The man with a hat.
    b. The man who wore a hat.
    c. While Katy attends the show.
    d. Bob holds the school record.
    e. Bob, who holds the school record.
    f. What Candice found.
    g. Skating over the cold, hard ice.
    h. Although we cheated.
    i. Eagerly and sweetly.
    j. The car driven with skill.
2. In the following, identify each dependent clause by underlining it once, and each independent clause by underlining it twice.

Example: <u>He bought a dog</u> that had a fierce bark.

    a.   When I saw the rat, I ran for the stairs.

    b.   Since the movie was dull, we went out for drinks.

    c.   The foreman complained of her laziness, and she filed a grievance.

    d.   Buying an artificial tree seemed inappropriate to them.

    e.   They left after the fight broke out.

    f.   The summer vacation seemed too short, especially since it rained nearly every day.

    g.   There were six persons to feed, each being very hungry.

    h.   The cost of airline tickets dropped, but not low enough for us to afford the trip.

    i.   Although the woman answered the question, no one heard her.

    j.   While the teacher was out of the room, she missed an argument.

Appendix B

Writing
the Research Paper

Writing a research paper, like writing any other essay, involves planning, developing supporting material, and revising. It may seem more complex because, as the name implies, "research" means working with outside sources of information. Some inexperienced writers become so involved with locating and using this information that they forget many of the principles they normally apply to an essay. You can overcome this difficulty, however, by thinking of a research paper as a partnership between the information and you, and by remembering that the effectiveness of the finished product depends on how well you have shaped, arranged, and presented that information.

The purpose of this appendix is to help you avoid getting mired down by the problems common to writing a research paper. It begins with a brief review of the process of selecting a topic. It then illustrates the process of researching material, planning the use of that material, and documenting sources. The chapter concludes with a sample research paper.

ARRIVING AT A TOPIC

Resist the impulse to begin a research paper at the library; to do so without first having a clear idea of what you will write about will cause you to waste much time. Instead, begin as you would any other essay: by transforming a general subject into a manageable topic. Assume, for example, that you have been assigned a 2,000-word research paper by your biology instructor on the broad subject of "digestive systems." Your major objective is to explain, but you realize that addressing such a broad subject would result in a paper so general as to have no value. Thus, you apply the principle of ever-narrowing focus to the subject. In abbreviated form, this might be illustrated as follows:

<u>SUBJECT</u>

D				
I		<u>TYPES</u>		
G				
E		human	<u>INSECTS</u>	
S		animal		
T		insect	nonflying	<u>COMPONENTS</u>
I		reptile	worms	
V		vegetable	centipedes	pincers	<u>TOPIC</u>
E		floral	ants	thorax	
			fire ants	enzymes	The function
S			South African	mandibles	of the
Y			fire ants		mandibles in
S					the South
T					African fire
E					ant
M				
S				

Naturally, the more you know about a subject area, the easier it will be to arrive at a topic. But even if you have been assigned a subject you know very little about (a rare occurrence in college), a short period of thought will enable you to place some commonsense limitations on it, thereby simplifying your task when you do visit the library. For obvious reasons, researching material on brass-faced, mid-eighteenth-century English long-case clocks is considerably less complicated than researching material on clocks or even English clocks.

The assigned length of your research project—and the amount of time available to you—will also help you in limiting the topic. A 10,000-word paper would obviously enable you to cover a wider area and provide a corresponding breadth and amount of supporting detail than would a 3,500-word paper. For example, if you begin thinking about the general subject of "war," you may narrow your focus to "Napoleonic Wars," further narrow it to "Napoleon's strategy at the Battle of Waterloo," and finally arrive at "Napoleon's pincer tactic against the Russians at the Battle of Waterloo." The subject "war" is far too broad for even a hundred books, and the "Napoleonic Wars" might require ten volumes. But "Napoleon's strategy at the Battle of Waterloo" could be explored in a 10,000-word paper, and "Napoleon's pincer tactic against the Russians at the Battle of Waterloo" could be treated in 3,500 words.

Do not assume that a short research paper should have less depth than a long one. As with any essay, a successful research paper depends on evolving a topic that can be treated thoroughly within specified limits.

RESEARCHING MATERIAL

Once you have narrowed your focus as much as possible and you have arrived at a relatively clear idea of what you will write about, the library will provide the necessary resources and most materials for your research. Preliminary reading in specialized reference works may enable you to continue the narrowing process as you become increasingly familiar with the components of your topic. Subsequent research will acquaint you with the breadth of study and scholarship devoted to your topic. And as you immerse yourself in sources of information, you may refine your topic or even completely alter your point of view.

To derive maximum benefit from the library, you must know what it offers and how to use it. This section is therefore designed to familiarize you with the arrangement of materials in the library and the major resources that will aid your research.

Library Classification Systems

Materials are arranged either by the Dewey decimal system or by the Library of Congress system. Some libraries use both. Learning the basics of each system will aid you in locating material.

The following lists the major subject divisions and corresponding classification numbers for the Dewey decimal system:

000	General Works
100	Philosophy
200	Religion
300	Social Sciences
400	Language
500	Natural Sciences
600	Technology and Applied Sciences
700	Fine Arts
800	Literature
900	History and Geography

The following lists the major subject divisions and corresponding classification letters for the Library of Congress system:

A	General Works
B	Philosophy and Religion
C	General History
D	Foreign History

E-F   American History

 G   Geography and Anthropology

 H   Social Sciences

 J   Political Science

 K   Law

 L   Education

 M   Music

 N   Fine Arts

 P   Language and Literature

 Q   Science

 R   Medicine

 S   Agriculture

 T   Technology

 U   Military Science

 V   Naval Science

 Z   Bibliography and Library Science

Resources for Research

The library contains three broad resources for research: (1) general reference materials; (2) periodical indexes; (3) a list of the library's holdings. Knowing how to use each of these will allow you to save considerable research time.

GENERAL REFERENCE MATERIALS

General reference works provide background on a variety of subject areas, and include encyclopedias, dictionaries, yearbooks, bibliographies, atlases, and gazetteers. These materials are appropriate sources to consult when you *begin* your research. Because their information is simply a compendium of research done by others, however, they should never form the substance of your paper.

There are several works that will direct you to general reference material especially appropriate to your topic. A particularly good starting point is the *Guide to Reference Books,* edited by Eugene Sheehy, which provides an index of bibliographies and reference works on areas ranging from special dictionaries and government publications to specific disciplines within the humanities, social sciences, history and area studies, and the pure and applied sciences. Your library is likely to contain a number of other listings of general reference works. Here is a brief list of some of the best-known general reference works that may be of assistance as you begin your research:

HUMANITIES

Encyclopedia of World Art
Harvard Dictionary of Music
Dictionary of Philosophy
Literary History of the United States
Oxford Companion to American Literature
Oxford Companion to English Literature
Encyclopedia of Philosophy
International Encyclopedia of Film
Encyclopedia of Dance and Ballet
Grove's Dictionary of Music and Musicians

SOCIAL SCIENCES

Social Science and Humanities Index
Encyclopedia of Education
Encyclopedia of Economics
Dictionary of Social Sciences
International Bibliography of Sociology
International Bibliography of Social and Cultural Anthropology

SCIENCES

Universal Encyclopedia of Mathematics
Guide to Mathematics and Physics
Encyclopedia of Chemistry
Encyclopedia of Computer Science
Computer Dictionary and Handbook
Bibliography of North American Geology
Bibliography of Agriculture

Periodical Indexes

Any magazine, journal, or newspaper published on a regular basis constitutes periodical literature. Your library will have a list or a file of the periodicals it contains.

Because of the large number of periodicals available and because many of them are aimed at specialized segments of the reading public, *periodical indexes* are published to aid research. There are many such indexes, each of which lists articles published in periodicals concerning a particular subject or professional area. The following is only a brief sampling of the many indexes available to you:

Art Index
Business Periodicals Index
Index Chemicus
Index of Economic Journals
Education Index
Engineering Index Monthly
Humanities Index
Index Medicus
Applied Science and Technologies Index
General Science Index
Social Sciences Index

Many newspapers also produce indexes of articles that appeared in their pages; these indexes are particularly helpful in locating especially current material. Among the leading newspaper indexes are those published by the *New York Times,* the *Washington Post,* the *Wall Street Journal,* and the *Christian Science Monitor.*

The *Reader's Guide to Periodical Literature* deserves special mention. This index surveys many general magazines and journals, from *Computer World* to *Time* to the *Education Digest.* Published bimonthly, the *Reader's Guide* contains information that is always current. Like most periodical indexes, it is easy to use because it includes at its beginning a list of the periodicals that it surveys and a list of the abbreviations that it uses. Articles are indexed in the *Reader's Guide* by both subject and author.

The following annotations will familiarize you with the abbreviations common to the *Reader's Guide.* The first is a subject entry:

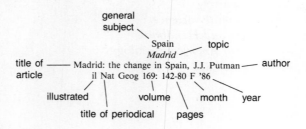

This is an author entry:

SKOW, John
  Call of the champion. il por Outdoor Life 157:
  54-7+ F '76

Like any index, the *Reader's Guide* contains cross-references which guide you to additional information under separate headings. Here is a sample cross-reference entry:

> SKILLED labor
> *See also*
> Trade unions—Skilled labor

List of Library Holdings

The list of library holdings is a file of all the books, pamphlets, and nonprint materials (such as films, videotapes, audiotapes, pictures, and maps) that the library possesses. It consists of a three-part system of entries arranged alphabetically under (1) the subject(s) of the book (or other holding), (2) the title, and (3) the author's name (last name first). The list is usually housed in a card catalog, but to save space, libraries increasingly are putting their lists of holdings on microfiche, microfilm, or Microcard. In addition, some libraries use computer data systems for storing their lists of holdings; you obtain access to a list through a computer terminal.

Whether you use a card catalog, microfiche, or computer, the basic three-part makeup of the list of holdings enables you to find relevant books without knowing specific authors or titles. For example, if you want to locate a book on tropical fish but you cannot remember the author or title, you can still find the book by thinking of subjects that the book is likely to embrace: icthyology, fish, tropical fish. One of your subject headings probably will correspond to a heading in the list of holdings.

You will note that a specific reference in the list contains considerable information. Here, for instance, is a *subject* entry:

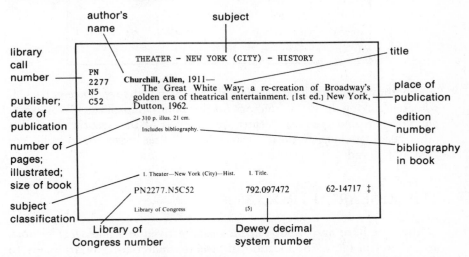

There are two other entries in the list for the same book: the *title* entry and the *author* entry. The title entry is identical to the subject entry except that the subject of the book is omitted and its title appears on the first line:

```
         The Great White Way
PN
2277
N5       Churchill, Allen, 1911—
C52           The Great White Way; a re-creation of Broadway's
              golden era of theatrical entertainment. [1st ed.] New York,
              Dutton, 1962.
                 310 p. illus. 21 cm.
                 Includes bibliography.




                 I. Theater—New York (City)—Hist.     I. Title.

              PN2277.N5C52                792.097472            62-14717  ‡

              Library of Congress                    [5]
```

The *author* entry is the same as the subject and title entries except that it omits the subject and title lines:

```
PN
2277
N5       Churchill, Allen, 1911—
C52           The Great White Way; a re-creation of Broadway's
              golden era of theatrical entertainment. [1st ed.] New York,
              Dutton, 1962.
                 310 p. illus. 21 cm.
                 Includes bibliography.




                 I. Theater—New York (City)—Hist.     I. Title

              PN2277.N5C52                792.097472            62-14717  ‡

              Library of Congress                    [5]
```

The library's list of holdings will also contain *cross-reference* entries. If you are checking the list of holdings for books on "transmitters," for example, you will find "see also" entries at the end of this section. These list other headings that pertain to "transmitters": "see citizen band radio" or "see mobile radio."

THE RESEARCH PROCESS

After you have narrowed your focus and arrived at a manageable topic, and after you know the location of research materials, you are ready to begin active research. There are four steps in this process: (1) examining research materials; (2) compiling a working bibliography; (3) taking notes; (4) preparing an outline of the research paper.

Examining Research Materials

Effective research, like effective writing, requires method. The best method for research is one of ever-narrowing focus as you move from the general to the specific, just as you have done in moving from subject to topic.

Your first stop in the library should be at the general reference collection. Your examination of the appropriate guides and indexes will have made you aware of certain encyclopedias, special dictionaries, and bibliographies. These, in turn, will supply you with valuable background information that may enable you to limit your topic further. In addition, the general reference collection may provide you with clues for further research. You may notice, for example, that a particular book, article, or author is mentioned prominently in a number of these references, a signal that you should investigate this specific reference further.

The background information and clues furnished by the general reference collection should lead you to the appropriate periodical indexes. Do not yet attempt to locate specific periodicals; simply make a note of articles that, from what you gather in the indexes, might later prove useful. Do not be reluctant to use periodicals, for they have a number of advantages. First, because articles in periodicals are shorter than most books, the information they contain is often more accessible—it is easier, after all, to thumb through a 20-page article than a 400-page book. Second, many periodicals (particularly scholarly journals) cater to specialized groups and professions; thus, they are easily classifiable. Finally, periodicals are current, and this is particularly valuable when you are dealing with a timely topic or issue.

The background information and clues provided by the general reference collection also should lead you to titles, authors, and subjects in the holdings list that may aid your research. Again, do not attempt to locate specific books at this stage; simply make a note of works that may be of interest. Also, bear in mind that many books contain bibliographies of additional works on the same topic; the list of library holdings will tell you if a book contains a bibliography.

Compiling the Working Bibliography

A working bibliography is a list of articles, books, and, on occasion, nonprint material you plan to examine for information pertinent to your research. You compile the working bibliography as you consult the library's indexes and list of holdings. These contain all the information you will require for the working bibliography.

In compiling the bibliography, follow four commonsense guidelines. First, be selective. Look for the most timely and comprehensive works as suggested by titles, number of pages, bibliographies, and so on. Second, be practical. There is no sense in listing forty-five books on the same topic; again, be guided by those works that seem especially promising. Third, be critical.

For example, a book entitled *The Whole Truth about the US Space Shuttle Program* that contains only 175 pages may offer sketchy and simplistic information. Finally, be accurate. Make sure that each entry in your working bibliography contains all the essential information necessary for your final bibliography or List of Works Cited (see page 302–309).

There are a variety of methods for compiling the working bibliography, and your instructor may wish to offer specific recommendations. As a general rule, however, you may find that using 3"x 5" index cards to list your references will give you maximum flexibility and will enable you to organize your material effectively. With this method, use only one card for each reference; individual cards will later be keyed to correspond with the notes you will take from specific sources (see pages 296–297).

Each card for the working bibliography should contain the following information:

1. the reference call number (the number by which the book is shelved in the library) for a book.
2. a number that you assign to each work in your tentative bibliography keyed to correspond with the notes you will subsequently take.
3. author's name, last name first (if no name is given—as, for example, with a government pamphlet—begin with the title of the work).
4. title of a book (underlined, and including any subtitle), or title of an article (in quotation marks) and title of the periodical (underlined) that contains the article.
5. publication data: for a book, the edition (if other than the first), number of volumes (if more than one), place of publication, publisher, date of publication; for an article in a scholarly journal, volume number, date of publication, and page numbers containing the article; for an article in a newspaper, magazine, or nonscholarly periodical, date of publication and the page numbers of the article.

You may also want to add a note at the bottom of the card if the reference is illustrated, contains a bibliography, or has any other information useful for your topic.

Here is a sample working bibliography card for a book:

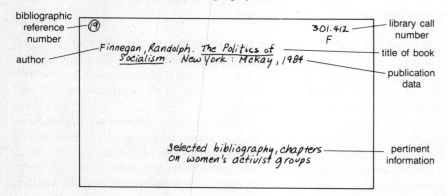

For an essay in a book:

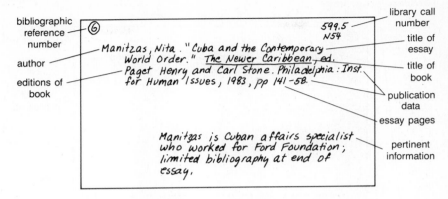

For an article in a newspaper:

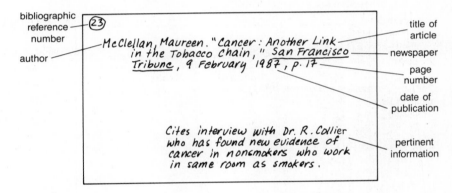

For an article in a scholarly journal:

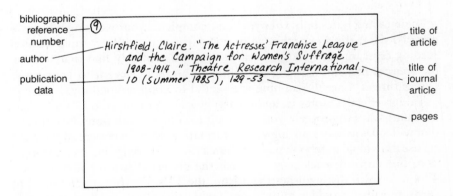

For nonprint material, you again include all the information in a working bibliography card that you will later need to compile the final bibliography or List of Works Cited. Here, for example, is a sample card for a computer software program:

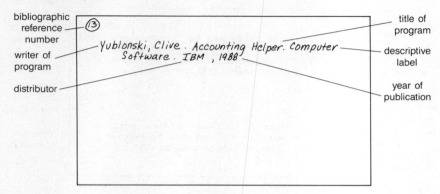

A recording:

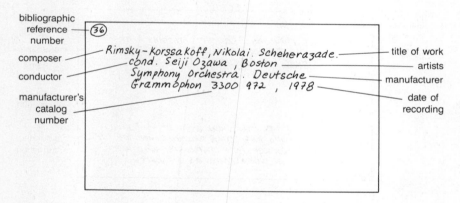

Taking Notes

Begin taking notes only after you have completed your working bibliography. To select the works that are particularly suited to your topic requires reading or scanning with great care. You will probably find that some of the sources in your working bibliography are not relevant to your topic. Discard them. Careful scanning is essential to good note taking.

Taking effective notes is, again, largely a matter of method. While there are many ways to proceed, you will want to compile your notes in a manner that will aid you in organizing your information. Most experienced researchers use individual notebook pages or index cards for compiling their information, one entry to each page or card; the preferred size for note cards is 4" x 6", which distinguishes them from the 3" x 5" working bibliography cards and also provides more room for writing. You will find that using individual pages or, perhaps even better, note cards, will enable you to shuffle and reshuffle your information until you have found the best way to organize it.

Each note page or note card should contain enough specific information so that you can locate its source card from your working bibliography with ease. Thus, at a minimum, at the top of the note you should write the author's full name and the complete title of the book or article. In addition, some researchers include a subject heading at the top of the card that identifies the basic content of the card, thereby facilitating the organization of their material. You may also consider including a number that corresponds to the bibliographic reference number in your working bibliography; this procedure helps ensure that you will be able to locate the source of your information even if you have omitted material from a note page or card.

Note pages or note cards should be compiled neatly and in an orderly manner so as to avoid factual and other errors. For ease in later reshuffling, you should avoid writing on both sides of the page or card; use two or three pages or cards for a single note that runs to some length.

The contents of your notes should reflect careful reading and deliberation. Your notes should contain facts, figures, and ideas as reflected in the specific sources of your research. Your method likely will involve *summary, paraphrase,* and *direct quotation.* In summarizing, you condense the major idea(s), substance, or point of view of a specific book or article; this method is especially suitable when you wish to encapsulate many pages of a source in a sentence or two. To paraphrase means to restate the substance of a sentence or paragraph in your own words; this method enables you to focus on and emphasize specific details as they appeared in the source without confining yourself to the source's wording. Finally, quoting means reproducing the words of the source exactly, even to the source's own punctuation; this method is especially effective when the source lends great authority to a particular point or when the quotation is so aptly or emphatically stated that too much would be lost in paraphrase. A note of caution here: inexperienced writers sometimes quote too frequently. If your use of quotations does not meet either of the above criteria, or if you quote excessively, you run the risk of letting your audience think that you have done little more than *copy* material.

Knowing how to use these three methods of taking notes will enable you to transfer your research material and data to your research paper quickly and efficiently. It will also help you avoid any problems with *plagiarism.* Plagiarism is a sophisticated term that means, quite simply, cheating. It occurs when you fail to credit information, ideas, or words that are not your own. In some instances, plagiarism is unintentional, and may reflect a writer's ignorance of the conventions governing academic honesty or of mistakes made in the note-taking process—another reason for taking great care when you are conducting your active research. Whether intentional or not, plagiarism in the academic world generally entails severe penalties, from a failing course grade to expulsion. In the business world, of course, plagiarism often results in law suits or other legal actions.

You will avoid any possible problem of this sort by bearing in mind that material summarized, paraphrased, or quoted must always be acknowledged. You can see how the following sample note cards make clear the researcher's indebtedness and also are presented in such a way as to make the information accessible and easy to use in the final research paper. Here is a note summarizing the points in an essay:

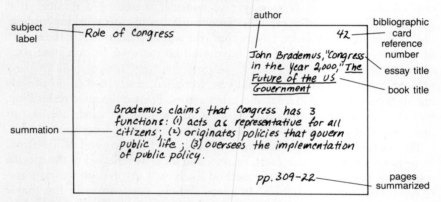

The following note is keyed to a working bibliography card on page 293 and contains a direct quotation from a scholarly journal:

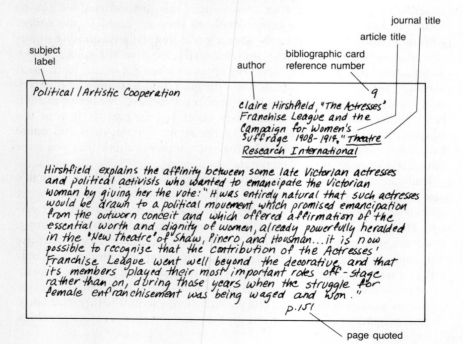

Here is a note paraphrasing the same passage:

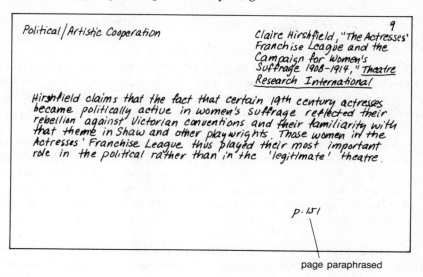

Political/Artistic Cooperation

9
Claire Hirshfield, "The Actresses'
Franchise League and the
Campaign for Women's
Suffrage 1908-1914," *Theatre
Research International*

Hirshfield claims that the fact that certain 19th century actresses became politically active in women's suffrage reflected their rebellion against Victorian conventions and their familiarity with that theme in Shaw and other playwrights. Those women in the Actresses' Franchise League thus played their most important role in the political rather than in the 'legitimate' theatre.

p. 151

page paraphrased

PLANNING THE RESEARCH PAPER

After you have completed your research and have, if necessary, modified and sharpened your topic and thesis statement, you are ready to plan the arrangement and presentation of the information your research has yielded. In devising a working plan, you may choose to employ an outline; in fact, your instructor may ask for an outline prior to your writing the paper itself. An outline can enable you to see, shape, organize, and develop your point as annunciated in the thesis and as supported by the research information you have uncovered.

Outlining

Many writers use outlines—some in the most casual of forms—for anything they write. An outline is particularly valuable for research papers, however, because it enables you to arrange your information in an orderly and logical manner. It also helps you to avoid being overwhelmed by the facts, figures, concepts, and ideas that you have noted. Outlining is thus a means of exerting control over your research information so that your paper will not simply be a compilation of material that you did not originate.

The following commonsense guidelines will assist you in outlining:

1. Do not attempt to make an outline before discovering your thesis; remember that an outline is a plan, not an idea.
2. View the outline as a means to an end, not as an end in itself; the purpose of

an outline is to help you accomplish what you intend to in your paper, not to produce a perfect outline.

3. Feel free to amend and improve the outline as you would any plan.

An effective thesis statement usually contains the main elements of an outline. As you examine your thesis, an organizational and developmental approach will begin to emerge as you decide how best to support and validate your main point. Assume, for example, that you have evolved the following thesis statement for a short research paper:

> A general historical overview of early and late medieval woman's status may help contemporary woman see just how far she has come—and how far she has to go. In the medieval era, women were paradoxically treated sometimes as ideals and at other times as mere beasts or property. The treatment of women in the twentieth century is perhaps also paradoxical, though the extremes are currently much less severe.

To support this thesis you must (1) discuss the status of medieval woman; (2) discuss the status of contemporary woman; (3) show how woman's lot has improved; (4) show that contemporary woman is nevertheless still subjected to indignities similar to those her predecessor suffered. These points will make up the various major parts of your paper, and the effectiveness of the paper will largely be determined by how well you use your research to validate your contentions.

Your first step in creating the outline will be to examine the subject labels on your note cards. This will enable you to group related information and to begin establishing an organizational framework of supporting research. Next, you may select from your information that which is especially appropriate to a given point. You will also want to decide which authors to quote or paraphrase, what material to summarize, which statistics to present, and which examples to cite. Finally, as you develop your outline, note as specifically as possible the various research information and sources you will use to support each of your points.

The following outline proceeds from a thesis statement, illustrates how each point will be developed, and lists specific research information that will furnish appropriate support. Note that the outline contains an introduction and a conclusion, elements common to any essay or research paper. (The research paper that evolved from the outline appears on pages 319–324.)

```
              Woman and Society: the Sexual Paradox
          I.  Introduction/Thesis: Contemporary society tends  to
              glorify medieval woman. Mention of her  likely evokes
              visions of a luxuriously robed Queen Guinevere
```

presiding next to Arthur at a feast, or of Saint Joan
of Arc in shining armor valiantly leading a ribbon—
bedecked cavalry. But most women in the period were, of
course, neither saints nor queens, and the status of
woman in medieval times offers certain parallels to the
status of contemporary woman. A general historical
overview of early and late medieval woman's status
enables today's woman to see just how far she has come—
and how far she has to go. In the medieval era, women
were paradoxically treated sometimes as ideals and at
other times as mere beasts or property. The treatment
of women in the twentieth century is perhaps also
paradoxical, though the extremes are currently less
severe.

II. Status of women in early Middle Ages (Rowling quote,
note card eight)

A. Women's rights

1. Ownership of property

2. Social role in freeing slaves

3. Testimony in court (Whitelock quote, note card
nine) (Wilson, note card fourteen)

B. Nevertheless, woman's status inferior to man's

1. Forced marriages for political purposes (Brooke,
note card two)

2. Polygamy reflecting male ego (Cite Charlemagne's
many wives as explained by Munz, note card seven)

III. Status of woman after Norman Conquest of 1066

A. Upper—class woman viewed as ideal rather than as
person, according to concept of courtly love

1. Elevated, dignified, and idealized (Cite Bishop,
note card one) (Jackson, note card 11)

2. Enjoyed leisure and read poetic romances written
about her (Bishop, note card one)

3. Allowed to enter into social role for first time
(Bishop, note card one)

B. Upper—class woman still viewed as inferior, however

1. Still subject to politically or economically
expedient marriages (Brooke, note card two)
(Doig, note card seventeen)

    2. Efforts to stand up to men often resulted in physical abuse (Cite Bishop's reference to a knight's attack on his wife for embarrassing him in public, note card one)

    3. Responsibility still viewed mainly in terms of running household (Bishop, note card one)

  C. Middle- and lower-class women even worse off

    1. No legal standing

    2. Superiority of male illustrated by his ''right'' to inflict torture on wife, though not to kill her (Cite example of man breaking wife's legs for disobedience, Bishop, note card one)

    3. Law of Gascony giving men right to beat their wives and use of ducking stool (Rowling, note card eight)

    4. Some women completely dehumanized (Rowling notes female serfs ''regarded as little more than beasts,'' note card eight)

IV. Status of contemporary woman

  A. Today's woman remains a major part of social life

    1. Woman's friendship prized

    2. Opening of doors and other chivalric customs continue to be reflected

  B. Contemporary woman enjoys some equal rights with man

    1. May bring suit against husband for brutality

    2. Ownership of property

    3. Right to vote

  C. Vestiges of medieval inequality remain, however

    1. Polygamy still practiced (Cite instances in Western society, as well as countries such as Saudi Arabia and Kuwait, as noted by PBS TV production, note card ten and London Times, note card twelve)

    2. Politically/economically expedient marriages continue (Reflected in marriages of England's Prince Charles and Princess Diana, and Prince Andrew and Lady Sarah)

    3. Ongoing abortion fight meanwhile suggests woman

still denied ultimate responsibility over her own
body

4. Woman's role still focused on managing household
(Cite survey in Ferree, note card five)

5. Job discrimination against woman continues and
may be having a psychological impact on her (Cite
and quote Farbweather, who notes that many women
feel that even their jobs outside the home are
inferior to those held by men, note card four)

V. Conclusion: Women have come a long way, but the legal,
economic, and social patterns established in medieval
times continue, though at a vastly reduced level.
Nevertheless, it is instructive to remember that
Guinevere ended up in a convent after King Arthur's
realm was destroyed by civil war; Joan of Arc ended up
at the stake. Today's woman meanwhile faces job
discrimination instead of the convent or the stake and
the kitchen sink instead of the ducking stool. Thus,
although her lot may be increasingly less restrictive,
it remains just as unfair as it did centuries ago.

Such an outline may seem somewhat elaborate, but because it represents careful planning and thought, it will facilitate the actual writing of the paper. In addition, remember that the outline is only a tool, and that its form is therefore much less important than its function, that is, to help you organize and present the product of your research.

DOCUMENTATION

To *document* a research paper is to give credit to sources. This enables you to indicate which information and ideas are the products of your research and which are your own. Documentation assists your audience in assessing the effectiveness of your supporting detail and evidence. It also provides the audience with valuable information should it decide to do some research on the same topic.

You document in two ways: (1) by compiling a List of Works Cited and (2) by providing parenthetical references in your text that are keyed to the list. It is important to note that the format and procedures for documentation in this text conform to guidelines established by the Modern Language Association, whose style guide is generally accepted in the humanities. There are a variety of other style guides for other disciplines. Some of these are listed in the *MLA Handbook for Writers of Research Papers,* 2nd ed. (New York: MLA, 1984). See also John Bruce Howell, *Style Manuals of the English-Speaking World* (Phoenix: Oryx, 1983).

List of Works Cited

The List of Works Cited is a catalog of the sources you have used in compiling your research paper. The list appears at the end of the paper on a separate sheet or sheets, with each of these sheets numbered consecutively from the last page of text. Compiling the list as you do your research will enable you subsequently to provide appropriate parenthetical references in your text.

Follow these rules for preparing the List of Works Cited:

1. Alphabetize all references by author (last name first); if you are dealing with an anonymous work, alphabetize by title (excluding the article—"a" or "the"—that appears as the first word in the title).
2. Place the first line of each reference flush left with the margin; indent the second and subsequent lines five spaces.
3. Do not number references.
4. Double-space reference information within each entry; double-space between entries.

Books in the List of Works Cited

A reference for a book should include the following basic information:

1. Author's name exactly as it appears on the title page but with last name first
2. Full title, including subtitle, underlined with a continuous line
3. Place of publication (cite only the first if more than one place appears on the title page)
4. Publisher (name shortened or abbreviated as explained below)
5. Date of publication (use the original publication date if the book has had more than one printing by the same publisher)

Note the annotations in the following sample entry:

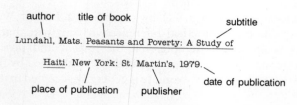

The annotations explain most of the above. Note, however, that the publisher's name has been shortened (from St. Martin's Press, Inc.). You may omit descriptive terms (such as "Press" or "Publishers"), except in the case of university presses that are indicated with a "P" (Kent State UP) to distinguish what they publish from what the university they are associated with publishes independently. You may also drop the publisher's first name ("Knopf" instead of "Alfred A. Knopf, Inc."). If the publisher's name includes the surnames of more than one person, provide only the first of the surnames ("Little" instead of "Little, Brown, and Co."). If the publisher's name is commonly abbreviated, reproduce only the abbreviated form ("MLA" for "Modern Language Association). Make sure that your efforts to shorten or abbreviate do not confuse and that you provide your audience with sufficient information so that the publisher may be traced in *Books in Print* or in any of the other literary guides.

There are certain conventions involved in entering books in the List of Works Cited. The following sample entries detail and explain these conventions.

▶ One author:

> Keillor, Garrison. Lake Wobegon Days. New York: Viking,
> 1985.

▶ Two or more books by the same author:

> Nichols, David. From Dessalines to Duvalier: Race, Colour
> and National Independence in Haiti. Cambridge, Eng.:
> Cambridge UP, 1979.
> ---. Haiti in Caribbean Context: Ethnicity, Economy and
> Revolt. London: Macmillan, 1985.

(The three hyphens substitute for repeating the author's name. Note also in the first Nichols entry that the abbreviation for England follows the city of publication to avoid possible confusion with a city in the United States.)

▶ Two authors:

> Hennipen, Leo, and Maria Muntz. Edible Fungi. New York: St.
> Swithins, 1986.

(Only the first author's name is reversed and followed by a comma.)

▶ Three authors:

> Wallace, Helen, William Wallace, and Carole Webb. <u>Policy-</u>
> <u>making in the European Communities</u>. London: Wiley, 1983.

(Again, only the first author's name is reversed; note also that when you cite a book written by two or three authors you should give their names as they appear on the title page; occasionally, they will not appear alphabetically on the title page.)

▶ More than three authors:

> MacSwine, Horatio P., et al. <u>Life on the Farm: A Serious</u>
> <u>Inquiry</u>. Corncob Corner, Ind.: Chicken Press, 1986.

("et al." means "and others.")

▶ Corporate author:

> American Council on Paleography. <u>Secrets Uncovered: The New</u>
> <u>Fragments of the Rosetta Stone</u>. Washington, D.C.:
> Basalt, 1947.

(The council above takes the place of the author's name and would be alphabetized under "A".)

▶ Anonymous:

> <u>Parental Involvement in Public Education</u>. Washington, D.C.:
> NEA, 1983.

(When no author is given, start with the title and alphabetize the entry according to the first word in the title.)

▶ Author included in an anthology:

> Hellman, Lillian. <u>The Little Foxes</u>. <u>Twentieth Century</u>
> <u>American Theatre</u>. Ed. Gabriel Potter. San Diego:
> Seaman's, 1982. 119–83.

(Hellman is the author of the play, *The Little Foxes*, and Potter is the editor of a book that is a collection of plays; the play is underlined because it was originally published as a book, and you would follow the same procedure for a novel; titles of works not published as books, such as short stories or poems, would be placed in quotation marks. Note the reference of 119–83, which refers to the pages in the anthology containing the play.)

▶ Author of a multivolume work:

> Bowser, William T. Basic Photography. 2 vols. New York:
>   Delray, 1973.

(In the List of Works Cited, give the total number of volumes, not just the specific volume number that you consulted; you may give the specific volume number you cited parenthetically in the text of your research paper.)

▶ An edited edition:

> Anderson, Sherwood. Sherwood Anderson Selected Letters.
>   Ed. Charles E. Modlin. Knoxville: U Tennessee P, 1984.

(The above reference focuses on Chaucer, indicating that the researcher is dealing with the author and is merely acknowledging the editor, who put the collection of Chaucer's works together. If the researcher wanted to discuss the role of the editor, the focus would so indicate, as illustrated below.)

> West, Rebecca, ed. Selected Poems of Carl Sandburg. New
>   York: Harcourt, 1926.

▶ A translation:

> de Chardin, Pierre Teilhard. The Future of Man. Trans.
>   Norman Denny. New York: Harper, 1964.

(Acknowledge the translator of a work cited that originally was published in a foreign language.)

▶ A compilation:

> Singing Bee! A Collection of Favorite Children's Songs.
>   Comp. Jane Hart. New York: Lothrop, 1982.

(Acknowledge a compiler, provided that the name appears on the title page.)

▶ An article in a reference book:

> ''courtly love.'' New Columbia Encyclopedia. 1975 ed.

(Citing common reference books does not require full publication data, but give the year of publication and the edition used.)

▶ A pamphlet:

> Forbes, John D. Jamaica: Managing Political and Economic
>   Change. Washington: Am. Enterprise Inst., 1985.

(Follow the format for a book.)

▶ An anonymous pamphlet:

> Parental Involvement in Title I ESEA. Washington: GPO, 1972.

(No author is given for the above, so the citation begins with the title; note also the abbreviation for Government Printing Office, the publisher of most U.S. federal publications.)

▶ Pre-twentieth-century books:

> MacKaye, Percy. Fenris the Wolf. Philadelphia, 1899.

(Omit the names of publishers of books before 1900, and separate the place of publication and the date with a comma.)

▶ Missing information:

> Angus MacKenzie. The Lowlands of Western Scotland.
>   Edinburgh: Blackie, n.d.

(You can supply only the information available to you. The "n.d." in the above stands for "no date of publication given." You may use the following abbreviations and insert them in place of missing information: "n.p." for "no place of publication given"; "n.p." for "no publisher given"; "n. pag." for "no pagination given.")

Periodicals in the List of Works Cited

A reference for an article in a periodical—scholarly journal, popular magazine, or newspaper—should include the following basic information:

1. Author's name (last name first)
2. Full title of article in quotation marks
3. Title of periodical underlined with a continuous line
4. Volume number (for scholarly journals)
5. Date of publication
6. Pages on which article appears

Note the annotations in the following sample entry:

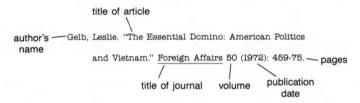

As with books, there are a number of conventions involved in entering periodicals in the List of Works Cited. The following sample entries illustrate and explain these conventions.

▶ From a scholarly journal:

> Hirshfield, Claire. ''The Actresses' Franchise League and
> the Campaign for Women's Suffrage 1908–1914.'' Theatre
> Research International 10 (1985): 129–53.

(This reference is for a journal that features continuous pagination throughout a volume year; note that this format requires citing the volume number followed by the year of publication, which is then separated from inclusive pages by a colon.)

> Squires, Sandra, and Julius Owen. ''Reflections on the
> Water Imagery in the Poetry of Wole Soyinka.'' Tamarind
> Review 7.3 (1986): 13–28.

(For journals that begin each issue on page one; this requires following the volume number with a period and then the issue number. Note also that a few journals use only an issue number; in such instances, put the issue number in place of the volume number.)

▶ From a popular monthly or bimonthly magazine:

> McFinn, Enos. ''The Karakul Love Song.'' Music Today June
> 1985: 10–16.

(Note that the month and year take the place of a volume and issue number; note also that there is no punctuation between the title and the month of publication.)

▶ From a newspaper:

> Connoly, Kathleen. ''Experts Fear Financial Collapse.'' <u>San Francisco Examiner</u> 17 Feb. 1931: 9–10.

(Day, month, and year take the place of volume and issue references.)

> Maudlin, Kelly T. ''Tourism Bonanza Underway.'' <u>Windsor Observer</u> [Neb.] 13 Oct. 1986, late ed.: C20.

(The city of publication does not appear in the paper's title and has therefore been added; indicate the edition of the paper when it is specified on the masthead; if the paper has more than one section, specify the section you are citing prior to giving the page number.)

Nonprint Sources in the List of Works Cited

Nonprint sources include computer software, material from a computer service, radio and television programs, and videotapes and audiotapes. As with print sources, citations for nonprint materials should provide as much information as possible about writer or composer, title of program, and publication. Each of the nonprint sources also has additional conventions. The most common of these are illustrated in the following annotated sample entries.

▶ Computer software:

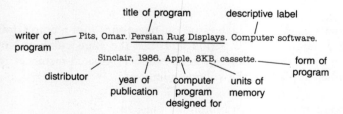

(It is not always possible to get all of the above information, but try to provide enough to enable the audience to locate the specific program.)

▶ Material from a computer service:

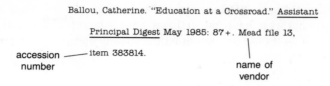

▶ Radio and television programs:

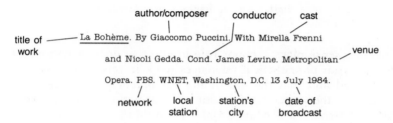

(If you are referring mainly to the composer rather than to the work, you would begin with the composer, in this case, Puccini.)

▶ Recordings:

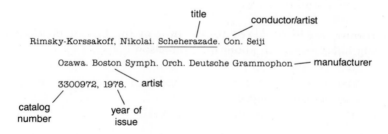

(Note the use of common abbreviations.)

▶ Movies and videos:

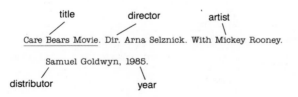

(If you are focusing on the work of either the actor(s) or director, the name should precede the title of the work.)

Parenthetical Documentation

Parenthetical documentation signals *indebtedness*. It tells your audience specifically what you have taken from your sources and exactly where you found it. You should use parenthetical documentation under the following conditions:

1. When you present a direct quotation
2. When you paraphrase or summarize material that is not your own
3. When you present facts that are not common knowledge
4. When you copy a chart, table, or diagram, or construct one based on someone else's research

Common sense plays a major role in effective documentation. Bear in mind that your parenthetical references work in tandem with the List of Works Cited and that the job of the parenthetical reference is only to show exactly the source and location of information. Consequently, most of your references will contain only the author's last name and a page number, as illustrated in the following example:

> Most public opinion polls suggest that only about one-
> quarter of the population has much confidence in big business
> (Samuelson 109).

This reference would be keyed to an entry in the List of Works Cited containing full information about the Samuelson book:

> Samuelson, Paul A.   Economics.   11th ed.   New York: McGraw,
>   1980.

You may sometimes have two or more books or articles by the same author in your List of Works Cited. To avoid confusion, add the title of the work (in a shortened form, if possible) to the parenthetical reference. Here, for example, is one such reference and the corresponding information in the list:

> The narrator frequently appears to admire the ability of
> others to explore the realms of woman, sex, and love (Snow,
> Conscience 7).

> Snow, C. P.   Time of Hope.   New York: Scribners, 1949.
> ---.   The Conscience of the Rich.   New York: Scribners, 1958.

Confusion may also occur when two or more separate authors with the same surname appear on your list. In such a case, include the first name in your parenthetical reference.

> Mussolini was blunt about the authority of the state as an absolute and thus saw it as the force that defines and subjugates all individuals (Anthony Smith 52).

Such specificity ensures that the audience does not confuse either of the following works in the list:

> Griffith, Thomas. The Waist-High Culture. New York: Harper
> & Row, 1959.
> Griffith, Eleanor. The Aims of Lyric. Chicago: Plains
> Press, 1986.

Parenthetical documentation aims to clarify and simplify. If references intrude on your text or in any other way distract the audience, however, your efforts will be counterproductive. Commonsense guidelines are again the best means of ensuring the smooth and clear integration of parenthetical documentation. First, place your parenthetical references at the end of sentences whenever possible or, at the very least, at the end of clauses. Second, use parenthetical references sparingly. For example, a single paragraph of your text that refers to only one source but in three or four separate citations is likely to distract the audience; one citation (even with multiple page references) at the end of the paragraph should suffice. Third, when possible, integrate the author's name into your text; this may serve to emphasize his or her authority, give your text greater stylistic breadth, and enable you to omit the name from the parenthetical reference. Note how this practice operates in the following examples:

> One critic argues that efforts to show an exact correlation between class size and academic achievement in high school students have been unconvincing (Chiselko 131-2).

> As Chiselko notes, efforts to show an exact correlation between class size and academic achievement in high school students have been unconvincing (131-2).

> Efforts to show an exact correlation between class size and academic achievement in high school students, according to Chiselko, have been unconvincing (131-2).

Like other aspects of the research paper, parenthetical documentation acknowledges a variety of conventions. The following examples illustrate and explain these conventions.

▶ Reference to a single-author work:

> The houseplant, according to a leading horticulturist, offers contemporary man a fleeting glimpse of his primordial origins (Fitch 17).

▶ Reference to two or three authors in a single work:

> Tyrell and Jones charge that ''any effort by an individual to question the price-setting policies of US airlines is met with evasion or silence'' (15).

▶ Reference to more than three authors in a single work:

> Even today, despite intimate links to English history and contemporary government, polls taken in Cardiff suggest that most Welshmen see their loyalties to Wales, not London (Rowe et al. 163).

▶ Reference to an entire work:

> Carlos Baker's biography of Hemingway continues to be the standard by which all other studies of Hemingway are measured.

(As a general rule, integrate the author's name into your text; because the reference is not to a specific part of the work, no page reference is necessary.)

▶ Reference to a multivolume work:

> Despite the dramatic potential inherent in the Civil War, the postwar theater generally returned to the safety of melodrama (Quinn 1: 357-60).

(The number after the author's name refers to the volume; the colon separates it from the pages summarized. Should you wish to refer to the entire volume, follow the author's name with a comma and "vol" [Quinn, vol. 2].)

► Reference to a work by a corporate author:

> A recent report by the National Council of Lawyers concluded
> that widespread discrepancies exist between northern and
> southern states regarding penalties for drug abuse (87).

(To include the council's name in the parenthetical reference would be cumbersome and intrusive; it is generally best to include the name of a corporate author in your text.)

► Reference to a work without an author:

> The castle ''was fortified in 1067 and became one of the
> principal strongholds of the realm'' (<u>Winchester Castle</u> 1).

(The title takes the place of the author's name; if you are citing a nonprint source or a one-page article, no page reference is necessary.)

► Reference to a nonoriginal source:

> Hitler viewed man living in a brutal world where ''One
> creature drinks the blood of another. The death of one
> nourishes the others. One should not drivel about humane
> feelings'' (qtd. in Smith 76).

(It is best to cite from the original material; when this is impossible, you may use an indirect source in which a writer quotes someone else. In such an instance, use the abbreviation "qtd. in" to signify your indebtedness to a nonoriginal source.)

► Reference to multiple sources:

> Two leading archaeologists are convinced that the west of
> England was indeed the location of Camelot (Ashe 17; Alcock
> 123).

(Cite each work as you normally would, but separate them with a semicolon.)

Additional Conventions and Guidelines

There are a variety of other issues having to do with format and style in the research paper. The next section discusses the most common of these.

USING QUOTATIONS

Directly quoting the words of others can be extremely effective if you use this technique judiciously. The following conventions will assist you with presenting quoted material:

1. Keep quotations as short as possible. Avoid, for example, a 200-word quotation in a 1,500-word paper; it would be better to summarize such a quotation.
2. Incorporate prose quotations of four lines or less (as they appear on *your* paper) directly into the body of your text and indicate them with quotation marks. For example:

> Whitman's pronouncement in the 1850s that ''Americans are going to be the most fluent and melodious-voiced people in the world, and the most perfect users of words'' seems today to border on the ludicrous.

3. Begin quotations of more than four lines (as they appear on *your* paper) on a new line, indent it ten spaces from the left margin, and omit quotation marks. Do not indent the first line if the quotation is taken from a single paragraph. Establish the context prior to beginning the quotation, as in the following example:

> Few visitors to eighteenth-century American shores were more impressed with the possibilities of the New World than St. Jean de Crèvecoeur, who approached euphoria in his <u>Letters from an American Farmer</u>:

> > No sooner does an European arrive, no matter of what condition, than his eyes are opened upon the fair prospect; he hears his language spoke, he retraces many of his own country manners, he perpetually hears the names of families and towns with which he is acquainted; he sees happiness and prosperity in all places disseminated; he meets with hospitality, kindness, and plenty every where; he beholds hardly any poor; he seldom hears of punishments and executions; and he wonders at the elegance of our towns, those miracles of industry and freedom. He cannot admire enough our rural districts, our convenient roads, good taverns, and our many accommodations; he involuntarily loves a country where every thing is so lovely.

4. Insert [sic] into a quotation to indicate that you are exactly reproducing that quotation; [sic] points up that the error or outdated usage appears in the original.

   ''The Order of Battle is given to evry [sic] commander of a
   Regiment or Squadron.''

5. Use brackets to clarify references within a quotation. For example:

   ''The use of this new weapon will end civilization as we know
   it.''

   ''The use of this new weapon [the titanium bomb] will end
   civilization as we know it.''

6. Indicate words omitted from the middle of a quoted sentence with three spaced dots (ellipsis points). For example:

   ''When 24 percent of our children fail to graduate from high
   school, the schools must be at fault.''

   ''When 24 percent . . . fail to graduate . . . the schools
   must be at fault.''

7. Indicate words omitted at the end of a quoted sentence with four ellipsis points with no space before the first (one to signal the end of the sentence). For example:

   D. K. Elkins states, ''The use of this new weapon will end
   civilization. . . .''

8. When omitting words from a direct quotation, make sure that the omissions do not alter the original meaning of the quotation. For example:

   The noted Broadway critic said of the play, ''Miss Smith is
   marvelous but the play is a disaster.''

   The noted Broadway critic said of the play, ''Miss Smith is
   marvelous. . . .''

9. When quoting poetry or verse, incorporate a single line within your text and highlight it with quotation marks. For example:

> In his epic <u>Idylls of the King</u>, Tennyson announces that his
> intention is to study the moral realm, with ''Sense at war
> with Soul, ideal manhood closed in real man.''

Quotations of three lines or less may also be incorporated into your text by using quotation marks and slash marks to indicate where the lines end. For example:

> Milton, too, saw the moral as his theater in <u>Paradise Lost</u>,
> as he proclaims he will write ''Of man's first disobedience,
> and the fruit / Of that forbidden tree whose mortal taste /
> Brought death into the World. . . .''

Begin quotations of more than three lines on a new line ten spaces from the left margin (if possible); generally, the quotation should be introduced by a sentence that establishes context. Introduce the quotation with a colon. For example:

> Emerson's poem, ''Concord Hymn,'' presents a simple yet
> stately celebration of the American Revolution by
> contrasting the humble status of the fighters with the
> significance of the occasion:
>
>> By the rude bridge that arched the flood,
>>   Their flag to April's breeze unfurled,
>> Here once the embattled farmers stood
>>   And fired the shot heard around the world.

References to Literary Works

The variety of editions of great works of literature means that a quotation found on page eighty-six of one edition sometimes will not appear until page ninety-five of another. Literary scholars therefore frequently provide chapter numbers with their page references to assist an audience. For example:

> In <u>Moby-Dick</u>, the narrator, Ishmael, early on sounds the
> theme of alienation when he describes Captain Ahab as ''a man
> cut away from the stake, when the fire has overrunningly

```
wasted all the limbs without consuming them . . .'' (Melville
37; ch. 6).
```

When you are dealing with classic verse drama, you may as a general rule make references to act, scene, and, when available, line numbers. For example:

```
Shakespeare's Othello is among the most prideful of
protagonists, as he unwittingly reveals to us:
        Who steals my purse steals trash; 'tis something,
        nothing!
        'Twas mine, 'tis his and has been slave to thousands;
        But he that filches from me my good name
        Robs me of that which not enriches him,
        And makes me poor indeed (3.3; 147–51).
```

(The first number refers to the act, the second to the scene; as a general rule, use arabic rather than roman numerals, though you may wish to check with your instructor. Note the semicolon separating scene from line numbers in the above.)

Other Format and Stylistic Conventions

The following is an alphabetized list of some additional format and stylistic issues that frequently arise during preparation of research papers.

Dates: Write out centuries (the fourteenth century); decades may be written out or presented in figures (the 1950s).

Foreign Words: Write foreign words exactly as they are written in the original, including accent marks. Underline foreign words that have not become part of the English language.

Names: Give the complete name the first time you use it; thereafter, use the surname. Avoid titles (Dr., Commander, Professor).

Numbers: Write out one digit numbers as words; write all others as numerals. Use words and numerals for large numbers such as 7.9 billion. In sentences with a series of numbers, use only one form. ("In Padua County, there are 7 precincts, 41 towns, and 1.1 million people.")

Titles: Capitalize the first words, last words, and all major words; do not capitalize all letters in each word. Underline the titles of books, magazines, journals, pamphlets, newspapers, long poems, plays, films, audiotapes and videotapes, works of art, and performances; never underline the title of your own research paper. Use quotation marks to designate titles of short stories, poems, articles, songs, and all other elements originally published within a larger work. Religious books or their parts (such as the Bible, Old Testament, Talmud, and Koran) take neither underlining nor quotation marks.

A SAMPLE RESEARCH PAPER

The following sample research paper, largely based on the outline earlier in this chapter, illustrates the principles and conventions of the research process. Note in particular the limited topic, the integration of sources into the text, the establishment of context prior to quoting and paraphrasing, and the form of both parenthetical documentation and the List of Works Cited. As in any effective essay, the paper proceeds from a clear thesis statement, guides its development through topic sentences, and uses transitions to move smoothly from one point to another.

Woman and Society: the Sexual Paradox

Contemporary society tends to glorify medieval
woman. Mention of her likely evokes visions of a
luxuriously robed Queen Guinevere presiding next to
Arthur at a feast, or of Saint Joan of Arc in shining
armor valiantly leading a ribbon-bedecked cavalry. But
most women in the period were neither saints nor queens,
and the status of the woman in medieval times offers
certain parallels to the status of contemporary woman. A
general historical overview of early and late medieval
woman's status enables today's woman to see just how far
she has come—and how far she has to go. In the medieval
era, woman were paradoxically treated sometimes as
ideals and at other times as mere beasts or property.
The treatment of women in the twentieth century is
perhaps also paradoxical, though the extremes are
currently less severe.

The status of medieval woman, as Marjorie Rowling
has noted, was ''perpetually oscillating between a pit
and pedestal'' (72). Between the years 500 and 1,500,
however, her dignity and rights were gradually eroded,
and her status became increasingly dependent on male
whim. During the early medieval period, in fact, woman
had the right to hold and sell land, to defend herself
in court, to testify to the innocence of others, to make
religious donations, and to free slaves (Wilson et al.
423-5).

Despite these rights, woman's station in the early
Middle Ages was vastly inferior to man's. A woman was
subject to being married for political expediency, if a
father, brother, or uncle so ruled (Brooke 70-4).
Especially telling was the proliferation of polygamy,

which heightens the status of the male by subordinating the rights of several women to a single male ego. The custom was given particular legitimacy by the powerful ninth-century emperor Charlemagne, who had five wives (Munz 44-5).

Woman's difficulties in the early medieval period paled in comparison to her fate after the Norman Conquest in 1066. As Dorothy Whitelock concludes, she became increasingly dependent, losing many of her former rights and much of her dignity (94). The rise of the concept and ritual of courtly love, which depicted woman as an ideal rather than as an individual, was, ironically, the main culprit (Jackson 243-51). Morris Bishop highlights this paradox:

> The female sex gained status. Previously women had been merely unpaid domestic laborers or symbols of sin. Now they attained dignity and commanded respect. The concept of chivalry and the code of courtly love elevated women, or at least upper-class women. They had leisure to learn to read and to enjoy the long poetic romances that were written for them. Women's conversation was prized, their friendship sought. . . . Social life, as we understand the term, really began in the thirteenth century (37).

If, as both Bishop and Giles Doig suggest, it was only the upper-class woman who was elevated, a woman of such status had to live with the frustration of great inequality to the same men that were elevating her (46). That frustration was sometimes vented in the most unfortunate ways, and thus caused a male response that undercut the whole notion of woman as ideal. Bishop, for

3

example, cites the case of the wife of the knight of La
Tour-Landry, who, because she had scolded him in public,
suffered a broken nose when he kicked her in retaliation
(73). Other examples of abuse are provided by
Christopher Brooke's account of how upper-class women
were married off in ''a kind of dynastic game'' to
consolidate land holdings and political alliances (70),
a form of medieval power politics that even denied woman
control over her own body. Interestingly, however, no
one challenged her right to run the household, an
occupation that transcended class as it was assumed that
such was woman's rightful role (DePiero 126; Kreisler
17).

     Woman's rights appear to have further diminished
as she moved down the class scale. Bishop notes that in
many parts of Europe, middle-class woman had virtually
no legal status; for example, she was not allowed to
testify in a court or even to make a will (219). It was
not the lack of legal standing alone that made
conditions deplorable for a woman but rather the
physical power that a male relative-particularly her
husband-held over her. Apparently a husband could
subject his wife to nearly any kind of physical torture
as long as he stopped short of murder, as the following
account suggests:

          [One] fourteenth century writer, instructing
          his maiden daughters, warns them of the fate of
          a certain disobedient wife. Her husband
          consulted a surgeon and made a deal for the
          mending of two broken legs. He then went home
          and broke both his wife's legs with a pestle,
          remarking that in the future she wouldn't go
          far to break his commandment again (Bishop 271).

4

In addition, all wives in Gascony, regardless of their
class, were subject to a thirteenth—century law that
stated that ''all inhabitants of Villefranche have the
right to beat their wives, provided they do not kill
them thereby'' (qtd. in Rowling 72).

Lower—class woman appears to have faced the
greatest threats and enjoyed the least amount of hope.
''Village women,'' reports Rowling, ''who dared to rail
against their husbands were dowsed in the ducking stool
in the village pond. . . . Court rolls show that
villages were repeatedly threatened or fined for
failing to provide these punitive instruments'' (72).
Furthermore, a peasant woman probably remained unaware
of the codes of chivalry and courtly love, and had to
continue her daily drudgery in the fields with no hope
for anything better. That her suffering was largely
shared by lower—class men probably provided little
comfort, as her lot was accorded subhuman status. As
Rowling notes, ''The woman serf [was] regarded as little
more than a beast'' (74), an assertion given credence
by a poet of the day, who asked ''Why should the villein
[serfs] eat beef, or any dainty food? Nettles, reeds,
briars, peashells are good enough for them'' (qtd. in
Bishop 243).

When compared with the roles of contemporary woman
and the opportunities open to her, such sentiments seem
remote in the extreme. Today's woman is allowed to hold
property in this country, to defend herself in court,
and to vote——though that right is fairly recent, gained
in the early part of this century. At the same time, it
would be safe to generalize that society prizes woman's
conversation and seeks her friendship. Traces of

chivalric treatment remain; some men still will open a
door for a woman. And indeed, an upper- or lower-class
woman today need not fear being kicked in the face if
she were to challenge her husband in public--her
husband, should he break her nose, would face the
possibility of arrest.

Yet upon reflection, the past--with all its
''nettles, reeds, briars, and peashells''--may not seem
so distant. Polygamy, according to a recent television
broadcast, continues in some Middle Eastern countries
(Death of a Queen); it was even practiced up through the
last century by certain groups in the United States
(Hosenball 31). Meanwhile, the ''dynastic game'' of
marriage for political alliance and consolidation of
land holdings is still in effect today, with the royal
families of England, Spain, and Monaco generally
continuing to spurn alliances with commoners and the
less class-conscious American dynasties seldom looking
outside their own moneyed circles. In fairness, there
are surely many exceptions to wealthy persons marrying
other wealthy persons; nevertheless, such marriages are
still common enough among the upper classes that it is
tempting to argue that de facto marriages of political
and economic convenience are still strongly encouraged
if not, as in the Middle Ages, forced.

Perhaps most tellingly, woman's main occupation--
that of managing the household--remains unchanged for
the majority of contemporary women. According to Myra
Marx Ferree, this includes women who hold jobs outside
the home (76), suggesting that women have increasingly
come to accept the role that history has handed them.
The psychological ramifications of such a self-image
are suggested in a recent survey conducted by a

6

sociologist, who found that most women working outside
the home ''wished their work was as important as their
husband's'' (Glendenning 47).

Women have nevertheless come a long way, but the
legal, economic, and social patterns established in
medieval times continue, though at a vastly reduced
level. It is instructive to remember, however, that
Guinevere ended up in a convent after King Arthur's
realm was destroyed by civil war; Joan of Arc ended up
at the stake. Today's woman meanwhile faces job
discrimination instead of the convent or the stake and
the kitchen sink instead of the ducking stool. Thus,
although her lot may be increasingly less restrictive,
it remains just as unfair as it did centuries ago.

                   List of Works Cited

Bishop, Morris. The Middle Ages. New York: American
     Heritage, 1970.
Brooke, Christopher. The Structure of Medieval
     Society. New York: McGraw, 1973.
Death of a Queen. Narr. Joel Smiley. Writ. and prod.
     Marsha Feinstein. PBS. WLLT, San Jose. 3 May 1983.
DePiero, Heather. ''Kingdoms and Castles: Sexual
     Politics in Medieval Europe.'' Sociology in the Age
     of the Plantagenets. Ed. Agnes Piłtowski. Denver:
     Prairie, 1986. 202–24.
Doig, Giles. ''Sex and Class in Norman England.''
     Economic Historian 6 (1984): 338–52.
Ferree, Myra Marx. ''The Confused American Housewife.''
     Psychology Today 10 (1976): 76 –80.
Glendenning, Wilma. ''Woman's Work Is Never Done.''
     Social Spectrum 13 (1985): 147–68.
Hosenball, Mark. ''Shockwaves on the Salt Lake.''
     [London] Sunday Times Magazine 30 March 1986:
     26–35.
Jackson, W.T.H. ''The De Amore of Andreas Capellanus
     and the Practice of Love at Court. '' Romantic
     Review 49 (1958): 243–51.
Kreisler, Carlyle N. Class and Nationalism Through the
     Ages. Manchester [Eng.]: Carpathian, 1936.
Munz, Peter. Life in the Age of Charlemagne . New York:
     Putnam's, 1969.
Rowling, Marjorie. Life in Medieval Times. New York:
     Putnam's, 1968.
Whitelock, Dorothy. The Beginnings of English Society.
     Baltimore: Penguin, 1952.
Wilson, Richard, et al. ''An Ancient Pattern.''
     Arthurian Age 5 (1986): 186–204.

Index